Writing Voyage

Writing Voyage

A Process Approach to Basic Writing

SEVENTH EDITION

Thomas E. Tyner
REEDLEY COLLEGE

THOMSON

WADSWORTH

Australia   Canada   Mexico   Singapore   United Kingdom   United States

THOMSON
————★———— ™
WADSWORTH

Writing Voyage, Seventh Edition
Thomas E. Tyner

Publisher, English: Michael Rosenberg
Acquisitions Editor: Stephen Dalphin
Sr. Developmental Editor: Cathlynn Rich
Sr. Production Editor: Maryellen E. Killeen
Director of Marketing: Lisa Kimball
Executive Marketing Manager: Carrie Brandon
Sr. Manufacturing Coordinator: Mary Beth Hennebury

Text Design, Composition, Project Management:
    Thompson Steele, Inc.
Photo Permissions Editor: Sheri Blaney
Cover Designer: Gina Petti, Rotunda Design
Cover Photograph: ©Peter Adams/Index Stock Imagery
Printer: Webcom

Printed in Canada.
2 3 4 5 6 7 8   06   05   04

For more information contact Wadsworth,
25 Thomson Place, Boston, MA 02210 USA,
or you can visit our Internet site at
http://www.wadsworth.com

For permission to use material from this text
or product, submit a request online at
http://www.thomsonrights.com

Any additional questions about permissions
can be submitted by email to
thomsonrights@thomson.com

ISBN: 0-8384-0679-3

Tyner, Thomas E.
    Writing voyage: a process approach to basic writing/
        Thomas E. Tyner.--7th ed.
            p. cm
    Includes bibliographical references and index.
    ISBN 0-8384-0679-3 (alk. paper)
        1. English language--Rhetoric. 2. English language--
Grammar--Problems, exercises, etc. 3. Report Writing
I. Title.
PE1408 .T96 2003
808'.042--dc21
                                            2003040249

CONTENTS

UNIT 2

WRITING ABOUT RELATIONSHIPS 35

UNIT 4

WRITING TO COMPARE 107

Unit 5

WRITING ABOUT PROBLEMS AND SOLUTIONS 151

APPENDIX 219

PREFACE

The purpose of this text is to provide an integrated writing experience for students. Textbooks often isolate basic elements of writing from the developmental process. Students are left with a fragmented approach to writing, in which it is difficult to make connections between textbook instruction and their writing.

Writing Voyage, Seventh Edition, incorporates these writing elements within the process so that students write papers and work concurrently on specific writing skills to apply at different stages of the drafting process. Students learn what elements of writing are most important at each stage of the process, and they understand that a mastery of a variety of skills is crucial to the effective communication of their ideas.

NEW TO THIS EDITION

This seventh edition of *Writing Voyage* contains a number of new and noteworthy features:

- Integration of professional readings within the writing process in each unit for purposes of modeling and discussion.
- New, improved writing emphases in a number of units, including the units "Writing about Relationships," "Writing about Opinions," "Writing about Problems and Solutions," and "Writing about Issues."
- New small-group collaborative activities throughout the text.
- New prewriting strategies introduced in a number of units.
- New student writing samples for analysis and modeling throughout the text.

The following features continue to make *Writing Voyage* a highly effective writing text.

FOCUS ON PROCESS

In each unit, students are taken through the process of prewriting, drafting, revising, and proofreading their papers. The text emphasizes that writing is a process that develops in general stages that most writers go through. As students progress through the book, they tailor the process to their needs and preferences. By the book's end they are well versed in the basic elements of effective writing and in command of a process that works for them.

CONTENT ORIENTATION

Throughout the text, the primary emphasis is on writing content: what the writer wants to communicate to his or her readers. All other elements of effective writing—organization of ideas, paragraphing, wording, correctness—are addressed as a *means* to communicate a writer's ideas most effectively. Substance is always emphasized before structure, and structure is evaluated by how it contributes to the reader's appreciation of the substance.

ROTATING FORMAT

Writing texts frequently introduce a subject in one unit and then virtually abandon it. From my teaching experience, students who have been taught parallel construction in the first unit may have forgotten what they learned by the third or fourth unit unless the topic has been regularly reinforced. Therefore, this text is designed so the basic elements of writing—prewriting, audience/purpose consideration, paragraphing, sentence structure, organization—are covered in every unit. Many students in basic writing courses have problems that cannot be solved with the traditional block-coverage textbook approach. *Writing Voyage* provides reinforcement of basic writing skills throughout the book.

EMPHASIS ON WRITING

On the assumption that students cannot learn to write well without writing often, the text provides constant writing opportunities: free writing, drafting essays, paragraph writing, sentence combining exercises, and a variety of sentence writing activities. In addition to the major assignments that students take through the writing process in each unit, there are numerous shorter writing assignments, each emphasizing a particular aspect of the process.

STUDENT WRITING SAMPLES

Throughout the text, students will find student writing samples that relate to the kinds of writing they are doing. The writing samples are interesting to read, provide realistic models for students, and supply material to be analyzed from a number of angles: thesis development, purpose, audience consideration, organization, paragraphing, style, originality, and overall effectiveness. Each unit also contains first-draft writing samples through which students can sharpen their revising skills. Throughout the text, students will analyze and learn from the essays of other student writers.

PEER EDITING

Often students share their writing with no one but their instructor. This text is designed for students to share their writing with classmates at each step in the process. They use their classmates as an audience, and they develop their critiquing and revising skills by helping other writers. Students learn to view writing as a shared communication, and they see the effects that their ideas have on readers.

SELECTED READINGS

A selection of essays by professional writers, including a number of new readings, appears in each unit. The readings and questions for discussion reflect the writing emphasis for that unit. These essays serve as models for structural and content analysis, provide a link between the related skills of writing and reading, and offer additional reading experiences that will benefit students.

FINAL EDITING

Grammar, punctuation, and spelling receive thorough treatment in each unit of the text, as well as in the Appendix, where students can work on particular problems they may have. All of the major problem areas—run-ons and fragments, comma usage, subject-verb agreement, pronoun-antecedent agreement, irregular verbs—are covered in detail. Each section, as well as the Appendix, contains a number of exercises for students to work through. Ideally, students will refer to the editing sections as they proofread and edit their papers throughout the text. Grammar and punctuation study should be linked to the editing process students go through with each writing assignment.

WRITER'S JOURNAL

A new feature in the sixth edition was the "Writer's Journal." Students will keep a journal of their writing experiences throughout the semester by making regular entries reflecting on different aspects of their writing process. The journals will have students writing regularly, thinking about how they write, and providing their instructor with insights into individual writing processes.

ON-LINE ACTIVITIES

The on-line activities send students to the website writing labs of different universities. Once there they find help and suggestions on specific aspects of writing such as prewriting tips, eliminating wordiness in first draft sentences, using descriptive language, and writing introductions and conclusions for a paper. The on-line activities accompany and supplement the text's coverage of a specific writing topic, and give students a glimpse into the growing on-line assistance available to writers.

READINGS

WRITING FROM EXPERIENCE

Writing is a voyage of discovery. As a writer, you discover more about yourself, others, the world you live in, and how you think and feel about different things. Through writing, you learn what it is like to be a writer and how your writing experiences are both personal and unique but also similar to those of other writers. For example, the thoughts and feelings you express on paper may be distinctly yours, but the process by which you develop ideas and craft your wording may be similar to others.

Already a writer of some experience, you bring to this course considerable skills and knowledge from your previous writing experience. The purpose of this text is to build on those skills and knowledge and to help you progress as a developing writer. Writers continue to develop their skills as long as they write, and as you write for this course, read and analyze your own writing and that of your classmates, and work through the text, your writing skills will undoubtedly continue to develop and improve.

Some of your most valuable writing experiences are those that lead to self-discovery, helping you to understand better the different influences that have helped to shape your thoughts and feelings, and that have contributed to the person that you are today. These insights may come from reflecting on events in your life, relationships with different people, choices that you've made, or changes in your life circumstances.

Your writing for this unit focuses on personal experiences that remain vivid in your mind. You will recall these experiences for yourself, as well as for your classmates and instructor, and analyze them to understand better the impact they had or may continue to have on your life.

Sharing life experiences through your writing is interesting and valuable for both writer and readers. You learn to re-create experiences in writing to make them real and vivid for your readers, and by reflecting on such experiences, you pass on to readers what you have learned, and connect with them through common experiences.

WRITING PROCESS

From your previous writing experiences, you probably know that writing is more of a process than a one-step operation. Over the past twenty-five years, writing researchers have studied how people write to try to discover characteristics shared by effective writers. What they did discover was that most writers do some similar things in their writing practices, and that they go through different stages or steps in the writing process, commonly identified as prewriting, drafting, rewriting (or revising), and editing.

During these stages, however, writers perform a range of thinking and writing operations, often different for different writers, and the stages tend to overlap and intermix, not following a neat linear path from start to finish. The writing process, then, is not a step-by-step formula for producing good writing, but rather a framework for understanding the different thinking and writing acts that writers go through, and the general progression that they tend to follow as they write.

When we talk about the writing process, we include the following characteristics discovered by researchers, reconfirmed by writers like yourself, that bond us together:

1. Writing is not easy for anyone. All writers, novice and experienced, struggle at times with what to write about, what exactly they want to say, and how to put their thoughts into words. All writers experience "writer's block" at times, where they are stumped on how to begin or how to continue their writing.

2. Most writers don't just sit down and begin writing. They spend time deciding what to write about and what they want to say. They may start with a rough outline, jot down a list of ideas, talk to other people, or plan in their minds. Whatever writers do to help them get started is called prewriting, and most writers do some form of it.

3. Writing is a recursive process, which means going back over something. Writers constantly go back over what they have written, rereading a previous paragraph, sentence, or part of the sentence they are working on. They do this to keep a train of thought going in their writing, to reword sentences or passages that don't sound right to them, to build momentum to continue their writing, and to help them decide what to write next.

4. Writing is a process of discovery. Writers seldom know everything they are going to write before they begin. The writing act itself helps writers to find out what they want to say, and to discover new ideas and connections they hadn't thought of previously. The process of writing is a way of creating meaning that the writer may have never consciously considered. Writing is a way of discovering new meaning and understanding.

5. Rewriting is an important part of writing. Seldom can any writer word his or her thoughts in the most effective way the first time. Initially, it is a challenge just to get a thought on paper in a comprehensible manner. Thoughts are often just partially developed in the writer's mind before he or she tries to put them on paper. Getting a thought down in writing gives a writer something to work with. It is not surprising that writers may revise a sentence several times before it means what they want, a meaning they may have discovered as they revised.

6. Writers generally write drafts of their work, which culminate in a final draft. For most writers, writing is too difficult a task to accomplish successfully in one writing. Writers will often write a first draft of a paper to get their thoughts down, then in subsequent drafts, reword, reorganize, and further develop those thoughts until they have a final draft that is ready to share with readers.

7. The use of computers for writing has changed the drafting process for many writers. Since it is much easier to revise on a computer than on a handwritten draft, they may do substantial revision as they write rather than waiting until they have completed a draft. While this may result in fewer drafts, it doesn't necessarily result in less revision. In fact, some studies have shown that writers revise even more on computers because of the ease of deleting and replacing words or phrases, or moving sentences or paragraphs around.

8. Before completing their final drafts, writers usually proofread (read over carefully) their draft for errors and edit their writing to correct any errors in spelling, punctuation, or grammar. While writers sometimes correct errors as they discover them during drafting, error correction is generally the last phase of the writing process after writers have made all the content, wording, and organizational changes.

PREWRITING

In the "Prewriting" section of each unit, you lay the groundwork for writing the first draft of your paper. Thinking about what you want to write, generating some ideas for a paper, talking to others, and doing some organizational planning are common prewriting steps for many writers.

However, having an entire paper "laid out" in your mind or in an outline is not feasible. Some of the best ideas and insights that you have on a topic may come to you as you write. Writing is a process of discovery and creation where one sentence or word may trigger an idea, an example, or a perspective you'd never thought of. Papers that are too "scripted" in advance may be dull and formulaic. Any prewriting plan should be flexible enough to allow for the process of discovery and creation that is an essential part of good writing.

TOPIC SELECTION

For your writing assignment for this unit, you will choose an experience from your childhood or early teens—something that happened to you or something you did—that stands out in your mind. Take some time to think about different experiences that you can recall. The following questions may help you remember particular experiences.

What is one of the most frightening experiences that comes to mind from your childhood?

What is one of the happiest times in your life that you can remember, when life seemed particularly good?

What is something that occurred in your school life that made you feel particularly proud?

What is something that occurred in your school life that made you feel terrible?

What particular event do you recall from your youth when you made an adult very mad?

What is one of the biggest changes in your life situation that you have had to deal with when you were young (moving, divorce, loss of a friend or relative, etc.)?

What was one of the most painful (physical or emotional) experiences from your childhood?

In selecting a topic for your paper, consider the following:

1. What particular experience stands out most strongly in your mind?

2. What particular experience do you have the most vivid memory or feelings about?

3. What particular experience do you want to explore to try and analyze its impact on you?

4. What particular experience would you like to share with readers, and why?

STUDENT SAMPLE
IDEAS

There's the incident in first grade when the dad of a girl I liked died and I got in trouble for making noise at her house a few days later. The memory is pretty fuzzy though. Then there was my first "fight" when I was in second grade. It really wasn't much of a fight, just a little wrestling match, but I remember I didn't enjoy it. Not sure I'd have much to write about. I don't even remember how it started.

Then there was the problem I had with a long-time friend in eighth grade, but I'd rather go back farther in my childhood. There was the time in third grade when I buried a neighbor kid's gun in a field and we never found it again. I remember that pretty well, including how mad the kid got and how scared I was. There were other neighbor kids around to see what was going on, and I remember my mom getting involved. Then I moved to another town and, of all things, this kid moves in right behind me. I may write about the gun experience because I remember it well, I remember the kid well, and I remember how I felt about my mom helping me. The experience bothered me for some time, and I still remember it.

TOPIC SELECTION ACTIVITY 1.1

Based on the suggestions presented for topic selection, come up with two or three experiences from childhood that you may want to write about. Think of things that happened to you at home, at school, with friends, with relatives, and at different times and places in your childhood.

SMALL GROUP ACTIVITIES

Throughout the course you will be doing various activities in small groups with your classmates. The small group activities will accomplish a number of things: help you get to know your classmates better, help you discover possible topics for writing, allow you to read and react to other students' writing, allow other students to read and react to your writing, and improve your writing as you learn to analyze more closely your own writing and that of your classmates.

Working in small groups may be new to you, and initially it may feel uncomfortable talking and working with people you may not know well. You may also feel reluctant to express your thoughts or share your writing, fearing how others might react. Such concerns are certainly natural, and the more you work in small groups, the easier it will become.

Other students have the same concerns as you, and working together, you will help each other overcome them and eventually enjoy the process.

GROUP ACTIVITY 1.2

In small groups, share experiences that you recall from childhood. Go around the group and give everyone an opportunity to talk about an experience or two. Feel free to ask questions about classmates' experiences. The purpose of this activity is to try out some of your topic ideas on your classmates and to get other ideas from listening to their experiences.

When you finish, reconsider the experiences that you have been thinking about, and decide on one specific experience to write about.

PREWRITING REFLECTION

To continue your prewriting work, once you have chosen a topic for your paper, you can reflect on the experience by thinking about the following questions.

1. What actually happened? Try to visualize the experience as accurately as you can remember it: where it took place, who was involved, what occurred, what was said. Run the experience visually through your mind.

2. What did you think and how did you feel? Try to recall your thoughts and feelings at the time of the experience. What different things went through your mind as the experience unfolded? How did you feel at different times?

3. What were the results of the experience? How did it turn out for you and for others involved? How did it affect your life?

4. Why is the experience so memorable or important? What significance might it have? Did you learn anything about yourself, other people, or life in general? Did you gain or lose anything from the experience? What might you be able to pass on to readers based on this experience?

STUDENT SAMPLE RESPONSE I remember I was just in kindergarten. There was the big dirt lot with the eucalyptus trees and the old rabbit hutches near the front. It was hot—summer vacation time—and the gang had gathered at the lot. Then I remember Brian coming with this big beautiful gun and everything that happened afterwards—my burying it, trying to find it later, going home to Momma, Brian coming over, Momma digging in the lot. I can see everything.

I felt envious when I saw that gun, and I didn't like Brian much anyway. Then I felt scared when I couldn't find the gun, and when Brian yelled at me in front of the others. Then I felt ashamed when I was home with Mom, and when she was digging in the lot trying to find the gun. Then I was relieved when Mom bought Brian another gun. Then when we moved and Brian moved to the house behind us, I was shocked and unhappy, like it was meant for me to suffer for what I did.

Everything turned out all right in the end for everyone, except that the experience stayed with me and made me feel ashamed and cowardly. I wasn't so sure of myself after that, and I knew what it was like to have an enemy. I think I learned I don't like people mad at me or making me look bad, and that has stayed with me my whole life. I also think maybe I was more of a momma's boy than I thought.

REFLECTION ACTIVITY 1.3

Write your reflections on the experience you have selected by briefly answering the questions just presented. The purpose of the activity is to help you recall the experience more clearly, to think about it more deeply, and to generate some ideas for writing your first draft.

AUDIENCE AND PURPOSE

Two important considerations for all writing that you do is your audience—the people you are writing for—and your purpose—why you are writing to them. Your audience and your writing purpose will help to determine what you write about a particular topic and how you choose to write it.

For example, let's say you are a writer on the student newspaper, and the college administration has decided to discontinue the newspaper the next school year for budgeting reasons. Assuming you want the newspaper to continue, you may be moved to write two letters on the topic: one to the school administration, and the other to the students of the college. Your purpose for the letter to the administration may be to persuade them to keep the newspaper going. Your purpose for the letter to students may be to get them upset over the possible loss of their newspaper and to move them to action. Because of the two very different audiences and your different purpose for each audience, your letters would be very different although your topic would be the same.

When you are thinking about your audience and your purpose for writing on a particular topic, consider the following:

1. What does my reading audience know about the topic? Are they knowledgeable about it, or will I have to explain some things to them? (For example, if you were writing about an experience using a lug bolt wrench, you'd probably have to explain to many readers exactly what that wrench is and what it does.)

2. What is my audience's attitude towards the topic? Do they care about it one way or another, are they basically neutral, or do they know enough about it to have an opinion?

3. How should the characteristics of my audience—age, gender, education level—affect the way I write to them? (For example, you may not write the same way to young children on the dangers of smoking as you would to high school students.)

4. Why am I writing to this particular audience about this topic? What is my purpose in writing to them? (For example, your purpose in writing to a young audience about the dangers of smoking may be to keep them from ever starting, while your purpose in writing to high school students may be to get them to stop.)

5. How do I want my audience to respond? How do I want them to feel or think, or what do I want them to do after reading my paper? (For example, you may want to leave your young readers frightened about what cigarette smoking can do to their bodies.)

PREWRITING ACTIVITY 1.4

Your audience for your personal experience paper is your classmates. Apply the five points on audience and purpose to your classmates, and think about how those considerations may affect what you write about your topic.

For example, are you writing about an experience that many of your classmates may have also gone through, or are you writing about a rather unique experience? Second, think about your purpose for writing to your classmates about this particular experience. Do you mainly want them to enjoy reading about the experience, to learn something from it that you learned, to understand you better based on the experience, or to feel through reading your paper the fear, joy, pain, excitement, or embarrassment that you may have felt?

STUDENT SAMPLE IDEAS   What I'm writing about is a pretty common experience, so I think my classmates will understand it without any problem. Some of them may have had similar experiences, or felt similar things when they were young—especially the guys in class, who may relate more than the girls. I want my classmates to enjoy reading about the experience. The part where the kid moves into my new neighborhood was a huge coincidence, and might be interesting to read. They'll also learn something about me, since I'm going to be pretty honest about being scared and relying on my mom. Maybe some classmates will understand that.

GROUP ACTIVITY 1.5

Throughout the text are essays written by professional writers, such as "The Woman Warrior" by Maxine Hong Kingston. While you may notice that the professionally written essays seem more polished, you will also notice similarities between the writings of professionals, the student writings in the text, your own writings, and those of your classmates.

Read the following essay by Hong Kingston. In small groups, discuss the following audience and purpose considerations for "The Woman Warrior":

1. Although we don't know for sure, what particular audience may "The Woman Warrior" have been written for, and why?

2. What do you think Hong Kingston's purpose may have been for writing "The Woman Warrior"? What did she learn from the experience, and what is she passing on to her readers?

The Woman Warrior
by Maxine Hong Kingston

My American life has been such a disappointment.

"I got straight A's, Mama."

"Let me tell you a true story about a girl who saved her village."

I could not figure out what was my village. And it was important that I do something big and fine, or else my parents would sell me when we made our way back to China. In China there were solutions for what to do with little girls who ate up food and threw tantrums. You can't eat straight A's.

When one of my parents or the emigrant villagers said, "Feeding girls is feeding cow-birds," I would thrash on the floor and scream so hard I couldn't talk. I couldn't stop.

"What's the matter with her?"

"I don't know. Bad, I guess. You know how girls are. 'There's no profit in raising girls. Better to raise geese than girls.'"

"I would hit her if she were mine. But then there's no use wasting all that discipline on a girl. 'When you raise girls, you're raising children for strangers.'"

"Stop that crying!" my mother would yell. "I'm going to hit you if you don't stop. Bad girl! Stop!" I'm going to remember never to hit or to scold my children for crying, I thought, because then they will only cry more.

"I'm not a bad girl," I would scream. "I'm not a bad girl. I'm not a bad girl." I might as well have said, "I'm not a girl."

"When you were little, all you had to say was 'I'm not a bad girl,' and you could make yourself cry," my mother says, talking-story about my childhood.

I minded that the emigrant villagers shook their heads at my sister and me. "One girl—and another girl," they said, and made our parents ashamed to take us out together. The good part about my brothers being born was that people stopped saying, "All girls," but I learned new grievances. "Did you roll an egg on my face like that when I was born?" "Did you have a full-month party for me?" "Did you turn on all the lights?" "Did you send my picture to Grandmother?" "Why not? Because I'm a girl? Is that why not?" "Why didn't you teach me English?" "You like having me beaten up at school, don't you?"

"She is very mean, isn't she?" the emigrant villagers would say.

"Come, children. Hurry. Hurry. Who wants to go out with Great-Uncle?" On Saturday mornings my great-uncle, the ex-river pirate, did the shopping. "Get your coats, whoever's coming."

"I'm coming. I'm coming. Wait for me."

When he heard girls' voices, he turned on us and roared, "No girls!" and left my sisters and me hanging our coats back up, not looking at one another. The boys came back with candy and new toys. When they walked through Chinatown, the people must have said, "a boy—and another boy—and another boy!" At my great-uncle's funeral I secretly tested out feeling glad that he was dead—the six-foot bearish masculinity of him.

I went away to college—Berkeley in the sixties—and I studied, and I marched to change the world, but I did not turn into a boy. I would have liked to bring myself back as a boy for my parents to welcome with chickens and pigs. That was for my brother, who returned alive from Vietnam.

If I went to Vietnam, I would not come back; females desert families. It was said, "There is an outward tendency in females," which meant that I was getting straight A's for the good of my future husband's family, not my own. I did not plan ever to have a husband. I would show my mother and father and the nosy emigrant villagers that girls have no outward tendency. I stopped getting straight A's.

WRITER'S JOURNAL

During the course, you will keep a Writer's Journal where you will respond to different writing process activities that you do in the text. The purposes of the journal writing are to give you writing practice, to get you thinking more about how you write and what you write, to provide your instructor with some understanding of your writing process, to give your instructor feedback on the benefits of different writing activities and, like everything in the text, to improve your writing.

JOURNAL ENTRY ONE

Under Journal Entry One in your notebook, relate how useful the prewriting activities have been in preparing you to write the first draft of your personal experience paper. What, if any, activities have been particularly useful? How have the activities prepared you to write your first draft?

FIRST DRAFTS

Now that you have selected a topic, reflected on your experience, and considered your audience and purpose for the paper, you are ready to write the first draft. When you write the draft, you are telling a "story." Keep in mind the following *narrative*—or story-telling—elements to help make your paper most interesting.

NARRATIVE ELEMENTS

1. *Setting:* In order for readers to visualize the experience, let them see where and when it took place. Include such details in your draft wherever they will help readers picture what is happening.

2. *People:* Include in your draft the people who are important to the experience. Help readers visualize these people (or this person), and tell readers what they need to know about them to understand their importance in the experience.

3. *Story:* The most important thing is the story you have to tell your readers. Tell your story—whatever happened to you or what you did in this particular experience—in the most realistic and interesting way you can.

4. *Resolution:* Conclude your paper by leaving readers with a sense of completion: How did the situation turn out for you? For others? What, if anything, did you learn, or what do you understand better? What thoughts do you want to leave your readers with?

Before writing your first draft, read the following student draft and notice how the writer handles the elements of setting, people, story, and resolution as he relates his experience.

The Lost Gun

On Saturdays, the neighborhood gang of five and six year olds gathered at the vacant lot to play cowboys. The open space was great for range wars, and the eucalyptus trees were used for hideouts. There were even some old rabbit hutches for locking up prisoners. As we gathered with our assortment of guns and holsters, Brian swaggered in with the biggest, shiniest gun I'd ever seen. It had a ten-inch barrel and an ivory handle. It made my gun look like a peashooter. It wasn't fair that the youngest, brattiest kid in the gang had the best gun.

Before we started, I asked Brian, a fat-faced kid with a smirk on his face, to let me see the gun. He reluctantly handed it over, and I told him I wanted to borrow it for a while. Since I was the big leader of the gang, he couldn't refuse. As soon as we broke up for cowboys and Brian was out of view behind the trees, I ran to a far corner of the lot and buried the gun in the soft dirt. I wanted to give Brian a scare.

Before long, the bad guys were rounded up, and Brian was demanding his gun back. I let him squirm awhile, then laughed and said I'd hidden it. He didn't laugh and demanded I find it. We all trudged across the lot to the corner, and I dug where I thought I'd buried it. No gun. I dug some more, and then I dug deeper and faster. Still no gun. Brian started yelling, "Find my gun!" and I started getting sick. I knew it was there somewhere, but the whole corner was looking the same to me. Everyone stood around and watched as I desperately dug at the ground. No one helped. Brian finally screamed, "My dad's gonna get you, you bastard!" My eyes started burning, and I knew I was going to cry. I took off running across the lot with Brian yelling, "You bastard! My dad will get you!"

That afternoon, I lay down with my mom for a nap, but I couldn't sleep. I felt terrible about what I had done, and I was frightened about what would happen to me. I hadn't told Mom a thing, but when I heard Brian calling outside the window, I told her everything. She calmly listened to me, then went out to the garage and got the shovel. We met Brian outside and the three of us returned to the lot.

By now it was very hot outside, and my mom dug in the heat for an hour. She turned up most of the dirt in that corner, but the gun was never found. I stood and watched helplessly, and I felt worse and worse as she worked and sweated because of me.

My parents bought Brian a new gun, so he was satisfied. But I wasn't the big shot of the gang any more. Little Brian had pushed me around that day, and the gang didn't forget. I was just one of the boys. I wasn't really that brave, and I still needed Mom to bail me out of trouble. Now I realize how lucky I was to have someone who stood up for me and loved me. I guess I realize I was more of a momma's boy than I like to admit.

We moved to another town forty miles away the next year, and of all coincidences, a year later Brian moved into the house behind the alley. His moving there was a constant reminder of what had happened. That one incident with the gun kept us from ever becoming friends although we were neighbors for five years. I could never get it out of my mind that he was still the little punk that had embarrassed me in front of my buddies. And I've carried that trait since then: having trouble letting go of grudges or forgiving people. I know I've worried a lot more about Brian than he ever did about me, and that's my problem. I need to learn to let go and move on.

GROUP ACTIVITY 1.6

In small groups, analyze "The Lost Gun" by applying the four narrative elements to the story. What are the details of setting? What do we learn about other people involved in the experience? Where does the writer express his thoughts and feelings? What features stand out in the way the writer tells his story? How is the experience resolved in the end? What did the writer learn? In addition, analyze how the writer paragraphed his paper. When does he move from one paragraph to the next?

DRAFTING ACTIVITY 1.7

Write the first draft of your paper, keeping in mind the elements of narration, your reading audience—your classmates—and your purpose for writing. As a general guideline, change paragraphs as you move to something new in your experience: a different time, place, or situation. (Paragraphing will be covered in some detail during the "revision" stage of the writing process.)

REVISIONS

Now that you have written the first draft of a paper, you have taken a major step towards your final draft, but there is usually more work to be done. As you reread your paper, you will probably find things that you want to change to make it more interesting, more complete, or clearer. It often helps to set the draft aside for awhile—a few hours or a day—so you can read it more objectively.

First drafts of personal experiences often have similar revision needs. The following suggestions will help you evaluate your draft and make effective revisions.

REVISION GUIDELINES

1. Read your draft to make sure that readers can visualize where the experience took place and when it occurred. (Please see the upcoming section on "Concrete Language" in this unit.)

2. Evaluate your draft to see if you have told the experience in a way that emphasizes the most important parts. (Sometimes writers spend too

much time leading up to the experience and too little time showing readers what happened.) Also make sure that readers know what you were *thinking* or *feeling* at critical times.

3. Evaluate your conclusion to make sure your readers understand why this experience was significant enough for you to write about, and what your purpose was for writing about it.

4. Reread each sentence to make sure it says what you want in a clearly worded way.

5. Review your paragraphing to see if you have changed paragraphs as you move to different parts of the experience. (Please see the upcoming section on "Paragraphing.")

REVISION ACTIVITY 1.8

In small groups, evaluate the following draft by applying the suggestions for revision. Make note of what the writer does well, and provide suggestions for possible revisions to improve the draft. Be prepared to share your group's analysis with the class.

Next, evaluate each student's draft in your group in the same manner. Your instructor may have you make copies of your draft for each group member.

The Accident

When I was a child at home with my brother and sister, I decided to wash the clothes in the washer, but it was not a normal washer like the ones we have now. It was an old washer, one that has the two rollers, you know the one that you put the clothes in the middle of the rollers to squeeze out the water before hanging up the clothes. When I put in the clothes, my arm got caught in between the rollers.

I started crying and screaming at the same time, and my sister came out of the house and she couldn't get my arm out. She ran to get Mr. Tatai, who was the owner of the apartments in which we were living. He got my arm out after it had been in there about thirty minutes. My arm was cut wide open and there was a lot of blood. It was hurting badly.

The ambulance arrived to take me to the hospital in Orosi. My mother was not there. She was in Texas at my grandpa's funeral, so they called my dad at work, so he went to the hospital with my grandmother.

At that time I was in the surgery room. The nurse called my dad to go in with me, but the nurse did not know that my dad gets very nervous when it comes to blood. So they started cleaning and disinfecting the area. Then the doctor performed the surgery.

After two long hours, the surgery was done. I was in so much pain that I told the nurse to give me some pain medication. So after two days, I got to go home with my family, and everyone came to visit and also brought flowers and balloons, and some sympathy cards. So I gave thanks to everyone for being there with me when I most needed it.

That was the most painful experience in my life, and my mother not being there for me made it worse. The only good thing was we got rid of the old washing machine with the rollers. But to this day, I have a long scar on my arm that reminds me of what happened. It was a horrible experience.

REVISION ACTIVITY 1.9

Write the next draft of your paper, including any changes you want to make based on your group's evaluation and your own. The purpose of revision is to make your paper more interesting, more informative, more complete, and clearer.

JOURNAL ENTRY TWO

In your journal under Journal Entry Two, relate the kinds of changes you made from your first draft to your second draft. How do you feel the revisions improved the paper? How did the group evaluation activity help you in revising your draft?

PARAGRAPHING

Effective paragraphing is based on common sense. Most readers don't prefer reading extremely long paragraphs or strings of very short paragraphs. Neither helps them to get the most out of what they are reading.

Readers also can become confused by a paragraph that jumps randomly from idea to idea, or by papers that change paragraphs for no particular reason.

If you remember the following common-sense points, you will paragraph your papers in ways that will help readers get the most out of them.

1. Don't run paragraphs on too long. When you reread an overly long paragraph—one that goes on a half page or more—you will usually find a natural break where you can begin a second paragraph.

2. Don't string several short paragraphs—two or three sentences each— together. If you are writing in very short paragraphs, you can usually combine paragraphs containing related information, or sometimes you need to develop a paragraph further by adding more information.

3. Make sure the sentences in a paragraph are related. In most writing, each paragraph contains a different aspect of the paper's topic: a different point, example, time, event, or idea. When a paragraph tries to combine two or three different points, incidents, or changes in time, readers can become confused.

4. As a general rule, change paragraphs as you move to something new or different in your paper: a different point, example, incident, time, or idea.

PARAGRAPHING ACTIVITY 1.10

Read the following essay by David Good and analyze its paragraphing. When does the author change paragraphs? How do the paragraph changes help the reader? In addition, discuss what Good learned from his experience, and what his purpose might have been for writing the essay.

Science
by David R. C. Good

This morning at breakfast my ten-year-old daughter said that mockingbirds make 117different sounds. She was working in her science book, doing her last-minute homework. "One hundred seventeen?" I asked. It seemed impossible at first; then the more I thought about it, the more I listened to the chatter-boxes (I could hear them right there from the sink), the more I began to believe it was true. I've always thought they were amazing birds.

"So what else does it say about them?" I asked.

"About what?"

"About mockingbirds and how many sounds they make."

"No, Dad," she said. "While I was lying in bed this morning, I counted them." She said what she was studying was intestines, large and small, and did I know that my small ones would unravel to equal my height.

I didn't know that.

Science has always baffled me. I took Earth Science, a general science class, when I was sixteen. Earth Science was the science required for those of us who weren't going to go anywhere. Most of my friends were going to go to Berkeley or UCLA to work in plastics and electricity, so they took chemistry and physics. As for the rest of us, those in Earth Science, I guess we were going to be working in dirt. Anyway, my complete memory of Earth Science is the day I had the class under my control. It was early in the spring semester and one of those rare moments in my life. I mean I could not make a bad joke. *No duds.* Of course the teacher didn't see it that way. You see he made the mistake of laughing at first. I don't remember his name, but I do remember he was young and inexperienced enough.

Anyway, we were studying astronomy, and things had gotten so bad that he finally had to stop the class to straighten me out. He threatened me with a trip to the dean or worse, and I could sense the guy was serious. I really never meant him any harm, and I knew when to quit. So I said I would and I meant it. Then he did the inexperienced thing and tried to draw me back into the discussion by asking in a most serious tone of voice a question related to his astronomy lesson.

"Now, David," he said. "What do we call the path a satellite follows around a planet when the path swings out wider at one end than the other?" He had me there, of course. I knew it was one of those questions to which he had just given the answer, an easy one, I guessed, but of course I hadn't been paying attention. I had been laying down one-liners. I had been preoccupied, and now the whole class was waiting, large gulps of laughter wallowing deep in their throats. They knew I was faced with the choice—give the simple answer and save my hide, or give the smart-assed one and see the dean.

"I can't say for sure," I said most seriously. The teacher was eyeing me for any sign of indiscretion, ready to cut me off at the first sign of a joke, "but I do remember you said it went around, not in a circle, but in the shape of a *frog's butt*." The moment was there, then. It was that perfect one, that moment of absolute stunned silence, that moment when everybody in the room knew the right answer, and I had led them all right up to it, so close that it took that special moment to realize what I'd said. Then the laughter began, and I walked out of the room to spend the rest of that day and every fifth period for the rest of the year in the dean's office. There I got to know the dean's secretary by name and within a week I was handling special deliveries of emergency passes, passes to counselors, and passes for athletes to be released early for away games.

As for science, I was given credit (for staying away?) and allowed to pass to the next grade. Of course I was glad at the time. However, in the years since, there have been times when I've wondered what I missed out on while running summons for the dean: elliptical orbits, the length of intestines, the number of songs a mockingbird can sing.

PARAGRAPHING ACTIVITY 1.11

Following the four paragraphing suggestions, mark the beginning of each new paragraph in the following personal experience papers. Change paragraphs as the writer moves to something new within the experience, and avoid overly long paragraphs or strings of very short paragraphs.

When you finish, review the paragraphing of your latest draft, and if necessary, make changes to improve it.

Humiliation

I remember first grade was going along well. I was having fun in school. I liked my teacher, I got to play the wood block in the percussion band, and I even had a girlfriend. Then a string of events happened that ruined the year for me. My girlfriend's name was Karen, a quiet, dark-haired girl with a shy smile. After school, we'd go over to her house and sit on top of the slanted shingle roof, enjoying the sun, the view, and just being together. We'd sit there day after day, sometimes holding hands, and I was very happy. Then Karen was absent from school for a while, and the teacher, Mrs. Bray, told us Karen's father had been killed in an electrical accident. I remember being shocked by the news. I'd never heard of anyone's father being killed; it wasn't something that happened. I wondered how Karen was doing, but I was afraid to go and see her. Then one day the entire class walked together to Karen's garage to pick up some old hobbyhorses and props Karen's mother was lending our class for a play. We were all in the dusty old garage collecting the wooden stick horses and everyone was pretty quiet. Then I blurted out something loudly, I don't remember why. I liked to be the center of attention, but why I picked that time to say something stupid is beyond me. When I did, Mrs. Bray really jumped on me. "Shut up, Ben!" she hissed angrily. And I didn't open my mouth the rest of the day. Walking back to school, I felt awful. Mrs. Bray had never scolded me before, and I now had done something so terrible that she told me to shut up. On top of that, I had been acting stupid at Karen's house only a week after her father died. That made me a doubly evil person, and even though Karen hadn't been in the garage with us, I knew she'd find out. I felt miserable. I never saw Karen again. She stayed home from school for a long time, and then apparently she and her mother moved away. I walked by her house a couple of times before she moved, but I never had the courage to stop. I really never recovered that year from the incident. Things weren't right again between me and Mrs. Bray; I always felt I'd failed her. We moved that summer, and since I never saw Karen again, I assumed she thought the worst of me, and I'd never believe otherwise. Thinking back on that year, I still feel sad some fifteen years later. It's an awful feeling to do something you feel is terrible and never be able to make amends. I just wish I could have seen Karen one last time and said, "I'm sorry."

Piano Recital

I'd always enjoyed playing the piano until my first recital in the fifth grade. I didn't mind playing for my teacher, Mrs. Scott, and I didn't mind playing for my family. But playing for a roomful of strangers and piano students was more than I could handle. We all gathered in Mrs. Scott's living room. There were about twenty folding chairs in rows across the room with sofas lining the walls. All the chairs and sofas were filled with parents and other students, and it felt as though a hundred people were packed in the hot room. Since I was the fifth student on the program to play, I sat stiffly and listened to the others. I wasn't too nervous at first, but as my time came closer, I got tense. The students before me were playing like angels, and the audience applauded for each one. I knew I wasn't as good as the others, and the more I listened, the more I wanted to escape. Finally, my turn came. Mrs. Scott introduced me and told the audience I would be playing "Country Gardens," a song I'd practiced a hundred times. I put my hands to the piano, and before I knew it, they were playing "Country Gardens." I didn't feel in control, and I was moving through the song mindlessly. I started to panic. My hands kept playing but I was blanking out. Finally, I stopped playing. I couldn't play another note. I sat paralyzed at the piano having no idea what to do next. Finally, I felt Mrs. Scott's arm on my shoulder. She asked me quietly if I'd like to start the song again. I told her I didn't. She tried to encourage me by saying how beautifully I played it. The audience started applauding for me. I didn't move a finger to the keyboard. I don't know how long I sat there, but Mrs. Scott finally took me back to my seat. The next student went to the piano, and the recital continued. I sat in a daze. I don't remember much of the rest of the afternoon. There was punch, and everyone tried to console me. I just wanted to go home. I knew this was my last recital. I did take lessons a couple more weeks, and then I quit. The recital had done me in. I still remember sitting at the piano like a zombie. That was the first experience I remember choking with the pressure on, and all my life I've tried to avoid situations where the pressure was more than I could handle.

Seeing Grandpa

A week after my grandfather died, my mother told me she saw him standing in our backyard. She said he had returned to speak to her and that he would be back again. Mother believed in dead relatives returning to visit loved ones before they finally rested, and she said he might visit me too. It scared me to think about it. Three nights later I awoke and saw Grandpa standing at the foot of my bed. There was no doubt that it was Grandpa: the tall, thin body, the tousled white hair, the big, watery eyes. He stood there and stared at me with those big, sad eyes, but he never spoke. It somehow seemed natural for him to be standing there, and he was such a kind, gentle man that I wasn't the least frightened. We just looked at each other for the longest time, and then he turned slowly and walked out my bedroom door. I crawled out of bed and followed him. He walked out the back door, and by the time I peeked out the back window, he was gone. It was the last time I ever saw my grandfather. I slept with my mother the rest of the night, and the next morning I told her about

Grandpa. She wasn't at all surprised or concerned. She said he was probably contented now and wouldn't return. We talked about the incident as though it was the most natural thing in the world. No matter how absurd it sounds, it seems like the right thing for my grandfather to have come back one last time. It made me feel good, and it must have helped him. Since the incident, I have had more respect for some of my mother's beliefs that I once thought were nonsense. There are some things that happen that logic can't explain. Grandfather's return was one of them.

SENTENCE REVISION

All writers share the task of revising first-draft sentences to make them smoother, clearer, or stronger. In this section, you learn to use concrete wording to bring your sentences to life.

CONCRETE LANGUAGE

Using concrete wording simply means to choose words that *most clearly and visually describe what is happening and how things look*. For example, the difference between "The drunken white-haired woman staggered down the darkened alley," and "The drunken woman walked down the alley" shows the difference between concrete wording that creates a picture in readers' minds and more general wording that doesn't.

Here are some suggestions for using concrete language in your writing.

1. Use the most specific word to refer to a particular thing. For example, you might use *German shepherd* instead of *dog, TWA 747* instead of *airplane, six-lane freeway* instead of *road, Buddhist temple* instead of *church,* and *lemon chiffon pie* instead of *dessert*.

2. Use vivid, descriptive verbs to make your sentences lively and interesting. For example, you might write, "The boxer *lurched* towards his opponent and *crumpled* in his arms" instead of "The boxer moved towards his opponent and then fell against him."

3. Make your writing as visual as possible. Use language that helps readers see and feel what you did. For example, compare the effectiveness of the sentence, "The huge man careened down the slope, crashed into a startled skier, and knocked her head-long into a snow bank," to, "The man went fast down the slope, hit another skier, and knocked her to the ground."

Here are some examples of vaguely worded first-draft sentences followed by more concrete, descriptive versions.

VAGUE   The tree in my yard is very colorful.

IMPROVED The pear tree behind the house is covered with pink blossoms.

Vague	Liquid comes out of my dog's mouth sometimes.
Improved	Slobber dribbles down my bulldog Murphy's mouth when he gets excited.
Vague	The girl moved across the ice in a nice fashion.
Improved	The tiny girl in pigtails glided smoothly across the ice.
Vague	The weather is terrible this morning.
Improved	It's five degrees below zero and the fog is wet and thick.
Vague	Bothered by a leg problem, the football player didn't move well.
Improved	Hobbled by a swollen ankle, the halfback ran at half speed.
Vague	That young person just left with my glasses.
Improved	That tow-headed ten-year-old just stole my sunglasses.

ON-LINE ACTIVITY: DESCRIPTIVE LANGUAGE

For further suggestions on using descriptive language, go on-line to St. Cloud State University's writing website LEO (Literacy Education Online): http://leo.stcloudstate.edu/.

When you arrive, scroll down and click on the topic "I want to work on developing my writing." Next, click on "I'd like to work on sensory details," which will bring up a number of suggestions for replacing vague, boring wording with strong, vivid detail. Read the examples carefully, and apply what you learn to the upcoming exercise and to your first draft.

REVISION ACTIVITY 1.12

Revise the following vaguely worded sentences by replacing general words with more specific ones and weak verbs with more vivid ones. Then review your latest draft and replace vague language with more concrete, visual words.

| Example | We left to go downtown and take care of some business. |
| Revised | My best friend and I left school at noon to order our class rings from the downtown jewelry store. |

1. There is a funny smell coming from one part of the garage.

2. Melissa has a very strange hairdo.

3. That man is strong for his age.

4. The horses left from the starting gate and moved down the track.

5. The moon is beautiful tonight.

6. The girl waited for her date to arrive.

7. The boxer put his right glove in the other boxer's face and then did it again with the other hand.

8. After a long hike, the boy didn't feel great at all.

9. Your relative is quite small for his age.

10. The bird went up to the top of the tree and sat on a piece of it.

FINAL EDITING

Now that you have revised your paper to improve its content, organization, and wording, you are ready to give it a thorough proofreading to locate and correct any errors in punctuation, spelling, or grammar. No matter how interesting or well developed a paper may be, if it is full of distracting errors, readers will not enjoy it as much.

PROOFREADING GUIDELINES

When proofreading a draft for errors, keep in mind the following general areas.

1. *Check to make sure that each sentence ends with a period.* A common problem among writers is to run pairs of sentences together rather than separating them with a period. (See the upcoming section on "Run-on Sentences.")

2. *Check to make sure you haven't left off any word endings.* Occasionally, writers will leave off an *ed* on a past tense verb, an *s* or *es* on a plural word, or an *ly* on an adverb such as "quickly" or "longingly." A quick check of word endings may uncover some omissions.

3. *Check your spelling carefully.* Misspelled words are the most common writing errors and the most troubling for readers. If you use a computer, learn to use the spelling check on your word processor. Also make a list of words that you frequently misspell, and work on spelling those words correctly. If you struggle with spelling, your instructor may refer you to the "Spelling" section in the appendix at the back of this book. The section gives you some basic spelling rules and includes lists of frequently misspelled words.

4. *Check your "internal" punctuation: the commas and apostrophes within your sentences.* Make sure you have inserted commas where you want readers to pause in a sentence, and apostrophes (') in con-

tractions (you're, isn't) and possessive words (John's car, a week's salary). (See the section on "Comma Usage" later in the unit.)

5. *Check your use of subject pronouns (I, he, she, you, we, they).* Writers sometimes write "Me and my brother went fishing" instead of "My brother and I went fishing," or "Marie, Harriet, and me are friends" instead of "Marie, Harriet, and I are friends," or "Me and her went to the mall together" instead of "She and I went to the mall together."

Of course, this checklist doesn't cover all of the types of errors you may run across in your writing, and it doesn't provide you with the rules and practice you may need to eliminate certain error tendencies. It does provide some direction in proofreading your drafts and correcting common errors. As you work through the book, you will learn the rules and gain the practice needed to eliminate most errors and to proofread accurately.

PROOFREADING ACTIVITY 1.13

In small groups, proofread the following student draft for errors in spelling, punctuation, or grammar, and make the necessary corrections.

Bloody Mary

When I was young, I was a little of a rebel. One day some of my friends came over and we were just hanging out chillin. One of my friends said let's go out late tonight and check out the cematery while my friends were excited I was a little intimated cause I knew all those storys about the cematery. I said I don't know if I can make it. They gave me a hard time, so I said what the heck, let's go to the cematery.

We snuck out of the house around 1:00 A.M. and walked all the way to the cematery. It was me, David, Jose, Frankie, and Mike. One friend said so what did we come here for. I said we came her to see if there was really Bloody Mary roaming the cematery, like we had always been told. One of my friends was really getting scared, he wanted to go home. We all agreed to stay strong, so started roaming the cematery we all had flashlights, thank God.

All of a sudden we could sense we weren't alone. Everyone wanted to go home, but we couldn't cause we were too scared and we were in the middle of the cematery. Then we heard an owl hooting. Everywhere we go, it looks like the owl is following us. Then all of a sudden we saw somebody on the other side of the cematery. Now this is too much for us to handle, so we just stayed still where we were for about twenty minutes. We all know what we saw, it was something white roaming the cematery we drop the flashlights and started running as fast as we can like an escape from prison.

Finally we made it home nobody mentioned what we saw, and the next day nobody wanted to talk about it. When someone said something, we go pale and stay silent for a while. Is there really a Bloody Mary? I don't know for sure, but on that day, something told me maybe those stories are true. I'll end by saying I'm a believer. Maybe I'll go once more to the cematery if I'm stupid enough, which I dout.

PROOFREADING ACTIVITY 1.14

Following the guidelines just presented, proofread your latest draft and correct any errors that you find. Your instructor may have you work through the upcoming sections on run-on sentences and comma usage before you proofread your paper. Also, exchange papers with a classmate and proofread each other's drafts.

When you finish correcting your paper, write or print out the final draft to share with your classmates and instructor.

JOURNAL ENTRY THREE

Under Journal Entry Three in your notebook, relate the kinds of errors you found in your draft and the corrections you made. What are some of your error tendencies to be aware of for future writing?

SENTENCE PROBLEMS

The most common punctuation problem comes from running pairs of sentences together. Two or more sentences run together without a period or capital letter are called a *run-on sentence*. In many cases, run-on sentences confuse readers and make writing more difficult to understand. The purpose of this section is to help you recognize the most common types of run-ons, to show you how to correct them, and to help you avoid them in the future.

RUN-ON SENTENCES

Here are some common features of run-on sentences:

1. A run-on sentence is usually two sentences run together without a period ending the first sentence or a capital letter beginning the second.

   EXAMPLE   June is a very spoiled child she expects to get her way at all times.

2. A run-on sentence sometimes contains a comma between sentences. A comma by itself does not separate sentences, and it does not replace a period.

EXAMPLE   We never go into town during the week, it is too far from our farm.

3. The sentences within a run-on are usually closely related in meaning.

EXAMPLE   Maria is doing well in algebra she has gotten B's on all her tests.

4. Most run-on sentences follow certain patterns. A pronoun that replaces the subject of the first sentence often begins the second sentence within a run-on: he, it, they, she, you, we, or I. The following common "introductory" words also frequently begin the second sentence in a run-on: the, then, there, that, this, these, and those.

Here are some examples of run-on sentences in which the underlined pronoun or introductory word begins the second sentence within the run-on sentence:

EXAMPLES   Ted's parents spoil him <u>they</u> give him money to brush his teeth.

Sylvia came to class early <u>she</u> wanted to study her notes.

The tides at the beach were unpredictable and very strong, <u>they</u> made swimming dangerous.

John went for a long walk around the lake in the park <u>then</u> he took a nap before going to work.

Getting to the museum is difficult, <u>there</u> is one route that I would recommend.

5. To correct run-on sentences, you either need to separate the sentences with a period and capital letter or combine them with a joining word. As a rule, you *separate longer sentences with a period and combine shorter run-on sentences with a joining word.* Here are corrected versions of the run-on sentences.

EXAMPLES   Ted's parents spoil him <u>because</u> they give him money to brush his teeth.

Sylvia came to class early, <u>for</u> she wanted to study her notes.

John went for a long walk around the lake in the park. Then he took a nap before going to work.

Getting to the museum is difficult, <u>but</u> there is one route that I would recommend.

RUN-ON ACTIVITY 1.15

Most of the following sentences are run together. Correct the run-on sentences by putting a period after the first sentence and capitalizing the second sentence, or by combining the sentences with a joining word. *As a general rule, separate longer run-on sentences with a period, and connect the shorter sentences with joining words.* When you finish, proofread your latest draft for run-on sentences and make the necessary corrections.

EXAMPLE   The bear backed into its cave, it was frightened by the flames.

REVISED   The bear backed into its cave because it was frightened by the flames.

EXAMPLE   I have tried to ignore your annoying habit of cracking your toes in class I must now ask you to stop before I go crazy.

REVISED   I have tried to ignore your annoying habit of cracking your toes in class. I must now ask you to stop before I go crazy.

1. The downtown bus is always late, I don't expect it to arrive for another twenty minutes.

2. Bill Clinton jogs regularly you couldn't tell by looking at him.

3. Fred and Hilda have something special in common they were born in the back of the same taxi cab exactly one year apart.

4. Howard is never late for work, for he has an alarm that plays reveille.

5. The hurricane hit at midnight it brought winds of eighty miles an hour.

6. Most children seem to perform best when praised they often don't do as well when they are criticized.

7. Fishing was slow on Sunday morning, the salmon had all been caught Saturday evening in the fishing derby.

8. Only five of the fifty contestants were selected to represent the college in the academic decathlon those five will compete on national television this spring.

9. The otter disappeared under the dam, then it surfaced fifty yards downstream in the middle of some lily pads.

10. The political science students were active in the gubernatorial election in their state there were over 500 students participating in phone banks.

COMMA USAGE

The purpose of using commas in your writing is to make the meaning of each sentence clear to readers. Proper comma usage establishes the reading rhythm of a sentence by indicating to readers where to pause and by separating words or phrases whose meaning would be ambiguous if they were run together. Improper comma usage, on the other hand, can destroy sentence rhythm and confuse readers.

BASIC COMMA RULES

The following basic comma rules will serve you well for punctuating sentences effectively. A few additional rules will be covered later in the book.

1. *Commas in series:* Three or more words or groups of words in a series should be separated by commas. Words in a series are usually joined by *conjunctions,* such as *and, but,* or *or.*

   EXAMPLES   I enjoy hiking, fishing, and reading.

   Marie likes to jog in the morning, after lunch, after work, or in the early evening.

   Jorge is excited about the debate, prepared to argue his case, and determined to do well.

   Samantha works on Saturdays but relaxes on Sundays. (No comma needed because there are only *two* groups of words joined by *but*: "works on Saturdays" *but* "relaxes on Sundays.")

2. *Commas in compound sentences:* In a sentence containing two complete sentences *(independent clauses)* joined by a *conjunction*— and, but, so, or, yet, for,—a comma goes after the word before the conjunction.

   EXAMPLES   Teddy is planning on going to the curriculum meeting after school, but she may change her plans if her tooth continues to ache.

   Those bugs on the ceiling are coming in through the broken window screen, so I think we'd better buy a new one.

   The rain has flooded all of the streets around the college, and it is impossible to park anywhere near campus.

3. *Introductory groups of words:* If a sentence begins with an introductory group of words, a comma sets off the introduction. Introductory phrases and clauses often begin with a *preposition* (in, on, by, with, between, through, for example), a *subordinate conjunction* (when,

while, as, unless, although, because, if, after, before), or a word that ends in *ing* or *ed* (working, hoping, troubled, amazed).

EXAMPLES   On your way out of the auditorium, please lock the double doors in the back.

In the middle of her greatest season, Maribel broke her pitching hand.

If you have finished mowing the lawn, please give me some help with the laundry.

Because I have over 100 pages of botany to read tonight, I can't go to the concert.

Looking at her watch every few minutes, Marcela waited impatiently for her date to arrive.

Alarmed at how quickly his hair was falling out, Marvin bought a wig.

Shouting at the top of her lungs, Tanisha attracted the judge's attention.

COMMA ACTIVITY 1.16

Insert commas in the following sentences where they are needed in series, in compound sentences, and after introductory groups of words. When you finish, proofread your latest draft for correct comma usage.

EXAMPLE   In the back of the bus, we found snakes, frogs, and lizards.

1. Andretti barreled down the straightaway braked on the curve and punched the gas on entering the backstretch.

2. Stealing chickens trespassing hunting on private property and tying cats' tails together were charges brought against Akins.

3. In the back of my mind I remember having traveled this stretch of Texas before.

4. Judith wanted to go on a hayride but she was allergic to hay.

5. In spite of everything you've heard about Claudine she's really a dangerous person.

6. We can cut the firewood this afternoon after school or we can wait and cut it on Saturday morning.

7. Because you have been so faithful to the team you've earned the Most Inspirational Chess Player award.

8. It's raining too hard to pick strawberries behind the house so let's do it another time.

9. After we take the subway to Main Street let's walk up to 55th and Broadway.

10. Our plans are to meet at Maria's go to the dance in one car eat at Feducci's go back to Maria's for our cars and drive home.

11. That small mangy feisty flea-bitten cat is all mine.

12. Practicing for the piano concert on Friday Marian got blisters on her thumbs pinkies and index fingers but that didn't prevent her from playing beautifully at the concert.

JOURNAL ENTRY FOUR

Under Journal Entry Four in your notebook, evaluate the writing process you used to write your main paper for this unit. What things did you find most useful in the process? What would you want to do similarly when writing your next paper? What might you do differently?

WRITING REVIEW

At the end of each unit, you will apply what you have learned to a final writing assignment. For this unit, you will write a second personal experience paper, this one based on a more recent experience.

To write your paper, follow the steps presented, which summarize the writing process for this unit.

WRITING PROCESS

1. Select an experience-related topic from your recent past. To select a topic, consider the following:

   a. What particular experience in my recent life really stands out?

   b. What experience did I learn something from that may be of interest or value to my classmates?

   c. What recent experience have I had that may be similar to something my classmates may have gone through, and to which they can relate?

   d. What recent experience would I most like to spend some time thinking and writing about?

2. When you have selected a topic, reflect on the experience before writing by considering the following:

   a. Picture the experience in your mind and recall when and where it occurred, who was involved, and what exactly happened.

   b. Try to remember your thoughts and feelings at different times in the experience in order to share them with your readers.

   c. Reflect on the significance of the experience. What did you learn that has helped you (or may help you in the future)? How can you best express what you learned to your classmates? What do you want them to take from the paper?

STUDENT SAMPLE IDEAS   I think I'll write about an experience during my freshman year in college. Actually, I'll have to include a few experiences within my freshman year, all of which I learned a similar lesson from. I'll tie all of these experiences together so they are parts of one bigger learning experience, which they were.

The experiences that stand out include a meeting in my dormitory, the first day of swim practice, a discussion in English class, and a freshman queen competition. All had the same effect on me: humbling. It was hard realizing I wasn't as popular, smart, talented, or good looking as I thought, and it was a hard lesson. It might be good to share with classmates who have had similar experiences.

3. After you have reflected on the experience, write the first draft of your paper following these guidelines:

   a. Your classmates are your reading audience for the paper. Keep them in mind as you write, and your purpose for writing about this particular topic: why are you writing to them about this particular experience?

   b. Write without great concern for your wording or an occasional error. In a first draft, don't labor with a sentence to get the wording "just write." You'll probably change it anyway in a future draft.

   c. Keep the elements of narration in mind as you write: providing a setting, including and bringing to life the important people, telling the story with your audience in mind, and concluding with the resolution: what you learned, gained, or lost from the experience or the relationship.

   d. Change paragraphs as you move to different parts of the experience: different times, places, or incidents.

College Experience

STUDENT DRAFT I went from a high school of one hundred and fifty graduating seniors to a college of twenty thousand students my freshman year. I had been something of a big wheel in high school, and I was about to get a real shock coming out of the shelter of my small-town life.

The first defining experience I recall was a meeting of my classmates on the same dormitory floor. We got together to elect floor officers and discuss rules and regulations. I was surprised by how confident and articulate many of the girls were. I felt overmatched by their brains and good looks, so I sat in a corner and kept quiet. Needless to say, I wasn't nominated for any office, and I left the meeting a bit shaken. I sure didn't feel like the former senior class president of my high school.

A similar experience occurred in an English class. We had all read the same short story by Flannery O'Conner, but students in the class came up with insights and connections I hadn't begun to make. It was a lively and interesting discussion, but I was frightened stiff that the instructor would call on me. No one would have recognized me as a top ten student at Grimly High School.

The old swimming pool was one place I could regain my confidence, I thought. No way. Being an all-league swimmer where I came from was nothing compared to the talent on the college team. Some of these girls were the best in the state. I was put in a lane with about ten other "B" level swimmers, and that was clearly where I belonged.

A final humbling experience was something I'd always looked forward to in high school—popularity contests. A number of freshman girls were nominated for something called "Dream Court" to be a part of college homecoming activities. Posters of girls nominated by different clubs and dorms started going up around campus, and needless to say, my face wasn't among them. I wasn't nominated or, to my knowledge, even considered for nomination by anyone. I wasn't that pretty or popular.

Needless to say, my freshman year was rough. My whole life I felt I had a pretty good idea of who I was, and one semester in college changed all of that. I lost all confidence, and for a long time I went into a shell. No one got to know me because I didn't know who I was myself.

Then after feeling sorry for myself for a long time, I went in the other direction and foolishly decided to make a name for myself. I joined everything that I could, kissed up to every popular girl and boy, tried to talk and laugh louder than anyone, and tried to be the life of the party by outdrinking everyone. After a couple months of this, one of the few friends I had on campus asked me the question that needed asking: "Who are you trying to be?" That really got me thinking.

My freshman year was a mess, and I'd never want to relive it. However, it was a year I had to go through to understand a few things. No matter where I'd gone to college, there would be people who were smarter, better looking, and more talented than me. My first two reactions to that realization—first, to go into a shell, and second, to try to be something that I wasn't—were I think pretty natural reactions. I don't fault myself for either because I learned from both.

What I learned were a few basic things that have helped me rediscover myself. First, I know I'm basically a pretty good person, and that's the most important thing. Second, although I'll never be the smartest, prettiest, or most talented, I know I have what it takes to be successful as long as I work at it. Third, I know I can be myself and make friends and enjoy life. It takes time to get to know people and make friends in a new environment, and I had wanted it all to happen overnight.

As a sophomore, I am a different person than as a freshman. Actually, I'm the same person with a year's experience and understanding. I may now appear as confident and sound as articulate as the girls that I met at the first meeting a year ago. I may even intimidate some of them as I was intimidated. Thousands of freshmen surely go through experiences similar to mine, and like me, most of them will have to learn the hard way. Maybe that's why I've become a peer counselor at the college. When I talk to a freshman who is down in the dumps, I can say to her in all honesty, "Hey, I've been there. I know how you're feeling. It's going to get better."

4. When you finish your first draft, evaluate it for possible revisions by applying the following guidelines. Next, exchange drafts with a classmate and make revision suggestions. Then write the second draft of your paper, including any revisions you feel will make it better.

   a. Can readers clearly picture where and when the experience took place, and what actually happened?

   b. Have you highlighted for readers the most important parts of the experience or relationship and shared with them your thoughts and feelings as the experience or relationship unfolds?

   c. In the conclusion, have you revealed the significance of the experience to your readers and passed on what you learned?

   d. Can you improve some first-draft sentences by making them more concrete (visually descriptive), more concise, smoother, or clearer?

   e. Does your paragraphing help readers move smoothly through the experience? Do you change paragraphs as you move to different times, places, or incidents, and have you avoided extremely long or short paragraphs?

5. After you have written your second draft, proofread it carefully for errors by covering the following areas.

a. Read each sentence to make sure you have a period at the end. Check in particular for run-on sentences that need punctuating.

b. Check your word endings, and in particular the *ed* endings on all regular past tense verbs.

c. Check your spelling carefully, and use the spelling check on your word processor.

d. Check your use of commas in words in series, in compound sentences, and after introductory groups of words; and make sure you have used apostrophes in contractions (don't, it's) and possessive words (cat's tail, Ralph's notebook). If you have included dialogue, make sure you have introduced the speakers (Julia said, Mike shouted) and put quotation marks (" ") around the spoken words.

e. Check your use of subject pronouns (I, he, she, we, they, you), and make sure you haven't begun any sentences incorrectly with "Me and my mother" or "The Gomez twins and me," or "Ralph and her," or "The Williamses and them."

6. When you have proofread your paper and corrected all errors, write or print out your final draft. Share copies with classmates and your instructor.

WRITING
ABOUT
RELATIONSHIPS

During our lives, we form relationships with a wide range of people: parents, brothers, sisters, grandparents, husbands, wives, children, friends, teachers, co-workers, neighbors, classmates, and so on. The quality of our relationships with people, particularly those most prominent in our lives, greatly influences how we view ourselves, how we think and feel about different things, how we respond to other people, and our general welfare and happiness.

Writers often write about people who have influenced their lives, and the impact that they have made. The person may have been a positive influence—a loving mother, an understanding priest, a protective big brother, a caring teacher, a lifelong friend—or a negative influence—an alcoholic stepmother, an absentee father, a school bully, an incompetent boss. Sometimes our relationships with others have both positive and negative aspects, which can complicate the situation.

In Unit Two, you will write about people in your life who have made or continue to make an impact. The purpose of your writing is to think more deeply about relationships with different people, to analyze the impact of those relationships on your life, to understand your role in the relationship, and to understand better other people's attitudes and behavior towards you.

Writing about relationships also gives you practice bringing people to life for readers by using examples and situations that reveal much about the relationship and the person. It provides rich opportunities for writers to fill papers with descriptions, examples, and *anecdotes*—real life incidents—that interest and captivate readers.

PREWRITING

Prewriting includes everything that you do before writing the first draft of a paper. For your prewriting for the personal experience paper in Unit One, you considered a number of different experiences to write about, shared experiences with classmates to get feedback and ideas, reflected on your experience to remember and understand it better, and considered your purpose for writing and how your reading audience would react. By the time you began your first draft, you had done considerable preparation.

Prewriting activities differ from writer to writer, and there are a number of different activities you will use in the text. You may already have a prewriting routine that you developed in other classes or through you writing experience.

PREWRITING GUIDELINES

For any prewriting work that you do, the following guidelines should help:

1. Think seriously about what you want to write about. Topic selection is crucial to writing a paper that you will enjoy working on and will turn out well. Spend time thinking about possible topics, and select one that interests you and that other people may be interested in reading about.

2. Come up with some ideas to include in your first draft. It's a good idea to dig into your topic a bit before committing to it. You may find you don't really have much to write, or that you have lots of ideas on the subject.

   Different prewriting activities for generating ideas include the following:

   Making lists of a few main points to include helps writers get started and continue their writing.

   Brainstorming ideas—considering any thought that comes to mind on a topic—is a useful individual or group activity for coming up with main ideas as well as details and examples.

Outlining a draft to include main ideas and some supporting material provides both an organizational framework and plenty to write about.

Mapping or clustering—an informal type of outlining by diagram—helps writers to analyze their topic in ever-increasing detail.

Free writing—writing whatever comes to mind about a topic without concern for order or logic—helps writers discover what they may know about a topic, or helps them find a topic to write about.

Asking and answering questions about the topic, such as who is involved, what happened, when did it happen, where did it happen, how did it happen, and why did it happen, can help writers generate a lot of material for a draft and analyze a topic in some depth.

You will have opportunities to try out different prewriting activities as you work through the writing assignments in the text. You may find one particular activity that suits you well, different activities for different kinds of writing you do, or a mixture of activities that become your personal prewriting routine.

3. Determine your reading audience for the paper—the people you think would enjoy or benefit from reading it—and your purpose for writing—why you are writing about this topic for this particular audience. Writers write for many reasons: to entertain, inform, influence, amuse, provoke, challenge, educate, or some combination of these. During your prewriting, consider what your purpose is for writing, and keep that purpose in mind as you write your draft.

In "real life" writing, of course, topic selection and audience are dictated by your circumstances. You will write, whether it be a friendly letter, a complaint, an editorial, a memo, or an application, for a purpose: to bring a friend up to date on your life, to get money back on a defective product, to support the school bond election, to get a job interview— and for a definite audience—the friend, the manufacturing company, the voters, the hiring employer. In real life writing, people usually write when they have a clear reason for doing so and a definite audience in mind.

TOPIC SELECTION

For this unit's writing assignment, you will write about a person that you know well and about your relationship with him or her. Select a person who has made or continues to make an impact on your life, whether good, bad, or mixed. This may be a person you love, respect, dislike, fear, envy, or admire, or have a range of feelings towards. Select someone who, for better or worse, has influenced your life.

I might write about my young daughter, who is the brightest spot in my life right now. She makes me want to keep going and try to succeed and be a good mother. My own mother is a big influence. Without her I don't think I could make it being a single mother, and she has always been there. My ex is someone who has influenced my life, but in a sad and bad way. I'd never get involved with someone who did drugs and alcohol again. My continuation school counselor also played a big role. I wouldn't be here if it wasn't for her encouraging me.

GROUP ACTIVITY 2.1

In small groups, talk about some of the people that have influenced your life. Feel free to ask questions to help classmates explore their relationships with other people. The purpose of the activity is to help you decide on the person you want to write about and consider some of the things you may want to say.

When you finish, select the person you are going to write about, or keep a couple of people in mind if you aren't sure yet.

ASKING AND ANSWERING QUESTIONS

Once you have selected a person to write about, your next prewriting task is to generate some ideas that you may include in your paper. The following questions will help you explore your topic and list some of the ideas you may include in your first draft.

1. In a sentence, how would you characterize your relationship with this person?

2. What are your feelings towards this person, and why do you think you feel this way?

3. What are three or four qualities or traits that this person possesses?

4. What is at least one example or incident that would show readers each quality or trait?

5. In what way or ways has this person made an impact on your life (for example, by pushing you to work hard, by always being there for you when you need help, by criticizing everything you do, by loving you the way you are, by giving you good advice, by constantly picking on you, etc.)?

6. What are some examples or incidents that would show readers the way or ways in which the person has made an impact on your life?

STUDENT SAMPLE
RESPONSES TO
QUESTIONS

1. My dad is the greatest person I know.

2. I really love and respect him.

3/4. Hard working (works two jobs, 12 hours a day)

Caring (always wanting to know how I am doing in school and sports)

Funny (always liked playing jokes on me, like sneaking up and scaring me)

Always has time (always played ball with me, let me work on cars with him)

5/6. I'm a hard worker (go to school and have a part-time job)

My job choice (I'm taking auto mechanics courses, and will go to work for my dad.)

Love of the outdoors (enjoy camping, fishing, hiking because of my dad)

Love of family (I know I will be a good father because of him.)

PREWRITING ACTIVITY 2.2

Write answers to the six questions provided to help you think more deeply about your topic and to generate some ideas for your paper.

AUDIENCE AND PURPOSE

Two things to consider for any writing you do are the people you are writing for and your purpose for writing. For your upcoming paper, consider the following:

1. Your reading audience is your classmates. As you write about this person in your life, what do you need to keep in mind about your readers that may influence the things that you include, or the way in which you write about him or her?

2. What might your purpose be in writing about this particular person for your classmates? Is there anything they might learn? Is there anything they might understand better about you? Or do you just want them to know something about this special person and why he or she is so special?

STUDENT SAMPLE
RESPONSE

I'm writing about my dad because I'm really proud of him, and I don't mind my classmates knowing about it. I think they will see what a great dad he is, and that's what I want to show, and also how having a great dad can make your life better and make you a better person. I will also let my dad read the paper.

GROUP ACTIVITY 2.3

In small groups, read the following essay by Donna Smith-Yackel and answer these questions.

1. What readers do you think Smith-Yackel may be writing for primarily? Do you think she is writing for a very general audience or a more specific group of readers?

2. What do you think Smith-Yackel's purpose(s) may have been in writing about her mother?

3. Although Smith-Yackel doesn't speak directly about her relationship with her mother in the essay, how do you think she feels about her, and what did she learn from her?

My Mother Never Worked
by Bonnie Smith-Yackel

"Social Security Office." (The voice answering the telephone sounds very self-assured.)

"I'm calling about . . . I . . . my mother just died . . . I was told to call you and see about a . . . death-benefit check, I think they call it . . ."

"I see. Was your mother on Social Security? How old was she?"

"Yes . . . she was seventy-eight . . ."

"Do you know her number?"

"No . . . I, ah . . . don't you have a record?"

"Certainly. I'll look it up. Her name?"

"Smith. Martha Smith. Or maybe she used Martha Ruth Smith? Sometimes she used her maiden name . . . Martha Jerabek Smith."

"Yes. . . ."

Her love letters—to and from Daddy—were in an old box, tied with ribbons and stiff, rigid-with-age leather thongs: 1918 through 1920; hers written on stationery from the general store she had worked in full-time and managed, single-handed, after her graduation from high school in 1913; and his, at first, on YMCA or Soldiers and Sailors Club stationery dispensed to the fighting men of World War I. He wooed her thoroughly and persistently by mail, and though she reciprocated all his feelings for her, she dreaded marriage . . . .

"It's so hard for me to decide when to have my wedding day—that's all I've thought about these last two days. I have told you dozens of times that I won't be afraid of married life, but when it comes down to setting the date and then picturing myself a married woman with half a dozen or more kids to look after, it just makes me sick . . . . I am weeping right now—I hope that some day I can look back and say how foolish I was to dread it all."

They married in February, 1921, and began farming. Their first baby, a daughter, was born in January, 1922, when my mother was 26 years old. The second baby, a son, was born in March, 1923. They were renting farms; my father, besides working his own fields, also was a hired man for two other farmers. They had no capital initially, and had to gain it slowly, working from dawn until midnight every day. My town-bred mother learned to set hens and raise chickens, feed pigs, milk cows, plant and harvest a garden, and can every fruit and vegetable she could scrounge. She carried water nearly a quarter of a mile from the well to fill her wash boilers in order to do her laundry on a scrub board. She learned to shuck grain, feed threshers, shock and husk corn, feed corn pickers. In September, 1925, the third baby came, and in June, 1927, the fourth child—both daughters. In 1930, my parents had enough money to buy their own farm, and that March they moved all their livestock and belongings themselves, 55 miles over rutted, muddy roads.

In the summer of 1930 my mother and her two eldest children reclaimed a 40-acre field from Canadian thistles, by chopping them all out with a hoe. In the other fields, when the oats and flax began to head out, the green and blue of the crops were hidden by the bright yellow of wild mustard. My mother walked the fields day after day, pulling each mustard plant. She raised a new flock of baby chicks—500—and she spaded up, planted, hoed, and harvested a half-acre garden.

During the next spring their hogs caught cholera and died. No cash that fall.

And in the next year the drought hit. My mother and father trudged from the well to the chickens, the well to the calf pasture, the well to the barn, and from the well to the garden. The sun came out hot and bright, endlessly, day after day. The crops shriveled and died. They harvested half the corn, and ground the other half, stalks and all, and fed it to the cattle as fodder. With the price at four cents a bushel for the harvested crop, they couldn't afford to haul it into town. They burned it in the furnace for fuel that winter.

In 1934, in February, when the dust was still so thick in the Minnesota air that my parents couldn't always see from the house to the barn, their fifth child—a fourth daughter—was born. My father hunted rabbits daily, and my mother stewed them, fried them, canned them, and wished out loud that she could taste hamburger once more. In the fall the shotgun brought prairie chickens, ducks, pheasant, and grouse. My mother plucked each bird, carefully reserving the breast feathers for pillows.

In the winter she sewed night after night, endlessly, begging cast-off clothing from relatives, ripping apart coats, dresses, blouses, and trousers to remake them to fit her four daughters and son. Every morning and every evening she milked cows, fed pigs and calves, cared for chickens, picked eggs, cooked meals, washed dishes, scrubbed floors, and tended and loved her children. In the spring she planted a garden once more, dragging pails of water to nourish and sustain the vegetables for the family. In 1936 she lost a baby in her sixth month.

In 1937 her fifth daughter was born. She was 42 years old. In 1939 a second son, and in 1941 her eighth child—and third son.

But the war had come, and prosperity of a sort. The herd of cattle had grown to 30 head: she still milked morning and evening. Her garden was more than a half acre—the rains had come, and by now the Rural Electricity Administration and indoor plumbing. Still she sewed—dresses and jackets for the children, housedresses and aprons for herself, weekly patching of jeans, overalls, and denim shirts. She still made pillows, using feathers she had plucked, and quilts every year—intricate patterns as well as patchwork, stitched as well as tied—all necessary bedding for her family. Every scrap of cloth too small to be used in quilts was carefully saved and painstakingly sewed together in strips to make rugs. She still went out in the fields to help with the haying whenever there was a threat of rain.

In 1959 my mother's last child graduated from high school. A year later the cows were sold. She still raised chickens and ducks, plucked feathers, made pillows, baked her own bread, and every year made a new quilt—now for a married child or for a grandchild. And her garden, that huge, undying symbol of sustenance, was as large and cared for as in all the years before. The canning, and now freezing, continued.

In 1969, on a June afternoon, mother and father started out for town so that she could buy sugar to make rhubarb jam for a daughter who lived in Texas. The car crashed into a ditch. She was paralyzed from the waist down.

In 1970 her husband, my father, died. My mother struggled to regain some competence and dignity and order in her life. At the rehabilitation institute, where they gave her physical therapy and trained her to live usefully in a wheelchair, the therapist told me: "She did fifteen pushups today—fifteen! She's almost seventy-five years old! I've never known a woman so strong!"

From her wheelchair she canned pickles, baked bread, ironed clothes, wrote dozens of letters weekly to her friends and her "half dozen or more kids," and made three patchwork housecoats and one quilt. She made balls and balls of carpet rags—enough for five rugs. And kept all her love letters.

"I think I've found your mother's records—Martha Ruth Smith; married to Ben F. Smith?"

"Yes, that's right."

"Well, I see that she was getting a widow's pension . . . ."

"Yes, that's right."

"Well, your mother isn't entitled to our $255 death benefit."

"Not entitled! But why?"

The voice on the telephone explains patiently: "Well, you see—your mother never worked."

JOURNAL ENTRY FIVE

Under Journal Entry Five in your notebook, relate how prepared you are to write your first draft. What prewriting activities, if any, were most helpful in preparing you to write?

FIRST DRAFTS

Now that you have selected a topic and done considerable prewriting work, you are ready to write the first draft of your paper. Consider the following suggestions for writing your draft:

FIRST-DRAFT GUIDELINES

1. *Make use of your prewriting plans.* From your prewriting, you have a basic idea of what you want to write, something to help you get started and continue writing. However, feel free to add ideas that come to mind and to change other things that you aren't satisfied with. Your prewriting plan provides a general direction to follow rather than an unchangeable direction. You will probably discover new things to write as you go.

2. *Don't worry about perfect wording.* Get your ideas down using the wording that comes to you first. Don't labor endlessly over a sentence to make it "perfect." You will revise and improve your wording in the next draft.

3. *Don't worry about making some mistakes.* You can take care of a misspelled word or omitted comma when you edit your writing. Now is not the time to worry about mistakes. A first draft should flow fairly smoothly, and if you are constantly looking for errors to correct, you will spend more time than you need and not concentrate on the content of your writing, which is most important.

4. *Keep in mind that writing is a recursive process.* Writers continually go back and reread what they've written in the last sentence or paragraph to keep them on track, to help them generate new ideas, and to make sure their sentences follow logically one to the next. Often, ideas

that writers include in a draft are not in their minds when they start but come to them as they write. Much of the momentum for generating new ideas comes from going back and rereading what you've already written. All writers do it.

5. *Providing good examples is critical* for showing readers what the person you are writing about is like and your relationship with him or her. Each time you provide a quality the person possesses or something about your relationship, try to include an example.

6. *Keep in mind your audience and purpose.* Your reading audience for this paper is your classmates, and your purpose is whatever you want it to be. While you should have your readers and purpose in mind as you write your first draft, don't write every sentence with the thought, "What are my classmates going to think of this?" or "Does this sentence tie in to my purpose?" Such thoughts will slow your writing and perhaps keep you from writing what you really want. Remember, when you rewrite your draft, you can go back and make changes that you think will make your paper more interesting for readers or more true to your purpose, *which might even change as you write.*

Before writing your first draft, read the following student draft and notice how the writer uses examples to help the reader understand her situation.

Roommate

STUDENT SAMPLE DRAFT   I was really looking forward to going away to school and living in the dorms. I was lucky, or I thought I was lucky, to already know my college roommate. I didn't really know her well, she was from another town, but our parents were friends from childhood, and we had competed in volleyball against each other in high school, so I had spent some time with her. I soon discovered I didn't know her at all.

To say she was moody is not strong enough. She came to college with the idea that she would have this great social life. She showed me all the dresses she had brought for going out every weekend. When she didn't get dates and when the weekends started dragging, she would get very depressed and not want to talk at all. She would go into like a depression, and I had no idea what to do for her.

As the semester went on, and her social life wasn't great, she started getting more and more possessive of me. She wanted me to do everything with her and drop anything I was doing to spend time with her. I started making other friends in the dorms, and that bothered her. It was like I was betraying her or something. And when one of my friends visited for the weekend and I didn't include her in what we did, she screamed at me afterwards, and then pouted for days after my friend left. I couldn't believe it. I spent less and less time with her and starting hanging out with other girls.

Then things got weirder. I'd wake up at night sometime and she would be lying in bed just staring at me. I'd say "What's wrong?" and she'd just roll over and not say anything. It gave me the creeps. Other nights I'd wake up and she wasn't in the room. She'd come in the middle of the night and bang the door shut and I'd say, "Where were you?" "Just driving around," she'd mutter. I never knew where she went or what she did.

Like I said, she was moody, and after pouting and being mad at me, she'd turn around and cry and hug me and say I was her only friend. So I'd try to be nice to her, but it wouldn't take long before she started bugging me again. The friends I made didn't really like having her around because she was so unpredictable and into herself, and I quit spending much time in the room, avoiding her when I could.

It was the longest semester I'd ever had, and I was miserable a lot of the time because of my roommate. I kept thinking maybe all this was my fault because she'd lay such a guilt trip on me, like it was my fault she was miserable most of the time. I didn't know how to deal with it, and I think now that she really needed some counseling or psychological help, but all I knew was she was ruining my year.

The hardest thing I had to do was tell her I wasn't going to live with her the next semester, and even after all the signals I'd sent, she still went ballistic when I told her. She told her mom all kinds of lies about me and her mom called my mom and it was a mess. However, my mom knew the story, I'd talked to her a thousand times, and she supported me all the way.

I moved out next semester into an apartment with the girls I'd become friends with, and my life changed completely. Just coming home to our apartment every day was wonderful. Never again will I live with someone I don't know, and now I know how living with the wrong person can ruin your college experience, at least for a while. I also realize that I'm not responsible for making someone else happy. They have to figure that out for themselves. And I'm glad I finally confronted her and moved out. It was a hard thing to do, but it made me stronger.

After that semester I would see her once and a while at a party, and she was usually half drunk. We never spoke. I lost track of her after that year, and I hope that she got some help. She was in bad shape, but all I could think of was she wasn't making me miserable any more.

DRAFTING ACTIVITY 2.4

Write the first draft of your personal relationship paper. Divide your paper into paragraphs as you move to new areas: a new example, a different idea, a new quality or trait, etc.

REVISIONS

After you have written your first draft, set it aside for a while before reading it over. For whatever reason, it is much easier to see both the flaws and the strengths in a paper after you have distanced yourself from it for a while. Some sentences that looked fine to you when you first wrote them will suddenly seem rather awkward or wordy. You may find sentences or even paragraphs that seem out of place where they are located. Or you will discover a particular statement—*My uncle dresses strangely*—that is in need of a good example, or you will think of a better example than the one you used.

In each "Revision" section, you are provided a set of guidelines to help you analyze your first draft and those of your classmates. You also read and analyze a student draft in the text before working on your own draft. Next, you are given one or two "mini-lessons" in specific writing areas— "Paragraphing" and "Providing Examples" in this section—that will help you revise your draft. Finally, you look at some suggestions for improving the wording of your sentences, and apply those suggestions to your draft.

That may seem like a lot of revision activities for one paper. However, many of the things that are covered in the lessons and activities will become ingrained in your writing process, and before long you will analyze and revise your drafts effectively with little direction.

REVISION GUIDELINES

As you reread your first draft, apply the following revision suggestions.

1. *Additions:* Read your draft, looking for places where you might add an example or incident to help reveal to readers more clearly the person you are writing about or your relationship with him or her. (See upcoming section on "Providing Examples.")

2. *Improved wording:* Read each sentence to see if a change in wording would make it clearer or smoother. (See upcoming section on "Wording Problems.")

3. *Paragraphing:* Check to see if you have divided your paper into paragraphs as you move to new ideas in your paper. If you have not paragraphed your paper, read your draft and find places where you might end one paragraph and begin another: a new idea, a different point, an example, a conclusion. (See the upcoming section on "Paragraphing.")

4. *Improved organization:* Read your draft to see if any sentences or paragraphs seem out of place, and decide whether they would fit better somewhere else in the paper, with other sentences (or a paragraph) related to them.

5. *Audience and purpose:* Reread your draft with your reading audience—your classmates—and your purpose in mind. Consider making
changes that would make the paper more interesting or informative to
your classmates, and that would help you accomplish your purpose
for writing.

REVISION ACTIVITY 2.5

In small groups, read the following student draft and apply the suggestions
for revision, noting what you like about the draft, and the kinds of
changes that would make the next draft more effective. Next, provide
copies of your draft for your classmates to evaluate in the same manner,
and discuss each student's draft.

My Dad

STUDENT DRAFT I would like to write about a person who has been there for me in the bad
and the good times. I have known this person my whole life. This special
person in my life is my dad. I think I was blessed with the largest gift of
life by having such a loving and caring father.

As I was growing my, my dad was always there to help me out with
my schoolwork. Even though my dad read very little English, he did the
best he could to help me.

When I was in elementary I played the clarinet in the school band. I
remember my dad taking me to all my school concerts. I would get so
embarrassed when my clarinet squeaked, I had to stop playing for a
moment and look at my dad for a look of encouragement.

It is very hard for me to be away from my dad for a long period of
time. When I was a junior in high school, my parents and I went to
Mexico. When it came time for me to return to school after winter break,
our van didn't work. My dad sent me back to California with my uncle.

I cried and begged for him not to send me back. I didn't want to leave
without him. I was only sixteen and felt very frightened to be by myself
without his guidance. I felt like my whole life was falling apart. I was
scared and thinking the worst being that I came on an airplane.

I was in California for five weeks. I spent my seventeenth birthday
alone and felt very lonely and depressed because I had always spent my
birthday with my family.

When my family arrived from Mexico, my dad threw me a big surprise party. He bought me a small cake, and gave me two little teddy bears
hugging, symbolizing the father and daughter aspect. My dad promised
me he would never make me be without him again for a long period of
time.

My dad has been the strength in my life. I thank God every day for blessing me with a wonderful father. Without him I would not have been able to accomplish most of my short-term goals. I love my dad very much.

REVISION ACTIVITY 2.6

After considering your classmates' suggestions and your own evaluation, write the next draft of your personal relationship paper, including all changes you think will improve the paper. (Before rewriting, your instructor may have you work through the upcoming sections on "Paragraphing" and "Using Examples.")

JOURNAL ENTRY SIX

Under Journal Entry Six in your notebook, record the kinds of changes you made from your first draft to your second. How do you feel they improved your paper?

PARAGRAPHING

Among students in a class, experience with paragraphing varies greatly. You may already be quite sophisticated in your paragraphing skills, you may have some understanding of paragraphing but little experience, or you may vaguely recollect writing paragraphs in elementary or high school. Your instructor will determine how much time you need to spend on paragraphing instruction as he or she becomes more familiar with your writing.

Basic Paragraphing

Paragraphing is not an exact science. Two writers may paragraph the same paper in somewhat different ways. However, there are some general rules that apply to most paragraphing you will do.

1. *Develop one idea in a paragraph.* Generally speaking, all of the sentences in a paragraph relate to one idea. For example, if a paragraph begins with the sentence, "Training horses is hard work," the rest of the sentences in the paragraph would reveal how hard the work is. When the sentence "Although training horses is hard work, it can be quite profitable" appears, it is time to move to the next paragraph to develop the new idea.

2. *Change paragraphs when you move to something new in a paper.* A different point, a different event or time, a new step, a different example, or a different aspect of your topic usually triggers a new paragraph. For example, if you are writing about a good friend, you might devote a separate paragraph to each of his qualities or traits—good-natured, loyal, shy—and separate paragraphs to the ways he or

she has influenced your life—taught you to be loyal, helped you through some rough times.

3. *Although paragraphs vary in length, as a rule avoid writing overly long or short paragraphs.* Readers can get bogged down in paragraphs that run on too long and get little out of a paragraph of a sentence or two. Long paragraphs can usually be divided effectively, and short paragraphs can be combined with other paragraphs or lengthened through more development.

PARAGRAPHING ACTIVITY 2.7

In small groups, read the following essay "The Old Man" by Larry King, and discuss his paragraphing: what is contained in each paragraph, and why you think he changes paragraphs as he does. In addition, discuss the relationship between the writer and "The Old Man," and how you think it may have influenced King's life.

The Old Man
by Larry King

The Old Man was an old-fashioned father, one who relied on corporal punishments, biblical exhortations, and a ready temper. He was not a man who dreamed much or who understood that others might require dreams as their opium. Though he held idleness to be as useless and sinful as adventure, he had the misfortune to sire a hedonist son who dreamed of improbable conquests accomplished by some magic superior to grinding work. By the time I entered the troublesome teen-age years, we were on the way to a long, dark journey. A mutual thirst to prevail existed—some crazy stubborn infectious contagious will to avoid the slightest surrender.

The Old Man strapped, rope whipped, and caned me for smoking, drinking, lying, avoiding church, skipping school, and laying out at night. Having once been very close, we now lashed out at each other in the manner of rejected lovers on the occasion of each new disappointment. I thought The Old Man blind to the wonders and potentials of the real world; could not fathom how current events or cultural habits so vital to my contemporaries could be considered so frivolous,—or worse.

In turn, The Old Man expected me to obediently accept his own values: show more concern over the ultimate disposition of my eternal soul, eschew easy paths when walking tougher ones might somehow purify, be not so inquisitive or damn fool dreamy. That I could not (or would not) comply puzzled, frustrated, and angered him. In desperation he moved from a "wet" town to a "dry" one, in the foolish illusion that this tactic might keep his baby boy out of saloons.

On a Saturday in my fifteenth year, when I refused an order to dig a cesspool in our backyard because of larger plans downtown, I fought back: it was savage and ugly—though, as those things go, one hell of a good fight. But only losers emerged. After that we spoke in terse mumbles or angry shouts, not to communicate with civility for three years.

The Old Man paraded to a series of punishing and uninspiring jobs—night watchman, dock loader for a creamery, construction worker, chicken butcher in a steamy, stinking poultry house, while I trekked to my own part-time jobs or to school. When school was out I usually repaired to one distant oil field or another, remaining until classes began anew. Before my eighteenth birthday, I escaped by joining the army.

PARAGRAPHING ACTIVITY 2.8

Following the suggestions just presented, divide each of the following papers into paragraphs. Then reread the first (or second) draft of your paper, and make any paragraphing changes that you feel will improve the paper's effectiveness, including dividing overly long paragraphs and combining or developing very short paragraphs.

Being a Grandpa

At forty-five I didn't feel old enough to be a grandpa, but when my son and girlfriend announced that she was pregnant, I knew it was going to happen. My wife and I weren't happy about the situation, but there wasn't a lot we could do. So we did our best to accept the situation and be there when the baby came and they needed help. When I first saw the baby in the hospital, a little girl, I really didn't feel anything. I didn't get this feeling of being a grandpa or of her being a part of my life. But a couple weeks later, when I gave her her first bottle and she looked up at me, something happened. I guess they call it bonding. But whatever it was, I felt a closeness to this little baby that I hadn't expected. As the months went on, the bond got stronger. I enjoyed feeding her, walking around with her, and putting her to sleep, and I didn't even mind changing her diaper, which I hadn't done with my own kids. Pretty soon I'd make up excuses to come and visit her at my son and girlfriend's apartment. We also would baby sit for them once or twice a week, and I always looked forward to it. I was starting to like this idea of being a grandparent. Since then it has just kept getting better. Seeing her first smile and hearing her laugh, seeing her sit up, then crawl, then take her first steps, hearing her first words, and having her put her arms around my neck were all moments that I cherish. Baby and grandpa have become a real pair, and she loves being with me, probably because I let her do whatever she wants and spoil her all I can. To me that's part of being a grandpa. While I wasn't happy about my son's girlfriend getting pregnant and me becoming a grandpa, today I can say without a doubt that it was one of the greatest things to happen to me in a long time. I love that baby like my own, and fortunately I'm young enough to be able to enjoy many many years with her. There are some things about getting older that aren't so bad.

Apartment Hunting

Two weeks before school started, I started hunting for an apartment along with my future roommate. Actually, I ended up doing most of the looking because she was still working at an ice house. I went into Monroe at least five times looking for a two-bedroom apartment to rent, and I usually came home discouraged. Luckily, I found a pretty nice place to rent three days before school began. But shopping for an apartment with a limited budget is hard work. There are a lot of great apartments in Monroe, but they are all too expensive. I found a number of newer two-bedroom, two-bathroom apartments near the college with good-sized living rooms and kitchens, plenty of cupboard and closet space, and a swimming pool or Jacuzzi on the grounds. I'd ask the landlord the rental price, and it would always be somewhere from $375 to $450 a month. Since the maximum we could pay was $325 a month, the apartments were out of our range. It was depressing going through these nice apartments we couldn't afford. Then there's the problem of finding a good location. Obviously, the apartments nearer the college are the best located, but they are also the most expensive. Often when I'd find a decent-sounding apartment in the paper for $300, it would end up being halfway across town from the college or in some run-down neighborhood. The farther an apartment complex is away from the college, the less chance there is that it will have college students in it. We didn't want to end up in a complex with a bunch of older people or young married couples. I drove all over Monroe more than once tracking down a good-sounding deal, and usually the apartment ended up being beside a railroad track or a good twenty minutes from the campus. Then there's the problem of size. The larger apartments are naturally the more expensive ones. Many of the nicer apartments in our price range felt like dollhouses: tiny rooms and low ceilings. We had quite a bit of old furniture to move into an apartment, and we both slept on queen-sized beds. We needed adequate closet space for a semester's worth of clothes. We also planned on doing all of our own cooking, so we wanted a good-sized kitchen. Many of the apartments that sounded really nice turned out to be too small to consider. But as time began running out, I figured we'd probably end up taking a small apartment and stuffing everything into it that we could. Luckily, all of the effort finally paid off. After looking at at least twenty-five different apartments and rejecting all of them, I found an apartment complex that was being remodeled. It was an old complex that didn't look too hot from the outside, but inside, the remodeled apartments were like new. The apartments were good-sized and rented for $510 a month, and they were only ten minutes from the college. I put down a deposit immediately, and my search was over. What I thought would be an easy task had turned into two weeks of driving around, making phone calls, scanning newspapers, and finding a lot of places I didn't like or couldn't afford. Finding an apartment is hard work when you can't spend much money, and you need to plan on spending a lot of time looking.

USING EXAMPLES

The way in which writers often clarify their ideas and snare their readers' interest is to use examples. Examples often provide a human interest element to your writing and show readers exactly what you mean. A timely example will have readers responding, "Now I get it," or "That makes it clearer."

For example, a student may write, "My three-year-old daughter is a real character." What does that mean to readers? What does a "real character" do? Are people "real characters" in different ways? Notice how the following example personalizes and clarifies the student's statement:

My three-year-old daughter is a real character. For example, she likes to walk around with lampshades on her head. She also prefers walking backwards to forwards when there are people around to notice. She loves making strange sounds with her mouth and tongue, and she has at least twenty different grunting, chirping, cackling, and blowing sounds she makes. She also starts laughing wildly for no reason that I know of, until she has all of us laughing with her.

For another example, a student wrote, "Malcolm can intimidate people without even trying." What does that mean to readers? Maybe we think we can picture Malcolm, but we're just guessing. We need examples:

Malcolm can intimidate people without really trying. For example, when he walks into a room, all 6'5", 350 pounds of him, people tend to back up and stare. And when he talks in that loud, deep voice, he gets your attention. In addition, he has this scowl on his face a lot of the time, although it's just his normal look. Unless you get to know him, you wouldn't know Malcolm is one of the nicest people around.

Guidelines for Using Examples

The following guidelines will help you use examples effectively in your writing.

1. *Use examples to clarify general statements, statements that by themselves don't tell readers enough to get a clear picture or understanding.* For example, the following general statements need to be followed by examples:

   The swimming pool at my old high school is in terrible shape. (Describe it.)

My uncle has the weirdest sense of humor. (Give examples.)

It seems like Melinda can get away with anything. (Give an example.)

I would call Freddie a sly flirt. (Explain what you mean.)

A good back massage does wonders for me. (Describe what it does.)

2. *Use examples to help readers understand exactly what you mean:*

Vitamin C is truly a wonder drug. (Give examples of what it can do.)

The Arkansas State football program is a sleeping giant. (Explain what you mean.)

Aunt Thelma is a bridge junkie. (Give examples.)

3. *Use examples to help convince readers that you are right or correct:*

Six-cylinder engines can get better gas mileage than four-cylinder. (Convince us.)

The best time to buy stocks is during a recession. (Prove it.)

Drinking diet soda is as good for you as drinking water. (Convince us.)

This summer's heat wave is caused by global warming. (Give us evidence.)

REVISION ACTIVITY 2.9

Read the following paragraph, and insert examples in places where they would help clarify what the writer means and create interest for readers. Make up your own examples.

Uncle Rob was a scary old man to my sister and me when we were little. First, his face was sort of frightening looking. Second, he would scare us with stories about what happened to little kids who visited him. Third, he loved to hide behind doors and then jump out and say "boo" when we'd open them, make strange sounds when we were napping and then tell us the house was haunted, or jump up and down on the roof to make us think there were monsters up there. He just loved scaring us to death.

REVISION ACTIVITY 2.10

Reread your latest draft and see whether you have provided good examples to clarify general statements and make your paper most interesting. Add examples where you think they would help, or change examples if you think of a better one.

SENTENCE WORDING

Like most writers, an important part of your draft revision process is improving your sentence wording. When you first struggle to express a thought, the words seldom come out as smoothly or clearly as you may wish. Writers share the task of reworking first-draft sentences, and the result is usually a more clearly and concisely worded paper.

Wording Problems

The following wording problems are common in first-draft sentences.

1. *Wordiness:* using more words than necessary to express a thought. This often occurs in first drafts as writers get down their ideas in whatever words come to them.

FIRST DRAFT	I am late for school because of the fact that my car wouldn't start.
REVISED	I am late for school because my car wouldn't start.
FIRST DRAFT	The reason why I did well on my test was because I studied hard for it.
REVISED	I did well on my test because I studied hard.

2. *Awkward phrasing:* using words and phrases that don't tie together smoothly and logically. Awkward phrasing is again the result of writers trying out their ideas on paper for the first time.

FIRST DRAFT	Lunch could be had in the cafeteria hours between eleven and two o'clock.
REVISED	The cafeteria is open for lunch between eleven and two o'clock.
FIRST DRAFT	Although we went to the swap meet, but we didn't buy anything.
REVISED	Although we went to the swap meet, we didn't buy anything.

3. *Poor word choice:* not using the best word to express a thought. With first drafts, writers use some words that don't quite hit the mark, but for lack of a better word at the time, they move on and rethink the word during the revision process.

FIRST DRAFT	We were excited about a lot of different stuff in the intramural track meet.
REVISED	We were excited about participating in different events in the intramural track meet.
FIRST DRAFT	Jonathan had learned all his children to use a computer.
REVISED	Jonathan had taught all his children to use a computer.

ON-LINE ACTIVITY: ELIMINATING WORDINESS

If you have Internet access, there are some good suggestions for eliminating wordiness in your sentences at the on-line site for Purdue University's Resources for Writers. Go on-line to http://owl.english.purdue.edu/writers/by-topic.html.

When you arrive, click on Writing (Planning/Writing/Revising/Genres) General Writing Concerns and then scroll down to the "Effective Writing" section, where you will find the topic "Conciseness: Methods of Eliminating Wordiness." Click on that topic and read the suggestions for eliminating wordiness in your sentences. Then apply what you learn, along with the text's suggestions, to the upcoming exercise and to your first draft.

SENTENCE REVISION ACTIVITY 2.11

The following first-draft sentences need revising. The sentences have problems with wordiness, awkward phrasing, and poor word choices. Revise and rewrite each sentence to make it smoother and clearer. Then reread your latest draft and revise sentences to make them smoother and clearer, and to eliminate wordiness.

FIRST DRAFT   My goal is to lose six pounds of body weight.

REVISED   My goal is to lose six pounds.

FIRST DRAFT   On the left side of the ring my name is on it in initials.

REVISED   On the left side of the ring are my initials.

1. It was a Wednesday afternoon, and I noticed in my computer class a number of foreign students.

2. Being an only child is a very lonely moment in your life.

3. John's friends envy him due to the fact of the attention he receives, the possessions he possesses, and the privileges he is privileged to have.

4. The day was a total learning process of inestimable value to myself.

5. You will get a lot of responsibility for college.

6. The tables are round and square and setting on a carpet that is indoor and outdoor.

7. The pier has three microscopes planted on it, so you can see across the bay with those microscopes.

8. Working outdoors makes welding a difficult place to work.

9. The feasts on, before, or around Christmas day can be very fulfilling.

10. My room is a fifteen-by-twenty-foot square, and it is white in color on the walls and ceiling.

FINAL EDITING

Now that you have revised your paper for content and wording improvement, you are ready to proofread the latest draft for any remaining errors. When proofreading, pay particular attention to those areas where writers typically have problems, such as run-on sentences, misspellings, or comma omissions. Your goal is to identify and correct any errors to produce an error-free final draft for readers.

PROOFREADING GUIDELINES

As you check your paper for errors, be sure to cover the following areas.

1. *Make sure you have a period at the end of each sentence.* Look in particular for sentences that are run together without a period or that are separated by a comma instead of a period. If you have problems with run-ons, review the upcoming section on run-on sentences before proofreading.

2. *Make sure you haven't left off any word endings.* Since your paper is probably written in the past tense, check to make sure you have an *ed* ending on all regular past tense verbs. If you need some work on *ed* endings with past tense verbs or on spelling irregular verbs correctly, refer to the "Correct Usage" section in the Appendix at the back of the book, which deals with regular and irregular past tense verbs.

3. *Check each sentence carefully for misspelled words.* Check the spelling of any word that doesn't appear right to you, and check your use of homonyms such as there/their/they're, its/it's, and your/you're. Use the spelling check on your word processor.

4. *Check the internal punctuation of each sentence.* Make sure you have used commas in series of three or more words or groups of words, before conjunctions (and, so, but, or, for, yet) in a compound sentence, and after introductory groups of words. Also make sure you haven't inserted commas where they aren't needed. If you included any conversation in your paper, check your use of quotation marks. (See the section on "Quotation Marks" in this unit.)

5. *Check your use of subject pronouns.* Make sure you have used the proper subject pronouns—I, he, she, they, we, you—and haven't begun sentences with "My sister and me," "Me and my cousins," "Frances's mother and her," or "The Smiths and them." (See the section on "Subject Pronouns" in this unit.)

EDITING ACTIVITY 2.12

Following the guidelines presented, in small groups proofread the following student draft for errors and make the necessary corrections.

My Girlfriend

STUDENT SAMPLE
DRAFT

I met the most special person in my life when I was in second grade. She use to sit next to me in class, but I didn't talk to her because I was to shy and scared. We didn't talk or anything we didn't even become friends until the seventh grade when I started to hang out with her brother Charles. We were good friends back then, now he's in jail. I ended up going out with Tamyra in the seventh grade, we lasted two weeks until she left me. I ended up hating her for leaving me but I couldn't do anything about it.

Our first year in high school we started going out again. We became good friends as well. I don't know why she went out with me, that was when I started getting in trouble. I started drinking and partying with an older crowd, which was a big mistake. I didn't care about anything at the time.

Tamyra left me again because she seen the way I was. I told her lies to get her back and it worked. I lied a lot to her and she kept coming back to me. I'm not proud of that but I didn't want to lose her. I kept doing all those bad things behind her back. We stayed that way for a long time until she found out again. That's when she told me t hat I had to choose between her and my friends. I didn't know what to do at the time so I left for a few months.

When I came back six months later a lot of my friends were in jail or getting out of jail. That's when I made my decision. I had decided not to end up like my friends and chose to stay with my girlfriend. She looked out for me more then my friends did anyway.

Now I have new friends and a better life. It's been five years and I'm still with Tamyra. If she had never made me chose between her and my friends I don't think that I would be here today. I would probably be out getting into some kind of trouble.

EDITING ACTIVITY 2.13

Proofread your latest draft for errors and make necessary corrections. Your instructor may have you go over the upcoming sections on punctuation and pronoun usage before proofreading.

When you have corrected any errors, write or print out the final draft of your paper to share with classmates and your instructor.

JOURNAL ENTRY SEVEN

Under Journal Entry Seven in your notebook, record the kinds of errors, if any, you identified and corrected in your draft. What particular kinds of errors do you still need to work on eliminating in your writing?

SENTENCE PROBLEMS

This section reviews what you learned about run-on sentences in Unit One. Because run-on sentences are an ongoing problem for many writers, they will be covered at different times throughout the text.

Run-on Sentences

Here is a summary of points on run-on sentences presented in Unit One.

1. A run-on sentence is usually two sentences run together without a period. (Sholanda doesn't need to work on run-on sentence correction she never runs on sentences in her writing.)

2. Often sentences within a run-on are separated incorrectly by a comma. (Jules enjoys long walks in the morning, he usually takes his cocker spaniel with him.)

3. A pronoun (I, he, she, you, we, they, it) most frequently begins the second sentence within a run-on sentence. The following introductory words also begin the second sentence of many run-ons: there, then, the, that, this, those, these.

4. To correct run-on sentences, put a period after the first sentence or combine the sentences with a joining word, such as and, but, so, yet, because, until, before, although, unless. As a general rule, separate longer run-on sentences and combine shorter ones.

RUN-ON ACTIVITY 2.14

Most of the following sentences are run together. Correct the run-ons by separating complete sentences with periods and capital letters and by combining sentences with joining words (and, or, but, so, for, yet, because, until, when, if, as, unless, since, while, where). Use your judgment on when to separate sentences or join them. When you finish, proofread your latest draft for run-on sentences.

EXAMPLE   Freda tried out for the track team, she wanted to get in shape.

REVISED   Freda tried out for the track team because she wanted to get in shape.

EXAMPLE   I have tried to reason with Melissa about buying a new car that will put her in debt, she is determined to buy the car despite the consequences.

REVISED   I have tried to reason with Melissa about buying a new car that will put her in debt. She is determined to buy the car despite the consequences.

1. Taxes are devouring middle-class incomes people are looking for tax shelters.

2. Please take your tools home today before you do, please clean them well.

3. Tad never stopped to ask the price of cantaloupes at the fruit stand he assumed they were very expensive, he was right.

4. Allie has thirty minutes to read and answer one hundred test questions, she'll have no trouble finishing her mind works like a computer.

5. The tamales in this restaurant are terrible they have a mushy potato filling.

6. Sometimes the combination to the vault works perfectly, it clicks open without a problem other times it doesn't work at all we have to call a locksmith.

7. I'd like to put down a large payment on the braces I'll be getting in October I have the money now I might not have it two years from now when the braces come off.

8. The doctor was weary after doing eight hours of open-heart surgery although he was scheduled to continue on the night shift, he was relieved by his supervisor.

9. Mira has the skill to be a great pianist many people question her dedication, she only practices an hour a day she should be practicing at least five.

10. Fred is always in trouble with his probation officer he continually forgets to check in, Sheila has no problems with hers.

11. Harvey is doing well in plant science although he originally intended to major in business, he may change his major to ag-business, his father, a prune farmer, will be pleased.

12. The old high school gang broke up after graduation, some of them went away to different colleges others stayed home and went to the local community college others enlisted in the service or went to work at the garment factory.

PUNCTUATION

Because you may have included some dialogue (conversation) in your personal relationship paper, check the proper use of quotation marks in this section.

Quotation Marks

In any paper you write, you may on occasion want to include the actual words that someone said to add interest to your paper. Another time, you may want to quote an expert on a subject to provide support for a position you've taken. To show that a person is talking in your paper, you need to do two things:

1. Put *quotation marks* (" ") around the spoken words.

2. Make reference to the person speaking.

Here are some examples of direct quotations correctly punctuated.

EXAMPLES   John said, "Where are you going with my hammer?"

"I don't want to go shopping in these curlers," said Harriet. Alvin interrupted Mary by saying, "Stop telling those flattering lies about me."

My mother said, "You have always had a bad temper. Remember the time you threw your brother out the window?"

"I want you to go," Mike insisted. "We need you to liven up the party."

"Alice's biggest weakness," her sister admitted, "is that she can't say 'no.'"

Here are the basic rules for punctuating direct quotations, as demonstrated in the example sentences, and a word about indirect quotations.

1. Quotation marks go around only the spoken words: John said, "Where are you going?"

2. Quotation marks always go *outside* of end marks: Maria replied, "I am going home."

3. The reference to the speaker may come at the beginning, in the middle, or at the end of a quote. A comma always separates the reference to the speaker from the quote itself: "I don't believe," said Mark, "that we have met."

4. If a quote contains two or more sentences together, the quotation marks are placed in front of the first sentence and after the last sentence only: Juan said, "I am very tired. I am also hungry and thirsty."

5. A comma comes after the last word in a quote only if the sentence continues after the quote. Otherwise, an end mark is used: "You are a good friend," said Julia.

6. If the reference to the speaker is in the middle of a quote, the quoted words on both sides of the reference are in quotation marks. (See rule 3.)

7. When you change speakers in a paper, you usually begin a new paragraph.

8. Direct quotations are the exact words of the speaker. An *indirect quotation* tells what the speaker said *as told by the writer:* Jack said that he needs a second job. Mary told me that she was tired of school. Indirect quotations are *not put in quotation marks* because they are not the words of a speaker.

QUOTATION ACTIVITY 2.15

Most of the following sentences are direct quotations that need punctuating with quotation marks. Punctuate the quotations correctly following the rules just given. If a sentence is an indirect quotation, don't put it in quotes. When you finish, check your latest draft for correct usage of quotation marks.

EXAMPLE   If you don't stop biting your nails, you'll draw blood said Claire.

REVISED   "If you don't stop biting your nails, you'll draw blood," said Claire.

1. Hank said Please bring me a glass of Alka-Seltzer.

2. The trouble with school said Muriel is the classes.

3. I know what I'm going to do after my last final whispered Allyson.

4. Freda admitted I have very oily hair. I have to wash it twice a day.

5. That's a beautiful ring exclaimed Bob Where did you buy it?

6. No one said Millie is leaving this house. We have a mess to clean up!

7. Charlotte said that her nephew from Miami would arrive by bus.

8. Teddy said My niece will be on the same bus as your nephew.

9. Maria said that you would help me with my algebra.

10. Will you please help me with my lab report for botany? asked Freddie.

CORRECT USAGE

Each "Correct Usage" section presents some basic rules of grammar to help you eliminate problems you may have in a paper. Since your paper for this unit involves other people, this section covers the proper use of subject pronouns in your writing.

Subject Pronouns

The following basic rules will help you use subject pronouns correctly in your writing.

1. Subject pronouns are always the same: I, he, she, we, you, it, they.

2. The following pronouns are *not* used as subjects: me, him, her, us, them, myself, herself, himself, ourselves, yourself, themselves.

3. The most common subject pronoun errors involve compound subjects.

    INCORRECT   John and <u>me</u> went skating. Mary and <u>him</u> are a couple. The Ludlow family and <u>them</u> met for brunch. Felix, Katerina, and <u>her</u> look great together.

4. A good technique for selecting the correct pronoun form with compound subjects is to consider the pronoun by itself. For example, in the sentence "John and me went skating," would you say, "Me went skating"? In the sentence "The Ludlow family and them met for brunch," would you say, "Them met for brunch"? The incorrect forms stand out badly by themselves, and the correct forms—*I* and *they*—sound correct.

EXAMPLES   INCORRECT   Jonathan, Syd, and <u>me</u> like tuna sandwiches.

CORRECT   Jonathan, Syd, and <u>I</u> like tuna sandwiches.

INCORRECT   Samantha and <u>him</u> are excellent mechanics.

CORRECT   Samantha and <u>he</u> are excellent mechanics.

INCORRECT   Fran's mother and <u>her</u> don't want to go shopping in the rain.

CORRECT   Fran's mother and <u>she</u> don't want to go shopping in the rain.

INCORRECT   Alice, Alex, and <u>them</u> did well on the fitness test.

CORRECT   Alice, Alex, and <u>they</u> did well on the fitness test.

SUBJECT PRONOUN ACTIVITY 2.16

Underline the correct subject pronoun in each of the following sentences. Then proofread your latest draft for correct usage of subject pronouns.

EXAMPLES   Sue and (<u>I</u>, me) belong to the same business sorority.

I don't think that you and (<u>she</u>, her) really hate each other.

1. The Smiths, the Gonzaleses, and (we, us) will meet at the bottom of the mountain.

2. Shirley, (he, him), and (I, me) are studying together tonight.

3. Fred and (they, them) quit their jobs on the same day.

4. Do you think that Gladys, Thelma, and (she, her) are triplets?

5. I'm tired of wandering around the museum, but Gwen and (they, them) certainly aren't.

6. Are you and (they, them) still obligated to attend the supermarket opening?

7. Matty and (I, me) don't have anything in common.

8. Phil, my brothers, and (I, me) went ice skating at Mill Pond.

9. (We, Us) and (they, them) are archrivals in bocce ball.

10. (She, Her) and (he, him) don't see eye to eye on anything.

JOURNAL ENTRY EIGHT

Under Journal Entry Eight, relate how useful the grammar usage activities are for you. Can you apply the things you learn to your writing? Are you learning things that you didn't know or had forgotten, or are you just reviewing what you already knew?

WRITING REVIEW

At the end of each unit you apply what you have learned to a final writing assignment. For this unit, you will write a second personal relationship paper about a person who made a different impact on your life than the first person you wrote about.

WRITING PROCESS

To write your paper, follow the steps presented, which summarize the writing process for this unit.

1. Write about a person that has made a very different impact on your life than the first person you wrote about. Write about someone you know well and your relationship with him or her.

2. Once you have selected a person to write about, your next prewriting task is to generate some ideas that you may include in your paper. Answer the following questions to help you explore your topic and list some of the ideas you may include in your first draft.

   a. In a sentence, how would you characterize your relationship with this person?

   b. What are your feelings towards this person, and why do you think you feel this way?

   c. What are three or four qualities or traits that this person possesses?

   d. What is at least one example or incident that would show readers each quality or trait?

   e. In what way or ways has this person made an impact on your life (for example, by pushing you to work hard, by always being there for you when you need help, by criticizing everything you do, by loving you the way you are, by giving you good advice, by constantly picking on you, etc.)?

   f. What are some examples or incidents that would show readers the way or ways in which the person has made an impact on your life?

   g. What do I want to keep in mind about my readers (classmates) as I think about my topic, and what might be my purpose in writing to them about this particular person?

3. When you finish your prewriting work, write the first draft of your paper following these guidelines:

   a. *Make use of your prewriting plans.* From your prewriting, you have a basic idea of what you want to write, something to help you get started and continue writing. However, feel free to add ideas that come to mind and to change other things that you aren't satisfied with. Your prewriting plan provides a general direction to follow rather than an unchangeable direction. You will probably discover new things to write as you go.

   b. *Don't worry about perfect wording.* Get your ideas down using the wording that comes to you first. Don't labor endlessly over a sentence to make it "perfect." You will revise and improve your wording in the next draft.

c. *Don't worry about making some mistakes.* You can take care of a misspelled word or omitted comma when you edit your writing. Now is not the time to worry about mistakes. A first draft should flow fairly smoothly, and if you are constantly looking for errors to correct, you will spend more time than you need and not concentrate on the content of your writing, which is most important.

d. *Keep in mind that writing is a recursive process.* Writers continually go back and reread what they've written in the last sentence or paragraph to keep them on track, to help them generate new ideas, and to make sure their sentences follow logically one to the next. Often, ideas that writers include in a draft are not in their minds when they start but come to them as they write. Much of the momentum for generating new ideas comes from going back and rereading what you've already written. All writers do it.

e. *Providing good examples is critical for showing readers what the person you are writing about is like and your relationship with him or her.* Each time you provide a quality the person possesses or something about your relationship, try to include an example.

f. *Keep in mind your audience and purpose.* Your reading audience for this paper is your classmates, and your purpose is whatever you want it to be. While you should have your readers and purpose in mind as you write your first draft, don't write every sentence with the thought, "What are my classmates going to think of this?" or "Does this sentence tie in to my purpose?" Such thoughts will slow your writing and perhaps keep you from writing what you really want. Remember, when you rewrite your draft, you can go back and make changes that you think will make your paper more interesting for readers or more true to your purpose, *which might even change as you write.*

Uncle Prine

STUDENT SAMPLE DRAFT My family didn't visit Uncle Prine and his wife that often, but when we did it was always memorable. My brother and I were young when we visited them, between the years of six and twelve, when we still could be scared by adults. Uncle Prine was an expert at scaring children.

He must have been in his sixties, although he looked even older. He had a red face, big ears, a big nose with veins in it, a sly grin, and eyes that I can only describe as crazy looking: very blue but kind of wild looking like a crazy person. I remember he used to sit out on their old front porch in a rocking chair, and any time my brother and I went outside, we had to go past Uncle Prine.

He'd always call us over, that crazy look in his eyes, and I knew he was going to say something scary. I remember one time he said, "You kids watch out playing out back. There are snakes back there that crawl out from under the house and bite little kids. They'll get you!" We'd get all scared and stand very still and after a while, he'd let out this cackling laugh and say "Gotcha!" and just keep laughing. I guess we knew then that he was teasing, but he never said so, so we always played out back with an eye out for those snakes.

Another time my family had gone somewhere and come back to the house. I ran up to the house fast because I had to go to the bathroom. When I ran across the front porch, Uncle Prine said, "Where ya going sissy so fast?" "Gotta go to the bathroom," I said. "Wouldn't do that," said Uncle Prine. "There's a lion in the bathroom, he's been in there all morning, and he'll eat you up." Being young, I didn't think about how impossible that was, that a lion would somehow be in Uncle Prine's bathroom, but it scared me so bad that I just stood there and wet my pants. I started crying and Uncle Prine let out a hoot. My mother scolded him for scaring me like that, but Uncle Prine just sat there with that sly grin and those crazy eyes.

One day mom told us that Uncle Prine had passed away from cancer and we were going to see Aunt Sarah. We went, and it seemed strange not seeing Uncle Prine sitting in that chair on the porch waiting for us. I missed him in a way because as a kid, getting a good scare wasn't the worst thing in the world, and that was his way I guess of paying attention to us. Years later I still remember him very well because he gave me some of the best scares of my childhood, and what I also remember is how much he seemed to enjoy it and how he would laugh and laugh. I guess he was just like a big kid himself.

4. When you finish your first draft, set it aside for awhile, and then reread it, applying the following revision suggestions.

   a. *Additions:* Read your draft, looking for places where you might add an example or incident to help reveal to readers more clearly the person you are writing about or your relationship with him or her.

   b. *Improved wording:* Read each sentence to see if a change in wording would make it clearer or smoother.

   c. *Paragraphing:* Check to see if you have divided your paper into paragraphs as you move to new ideas in your paper. If you have not paragraphed your paper, read your draft and find places where you might end one paragraph and begin another: a new idea, a different point, an example, a conclusion.

   d. *Improved organization:* Read your draft to see if any sentences or paragraphs seem out of place, and decide whether they would fit better somewhere else in the paper, with other sentences (or a paragraph) related to them.

   e. *Audience and purpose:* Reread your draft with your reading audience—your classmates—and your purpose in mind. Consider making changes that would make the paper more interesting or informative to your classmates, and that would help you accomplish your purpose for writing.

5. Write the second draft of your paper, including all revisions that you feel will improve it.

6. When you've finished your latest draft, proofread it carefully for errors, applying the following guidelines for error correction, and make the necessary corrections.

   a. *Make sure you have a period at the end of each sentence.* Look in particular for sentences that are run together without a period or that are separated by a comma instead of a period. If you have problems with run-ons, review the upcoming section on run-on sentences before proofreading.

   b. *Make sure you haven't left off any word endings.* Since your paper is probably written in the past tense, check to make sure you have an *ed* ending on all regular past tense verbs. If you need some work on *ed* endings with past tense verbs or on spelling irregular verbs correctly, refer to the "Correct Usage" section in the Appendix at the back of the book, which deals with regular and irregular past tense verbs.

   c. *Check each sentence carefully for misspelled words.* Check the spelling of any word that doesn't appear right to you, and check your use of homonyms such as there/their/they're, its/it's, and your/you're. Use the spelling check on your word processor.

   d. *Check the internal punctuation of each sentence.* Make sure you have used commas in series of three or more words or groups of words, before conjunctions (and, so, but, or, for, yet) in a compound sentence, and after introductory groups of words. Also make sure you haven't inserted commas where they aren't needed. If you included any conversation in your paper, check your use of quotation marks. (See the section on "Quotation Marks" in this unit.)

e. *Check your use of subject pronouns.* Make sure you have used the proper subject pronouns—I, he, she, they, we, you—and haven't begun sentences with "My sister and me," "Me and my cousins," "Franny's mother and her," or "The Smiths and them." (See the section on "Subject Pronouns" in this unit.)

7. After you have corrected any errors, write the final error-free draft of your paper to share with your classmates and instructor.

WRITING
ABOUT
OPINIONS

Every day we make decisions and judgments based on our *opinions*: our beliefs about what is right or best, based on our experience and knowledge. Our opinions help us decide where to eat lunch, what to watch on television, what clothes to buy, what to do on a free night, whom to vote for, what jobs to apply for, and whom we choose to spend time with. Our opinions affect most of what we do and say.

Writing about opinions gives you the opportunity to accomplish a number of things: to consider seriously a particular opinion you hold; to provide support for an opinion to convince readers of its merit; to use effective examples to help provide that support; to employ opening, middle, and concluding paragraphs to introduce, support, and reinforce the opinion, to include a *thesis statement*, which expresses your opinion on a particular topic, and to organize your paper in a way that you will find useful for future writing.

For readers, the value of your opinion is often as great as the support you provide, and a well supported opinion can influence people. One objective of this unit is to help you learn to provide strong, believable support for your opinions. Other objectives are for you to understand the value of differing opinions, to respect opinions different from your own, and to evaluate and even reconsider your opinions when exposed to different viewpoints.

PREWRITING

For most writers, prewriting usually includes deciding on a topic and what to do with it. Prewriting often includes generating ideas for a paper and organizing them in some manner. Through prewriting thought and planning, writers often answer the following questions.

1. What am I going to write about?

2. What approach do I want to take?

3. What may I want to include in my writing?

4. How might I best organize my ideas?

5. Who should read my writing, and why am I writing for them (purpose).

While most writers consider these types of questions during prewriting, they don't all follow the same process. Some may deal with questions in tandem (such as deciding on the topic and approach together), others may give some questions much thought (such as topic selection) and other questions little or none (such as organization), and still others may not find answers to all questions during prewriting (waiting, for example, to discover the best writing approach during drafting). You create your prewriting process by discovering what works best for you, which may differ depending on your writing task.

Your prewriting activities for this unit include selecting a topic, generating a thesis statement based on your opinion about the topic, listing ideas to include in your paper, and considering how to organize your ideas most effectively. Rather than providing you with a rigid formula, the prewriting activities give you strategies to try as you continue to develop your prewriting process.

THESIS STATEMENT

The term *thesis statement* may sound more formal or imposing than it is. If someone asks you the point of your paper or your written opinion on a particular topic, he or she is asking for your thesis. *Thesis* is a basic writing concept that provides direction for all writers, whether writing a letter ("Just writing to let you know how finals went") or a lengthy research paper ("Based on extensive research, I have concluded that the hole in the ozone layer over the North Pole does not pose an environmental threat"). With much of the writing you do during college and beyond, you will need to have a clear writing focus for both you and your readers, which the thesis provides. To that end, it is useful to generate a tentative thesis statement early in the writing process.

The following points clarify what a thesis is and what it does.

1. A thesis expresses *the main idea* you want to develop on your topic. It often expresses your *opinion* on the topic.

2. Your thesis determines the way in which you develop a topic in a paper. You write your paper *in support* of your thesis.

3. Without a thesis, a paper may lack direction. A thesis provides a *controlling idea* to tie your thoughts together and to help readers understand your intent.

4. There is no right or wrong thesis; it reflects the way you think or feel about a particular topic. A paper's effectiveness rests strongly on how well you *support* your thesis.

Here are examples of thesis statements students have generated to express their opinion on a variety of topics. Notice that for the same topic, writers have come up with different thesis statements, which would lead to very different papers.

TOPIC	water beds
THESIS	Water beds are a health hazard to millions of users.
THESIS	Within ten years, water beds will make mattresses obsolete.
THESIS	To be kind to your back, buy a water bed.
TOPIC	daylight saving time
THESIS	I'd like to live on daylight saving time all year around.
THESIS	For a nocturnal person, daylight saving is a disaster.
THESIS	Daylight saving has both advantages and disadvantages.
TOPIC	gun control
THESIS	Gun control laws are a threat to every law-abiding American.
THESIS	Gun control is the only way to reduce violent crime in America.
THESIS	The only effective gun control is the elimination of handguns.
TOPIC	*Friends* TV series
THESIS	*Friends* is the best situation comedy of the '90s.
THESIS	The cast of *Friends* is a concoction of self-absorbed, juvenile-acting thirty-year-olds who need to get a life.
THESIS	*Friends* has been a great launching pad for the "big screen" career of many of its talented stars.

THESIS CONSIDERATION

Deciding on a thesis for your topic is an important part of the writing process. Not only does the thesis help you develop your paper, it reveals to readers how you think or feel about a topic. Whatever time you may spend deciding on a thesis is well spent.

When thinking about a thesis for a specific topic, consider the following:

1. *What is my opinion on the topic?* Don't worry about how other people may feel, or what you think readers might want to hear. Your thesis reflects your own belief.

2. *How could I best support my thesis in a paper?* No matter how strongly you feel about a topic, the effectiveness of your paper depends on how convincingly you can support your thesis. For example, although you may believe strongly that there are forms of life on other planets, you may find that it is difficult to support that opinion in a convincing way (or you may not).

THESIS ACTIVITY 3.1

Considering the questions just presented, write thesis statements that express your opinion on any five of the following topics. (Fill in each blank with your specific choice of topics.)

EXAMPLE

TOPIC   a particular hobby (writing songs)

THESIS   It takes little talent to write lyrics for country songs.

1. TOPIC   a particular town (_____)

   THESIS   _____

2. TOPIC   a particular team (_____)

   THESIS   _____

3. TOPIC   a particular TV program (_____)

   THESIS   _____

4. TOPIC   a particular job (_____)

   THESIS   _____

5. TOPIC   a particular holiday (_____)

   THESIS   _____

6. TOPIC   a particular school (_____)

   THESIS   _____

7. **Topic**   a particular type of music (_____)

   Thesis   _____

8. **Topic**   a particular pet (_____)

   Thesis   _____

9. **Topic**   a particular restaurant (_____)

   Thesis   _____

10. **Topic**   a particular book or movie (_____)

    Thesis   _____

TOPIC SELECTION

For your writing assignment for this unit, select a topic following these guidelines.

1. Choose a specific topic that interests you and that you have an opinion on. You may select a topic from the previous activity, or another of your choice.

2. Choose a topic that you are knowledgeable about.

3. Choose a topic that might interest your classmates, the reading audience for your paper.

TOPIC SELECTION ACTIVITY 3.2

In small groups, share with classmates different topic ideas and your opinion on each. Discuss differing opinions on the same topics, and analyze where these opinions come from: why people feel or believe the way they do. The purpose of the group activity is to help you decide on a topic, and to discuss and understand better differing opinions that people hold.

TOPIC SELECTION ACTIVITY 3.3

After you have finished the group activity, decide on a topic for your upcoming paper and the opinion that you want to support. After you have selected a topic, write a tentative thesis statement for your paper: a sentence expressing your opinion on the topic.

Student Sample   Since I returned to college after many years, I was interested in what college would be like twenty years later. I think I'd like to write about what college is like from my perspective as an older returning student. It might interest my classmates to view college through my eyes, whether they are my age or younger, and compare it with their own experience.

TOPIC   Returning to college as an older student.

OPINION   A lot of things have changed.

THESIS   In the twenty years since I last attended college, a lot of
STATEMENT   changes have occurred.

LISTING IDEAS

Now that you have selected a topic, formed your opinion, and written a
tentative thesis statement, you can consider the kinds of support you
might include in your paper. One way that writers generate support for a
thesis is to make a list of supporting ideas.

Listing your supporting points is beneficial in different ways:

1. You have a number of points to develop in your draft, which will help
   you get started and continue writing.

2. From your list, you can decide on an organization of your paper: the
   best order for presenting your supporting points in the draft.

3. After listing your supporting points, you can consider how you might
   develop each point in a paragraph, or you can come up with specific
   examples to use.

STUDENT SAMPLE   The returning student who wrote about what college is like listed the following points to support her thesis:

THESIS   In the twenty years since I last attended college, a lot of changes
            have occurred.

SUPPORTING POINTS

1. A more ethnically diverse group of students

2. A wider age range of students

3. Much better cafeteria food

4. The big impact of computers

5. My change in attitude

After listing these supporting points, she put them in the order she wanted
to present them in the paper, and she added some examples after each
point to include in her the first draft.

Supporting points in writing order, followed by examples:

1. A wider age range of students (students my age and older, students in
   their twenties and thirties, many married and working)

2. A more ethnically diverse group of students (more foreign students, especially from Asia and the Middle East, and more American-born African-American and Hispanic students)

3. The big impact of computers (all library files computerized, computers in composition and business classrooms, open computer labs around campus, Internet access)

4. Much better cafeteria food (more like a food court today, with all kinds of ethnic foods and franchised restaurants)

5. My change in attitude (more serious and motivated, more career direction than when I was young)

As you can see, by making a list of points, you generate ideas to support your opinion, you have some ideas to develop in individual paragraphs, you have an organizational plan for your paper, and you have some examples for developing each supporting point. A simple prewriting technique like listing can pay great dividends.

LISTING ACTIVITY 3.4

For your writing topic, do the following prewriting work.

1. Make a list of four or five points to support your opinion (thesis support).

2. Decide on the best order to present your supporting points in the paper, considering their similarity and relative importance (you might save the most important point for last, or lead and conclude with the most important points).

3. After each point, list some examples you might include in your draft.

AUDIENCE AND PURPOSE

Once again, your audience for your opinion paper is your classmates. When considering your reading audience, and your purpose for writing to them, keep these questions in mind:

1. How much do my classmates know about my topic? Can I write about it as if they have similar knowledge, or do I need to make sure and clarify some things that may be new to them?

2. What might my classmates' opinion be on my topic? Might some students feel very differently than I do? Might there be a range of different opinions on the topic? How might I take into consideration my classmates' opinions as I am presenting and supporting my own?

3. What is my purpose in sharing my opinion with my classmates? What do I want them to get out of the paper? Do I hope that they will learn something they may not know? Do I want to try and convince them of the merit of my opinion? Or do I want them to get to know me better by understanding my opinion on this topic?

STUDENT SAMPLE
RESPONSE

1. Since many of my classmates are younger than I am, they probably won't know what school was like twenty years ago, so I'll have to make sure and show the differences clearly.

2. Since many of my classmates are younger than I am, they probably don't have an opinion on this topic, or at least I'll assume that as I write.

3. I'm not really trying to convince anyone of anything, so I guess my purpose is to inform and to show students how much college has changed in some ways, but as I think about it, I think I will try to convince them in the ending that it has changed for the better. *In fact, I might change my thesis sentence to include that thought.*

AUDIENCE ACTIVITY 3.5

Discuss with a classmate your topic and opinion, and provide answers to the questions under "Audience and Purpose." Get feedback from your classmate, who is a representative of the reading audience for your paper.

JOURNAL ENTRY NINE

Under Journal Entry Nine in your notebook, relate how the prewriting activities for your opinion paper have helped you prepare to write. What particular activities, if any, did you find most useful?

FIRST DRAFTS

After selecting a topic, forming an opinion, generating a thesis sentence for your paper, listing and ordering supporting points, and adding examples under each point, you are ready to write your first draft. To write a paper in support of a thesis, consider the following suggestions.

THESIS-DIRECTED DRAFT

1. Write your draft in three parts: a beginning, a middle, and ending.

BEGINNING   In an introductory paragraph or two, introduce your topic, create some interest for readers (so they will want to continue reading), and include your thesis sentence expressing your opinion on the topic.

MIDDLE	Present the supporting points for your thesis, which tell *why* you believe as you do. As a general rule, present and develop each supporting point in a separate paragraph, using examples from your prewriting to help develop each paragraph.
ENDING	In a paragraph or two, conclude your paper by leaving readers with a sense of completion. You might reinforce your thesis in some manner, summarize your supporting points, or emphasize a particularly important point. Make sure through your ending that readers understand your purpose for writing.

2. As you write your draft, feel free to add ideas you didn't think of during prewriting, or to revise your organizational plan. Drafting is a process of discovery, and your prewriting work, while important, provides a general road map rather than a precise route to follow.

3. Keep your thesis in mind as you write. Everything in your draft should be related in some way to supporting your opinion expressed in the thesis sentence.

4. Keep your audience (classmates) and purpose in mind as you write: what do you want them to get out of the paper?

5. As with all first drafts, your goal is to get your ideas on paper, so don't be concerned about getting the wording perfect or writing an error-free draft.

ON-LINE ACTIVITY: PREWRITING TIPS

For further prewriting tips to help you get started with your writing, go to Purdue University's Resources for Writers on-line address **http://owl. english.purdue.edu/writers/by-topic.html.**

When you reach the website, click on Writing (Planning/Writing/ Revising/Genres) and scroll down to "Planning (Invention): When you start to write." Click on the topic, and you will find some general prewriting suggestions to apply to a range of writing situations. Read the suggestions and make note of those that seem particularly useful. Try applying them to your upcoming draft.

DRAFTING ACTIVITY 3.6

Before writing your first draft, read the following essay by Thomas Jones. In small groups, do the following:

1. Identify the opening paragraph(s) and the thesis sentence expressing the author's opinion. Discuss what is accomplished in the paper's opening.

2. Identify each supporting point in the middle paragraphs, and the examples clarifying each point.

3. Identify the concluding paragraph(s), and discuss what is accomplished.

Down with Jogging
by Thomas Jones

For a while, my neighborhood was taken over by an army of joggers. They were there all the time: early morning, noon, and evenings. There were little old ladies in gray sweats, sleek couples in matching White Stag sweats and Adidas shoes, pot-bellied, middle-aged men with red faces, and even my friend Alex, who'd never exercised more than his beer-hoisting elbow. "Come on!" Alex urged me as he jogged by my house every evening. "You'll feel great."

Well, I had nothing against feeling great, and I figured if Alex could jog every day, anyone could. So I took up jogging seriously and gave it a good two months of my life, and not a day more. Based on my experience, jogging is the most overrated form of exercise around, and judging from the number of defectors from our neighborhood jogging army, I'm not alone in my opinion.

First of all, jogging is very hard on the body. Your legs and feet take a real pounding running around a track or down a paved road for two or three miles. I developed shin splints in my lower legs and stone bruises in my heels that are still tender. Some of my old lower-back problems that had been dormant for years also started flaring up. Then I read about a nationally famous jogger who died of a heart attack while jogging, and I had something else to worry about. I'm sure everyone doesn't develop the foot, leg, and back problems I did, and jogging doesn't kill hundreds of people, but if you have any physical weaknesses, jogging will surely bring them out, as they did with me.

Secondly, I got no enjoyment out of jogging, and few people stick with an exercise they don't enjoy. Jogging is boring. Putting one foot in front of the other for forty-five minutes isn't my idea of fun. Jogging is also a lonely pastime. Some joggers say, "I love being out there with just my thoughts." Well, my thoughts began to bore me, and most of them were on how much my legs hurt. If I can't exercise and socialize at the same time, I'm not interested.

And how could I enjoy something that brought me pain? What's fun about burning eyes, aching lungs, rubbery legs, and heavy arms? And that wasn't just the first week; it was practically every day for two months. I never got past the pain level, and pain isn't fun.

Jogging can have other negative spin-offs, too. It can be very bad on relationships. Husbands and wives start out as friendly jogging mates until hubby runs away from wife in a macho surge and thereafter only runs grudgingly at a "woman's" pace. Then there's the time involvement. Joggers run once or twice a day, thirty minutes to an hour at a time, along with the jogathons that take up the weekends. You've heard of golfing widows? Try jogging widows.

A friend of mine named Mildred started out as a three-time-a-week jogger three years ago. Harmless exercise. Today, she jogs thirty miles a week, runs in jogathons twice a month, subscribes to *Jogger's Weekly*, spends thousands a year on equipment and travel, and, not coincidentally, is no longer married.

But forget everything I've said. What about the great benefits of jogging, the ones that allow you to live longer, lighter, and happier than any nonjogger?

From my perspective, jogging is really overrated in those areas. I ran for two months and didn't lose a pound. The calories burn off very slowly when jogging, and the appetite, in my case, increased. I got my heart and respiratory system in better shape, but what a torturous way to do it. So many other exercises, including walking, accomplish almost the same results painlessly, so why jog? And the happier part? Jogging did not make me feel better, period. I didn't have more energy, I didn't look forward to the next day any more, I didn't spring up wide awake each morning. Jogging made me tired, sore, and irritable. And I can be all of those things without jogging.

I don't jog any more, and I don't think I ever will. I'm walking two miles three times a week at a brisk pace, and that feels good. I also play tennis and racquetball occasionally, and I bicycle to work when the weather is good. I'm getting exercise, and I'm enjoying it at the same time. I could never say the same for jogging, and I've found a lot of better ways to stay in shape. Anyone care to buy a pair of slightly worn size-eight jogging shoes?

DRAFTING ACTIVITY 3.7

Write the first draft of your opinion paper.

REVISIONS

After writing your first draft, set it aside for a while before starting the revision process. After leaving it for a while, on return you generally view your draft more objectively and make more and better revisions. Set your draft aside for an hour or overnight, and you will find things to improve that you wouldn't have noticed otherwise.

REVISION GUIDELINES

As you read and evaluate your first draft, consider the following revision guidelines.

1. Evaluate your beginning. Have you introduced your topic, created some interest for readers, and included your thesis sentence? (See the upcoming section on "Openings and Conclusions.")

2. Evaluate your middle paragraphs. Do they provide strong supporting points for your thesis? Is each supporting point developed in a separate paragraph? Are there examples, details, or explanations you might add to improve any paragraph?

3. Evaluate the order in which you have presented your ideas. Would any sentence(s) or paragraph(s) make better sense in a different location? Would your supporting points be more effective in a different order?

4. Read each sentence and consider how it might be revised to improve its smoothness, clarity, or conciseness. Evaluate your sentence variety and make revisions, if necessary, to improve the variety. (See the upcoming section on "Guidelines for Sentence Variety.")

5. Evaluate your paragraphing to make sure that you have a distinct opening, middle, and ending to your draft; that you have developed your supporting points in separate paragraphs; that the sentences within each paragraph are related; and that you don't have any overly long or short paragraphs.

6. Evaluate your ending. Does it give readers a sense of completion? Does it help accomplish your purpose? Does it relate to your thesis statement in some way?

7. Reread your draft keeping in mind your audience (classmates) and purpose (what you want them to get out of the paper). What changes might you make to accomplish your purpose better or to make the paper more interesting or worthwhile for your readers?

REVISION ACTIVITY 3.8

In small groups, read and evaluate the following student draft by applying the revision guidelines. Be prepared to share your revision suggestions with the class.

When you finish, evaluate each group member's draft in the same manner and provide revision suggestions.

House Music

People enjoy listening to many different kinds of music. They listen to it in their car, while they're exercising, or even taking a shower and thinking that they're going to be the next American Idol.

There are so many different famous names out there, like Nelly, J-Lo, Garth Brooks, and Enrique Iglesias, and they all sing different kinds of music. Many people enjoy listening to these types of music, but my favorite kind of music is House or trans.

I need music that I can actually dance to and that I want to dance to. House music is really fast beats all going at the same time, so you always have to be moving, unlike rap. I don't know what kind of dance you do or even if there is a dance for rap.

A lot of people go to raves, which are all-age events that play house music all night long. They get very tiring though. Most of the clubs also play a lot of House music because it's a music that everyone dances to.

It's a kind of music that when I hear it, it will make me want to get up and dance. To some people, it gives them a big, fat headache. I tell them I could sleep to this kind of music. I guess everyone has a different taste in music, but House is my favorite.

REVISION ACTIVITY 3.9

Write the second draft of your paper, including all of the revisions you have noted for improvement. You may also find other things to revise during the drafting process. (Your instructor may have you go over the upcoming sections on "Paragraphing" and "Sentence Revision" before you write your next draft.)

JOURNAL ENTRY TEN

In your notebook under Journal Entry Ten, relate the kinds of changes you made from your first draft and how you feel they improved the paper. In addition, relate your revision process. Do you make revisions while you are reading the draft as you happen upon things that need changing, do you read all the way through the draft, highlight areas that you want to change, and then go back and make all the revisions, or do you use some other process?

PARAGRAPHING

Each unit presents some paragraphing instruction to apply to the paper you are working on. Since you are writing opening and concluding paragraphs for the current paper, this section gives you some help in those areas.

Openings and Conclusions

Two of the most important parts of a paper are its opening and its conclusion. If you get off to a good start, readers will continue to read your paper with interest. If you conclude strongly, they are left with a good final impression to take with them.

The following suggestions, and lots of practice, will help you begin and end your papers effectively. To write effective *openings*:

1. Motivate readers to read further by introducing your topic in an interesting way: through a brief personal experience, an anecdote, an interesting quotation, a provoking fact, or an example of how readers are affected (by the topic).

2. Let readers know what lies ahead by presenting your thesis: the opinion you are going to develop in the paper.

3. Keep your opening relatively short—a paragraph or two—since it is an introduction, not the heart of your paper.

4. Through your opening, you may "hook" or "lose" your readers' attention. Write your opening to capture their interest and ensure their understanding of your topic and opinion.

To write effective *conclusions*:

1. Leave readers with something you want them to remember: the importance of the topic, the importance of their involvement in something, your purpose for writing, a crucial point, a memorable example, a prediction for the future, a thought to ponder, a possible solution to a problem.

2. Your conclusion should follow logically from what has preceded it in your paper. Therefore, you may not decide how you will end a paper until you've written everything but the conclusion.

3. Give readers something new in the conclusion—more than just a summary of what has come before. Make the conclusion worth their reading.

4. Think of the conclusion as your "last shot" with your readers. If they remember little else other than the conclusion, what will they be left with?

5. A brief, hurried conclusion is a common first draft problem. You may want to take a break before writing it, return with a renewed energy, and give it the time and effort it deserves.

The following sample openings and conclusions reveal the variety of ways in which writers begin and end their papers, and may also give you some ideas for your own writing.

Buying Furnishings for a House
(written for future homeowners)

OPENING When my husband and I bought our first house, we were excited about getting rid of some of our junk furnishings and replacing them with nicer things. Our first acquisition was a beautiful entertainment center that we bought on sale.

When we put the three-piece unit in our family room, it swallowed up a lot of space. It made the room look tiny and took away from our seating space. Unfortunately, we were stuck with it because it was a "no return" sales item. That was one of many lessons we learned as we began to furnish our house. There are a lot of things to keep in mind when undertaking the costly task of furnishing a house.

(**Middle paragraphs** cover a number of points on furnishing a house wisely: taking measurements, taking into account the whole room, considering color schemes, considering decor themes, weighing deferred payment options, never purchasing non-returnables.)

CONCLUSION Above all else, make sure to take your time in furnishing your home. Most of what you buy may be with you for twenty years or more, so taking a few months to find just the right chair or picture is worth the effort. Furnishing a home is also expensive, so it makes sense to spread out your acquisitions over a few years rather than building up a huge debt. My husband and I now view furnishing our home as a longtime project; something that we will enjoy doing for many years. What a difference from those first months of shopping, when we made hurried and ill-advised decisions. We learned the hard way.

Recycling Paper
(written to a college audience)

OPENING Americans throw away millions of tons of paper a year: newspapers, magazines, paper bags, letters, and envelopes. All of this paper represents thousands of trees that are cut annually from our dwindling U.S. forest lands. Our national forests don't have to be devastated, however, if we recycle our paper instead of throwing it away. With the recycling programs that are available today throughout the country, no American should ever throw away a piece of paper again.

(**Middle paragraphs** cover a number of different paper recycling programs available in most towns, the profits individuals can make by recycling their paper products, and ways to start up paper recycling programs in towns that don't have them.)

CONCLUSION College students can make as big a contribution to saving our forests as anyone. Too often we throw away our notes, papers, handouts, returned tests, flyers, and student newspapers. Every college should have a number of paper "drop" stations on campus for recycling. The student council could be in charge of the program, and profits from selling the recycled paper could go to the student body. If your college doesn't have a recycling program, take the lead in getting one started, and once it is in place, carry the message to local K-12 school districts. Students can play a big role in helping to preserve U.S. forests for future generations.

Time for a Change
(letter to the editor of a local newspaper)

OPENING Coach Mabry has had three years to turn the college basketball program around, and the team isn't any better than when he came in 1992. The last two years he has had his own recruits to work with, so he can't blame the "carry-over" players that Coach Forney recruited previously. It's time for a change in basketball coaches because the current situation is producing some negative ramifications.

(**Middle paragraphs** cover the negative ramifications: poor attendance at games, disinterest in the program among students, lack of financial support from boosters, program in the red, and the program losing its previous national reputation.)

CONCLUSION Division I coaches are hired with the understanding that losing seasons bring about firings. That's the nature of the business and one reason that they are paid considerably more than other college instructors. No one should feel sorry for Coach Mabry. He has had his chance, he's made over $100,000 a year, and he hasn't produced. It's time to give someone else a chance before the college basketball program goes into cardiac arrest. There are plenty of excellent coaches in the country who would love the chance to revive our once outstanding program. It can be outstanding again, but not with Coach Mabry at the helm.

New College Drop Date
(written to a board of trustees)

OPENING The change in the college's semester drop date from the twelfth week to the sixth week was instituted quietly this fall and went practically unnoticed by students. Then when the sixth week of the new semester crept closer and teachers began notifying their classes, it began to sink in with students that the new date was going to create some serious problems. The six-week drop date is clearly not in the best interests of most students, and it should be changed back to the original twelve-week date.

(**Middle paragraphs** cover the reasons why the writer opposes the new drop date: not enough time for students to make up their minds, not enough testing at that point for students to evaluate their standing, negative effects on financial aid for students who drop classes that early, will lead to higher college dropout rate, will lead to poorer GPAs, and will hinder students' chances of transferring successfully.)

CONCLUSION   For all of these reasons, the six-week drop date is bad for most students and should be changed. It is not surprising that students were not involved in discussions on changing the drop date or on its effects. If we had been, I don't believe the date would have been changed.

True, the six-week drop date may make life easier for instructors, but does the board make decisions based on what is easy for instructors or what is best for students? Please reconsider this hastily made change and do what is best for students: return the drop date to the twelfth week. There is plenty of time to make that change for the fall semester of 1997. Thank you.

PARAGRAPHING ACTIVITY 3.10

Read the following essay "Long Live High School Rebels" by Thomas French. In small groups discuss the following:

1. What is accomplished in the opening of the essay?

2. What is the thesis for the essay—French's opinion on high school— and where is it found?

3. Identify the supporting points for the thesis and the examples that develop each point. How are the supporting points and examples paragraphed?

4. What is accomplished in the conclusion of the essay?

Long Live High School Rebels
by Thomas French

Ten years ago I was in high school. It was the most absurd and savage place I have ever been.

To listen to the morning announcements, you'd have thought the most pressing crisis in the world was our student body's lack of school spirit. Seniors were grabbing freshmen, dragging them into the bathrooms and dunking their heads in the toilets—a ritual called "flushing." Basketball players were treated like royalty; smart kids were treated like peasants. And the administrators worshiped the word "immature." Inevitably, they pronounced it "imma-tour." Inevitably, they used it to describe us.

The principal and his assistants told us to act like adults, but they treated us like children. Stupid children. They told us what we could wear, when we could move, how close we could stand to our girlfriends, how fast we could walk to lunch and what topics were forbidden to write about in our school newspaper.

When I went out for the tennis team, I remember, the coach told me to cut my hair. It was down to my shoulders and looked terrible, but I loved it. I asked the coach what was the point. Just do it, he said.

If we were taught anything, it was that high school is not about learning but about keeping quiet. The easiest way to graduate was to do what you were told, all of what you were told, and nothing but what you were told. Most of us did just that. I smiled at the principal, stayed out of trouble, avoided writing articles critical of the administration, asked only a few smart-alecky questions and cut my hair as ordered. I was so embarrassed afterwards that I wore a blue ski cap all day every day for weeks.

I admit to some lingering bitterness over the whole affair. I'd still like to know, for one thing, what the length of my hair had to do with my forehand. Maybe that's why, to this day, I almost always root for high school students when they clash intelligently with administrators. High school needs a good dose of dissension. If you've been there in recent years, and I have because I work with student newspapers around Pinellas County, you'd know it needs dissension more than ever.

A reminder of this came with the news that one day last month an assistant principal at St. Petersburg High was rummaging through a student's car in a school parking lot. When the assistant principal found three empty wine-cooler bottles and what was suspected to be some spiked eggnog inside the car, the student was suspended for five days.

Though the student has argued that the search was an unconstitutional violation of his rights, the incident should not have come as any huge surprise. High school officials around this country have been searching through kids' cars and lockers for some time. One day a couple of years ago, a teacher tells me, officials at Lakewood High allowed police to search for drugs with dogs. At the time, students were gathered at an assembly on God and patriotism.

Searches tell students plainly enough what administrators think of them. But in this county, such incidents are only part of a larger tradition of control. Some memorable moments over the years:

In 1983, a group of boys at Lakewood High decided it was unfair that they weren't allowed to wear shorts to school but that girls were allowed to wear miniskirts. The rationale for the rule was shorts—but not miniskirts—were too "distracting." To make fun of the rule, the boys began wearing miniskirts to school.

Administrators laughed at first, but once the rebellion began attracting publicity, the principal suspended the ringleader. When dozens of students staged further protest in front of the school and refused to go to class, the principal suspended 37 of them, too. Later, although close to 1,400 signatures were gathered on a petition against the rule, the Pinellas County School Board bore down and decided to ban shorts from all middle and high schools. Miniskirts, however, were still allowed.

"We need to set a moral standard for our children," explained board member Gerald Castellanos.

Last year, William Grey, the principal of St. Petersburg High, suspended a ninth-grader who dyed her hair purple. "I just don't think school is the place for multi-colored heads," Grey said. He did acknowledge that he allowed students to dye their hair green for special events—the school's colors are green and white—but he insisted that was different because it was "promoting school spirit."

Earlier this year at Pinellas Park High, two of the school's top students—they're number one and two in their class academically—were criticized by the principal when they wrote articles in the student newspaper pointing out that many of the school's students are sexually active and do not use birth control. I was working with the staff that year, and I know the two students wrote the articles in an effort to prevent teen-age pregnancies. But the principal called their work irresponsible—he disagreed with their methodology—and told the newspaper staff it should write more "positive" articles.

This fall, says a teacher at Pinellas Park, the administration cracked down on cafeteria infractions by warning that anyone caught leaving a lunch tray on a table would be suspended.

Last year, 16-year-old Manny Sferios and a group of other students from public and private high schools put together an underground magazine called *Not For Profit* and distributed several issues to students around the county. The magazine ridiculed apartheid, protested the proliferation of nuclear weapons and tried to prod students into thinking about something more than their next pair of designer jeans.

Not For Profit also contained a variety of swear words and ridiculed the small-mindedness of many school officials, and when administrators saw it, they began confiscating copies from kids and warning that those caught with the publication risked suspension.

Though the officials said their main objection to *Not For Profit* was its language, the magazine's activist stance also came under fire. Gerald Castellanos, the school board member, said he did not believe students were sophisticated enough to put together such a magazine.

"I sincerely sense the hand of some very anti-American, anti–free enterprise types in here," he said. "And I don't believe they're students."

Castellanos' attitude was not surprising. Too often the people who run our high schools and sit on our school boards are not prepared to accept or deal with students who think for themselves and stand up for themselves. It would mean a loss of some control, increased resistance to petty rules and a slew of hard questions for those officials who'd rather present a "positive image" than openly confront the real problems in our schools.

There are plenty of real problems that need confronting. Alcohol. Drugs. Broken families. Teen-age pregnancies. Not to mention what's happening in some of our classrooms.

While working on an article published earlier this year, I sat in a couple of classes at St. Petersburg High—the school run by William Grey, the principal who took a stand on purple hair—and what I saw were rows and rows of kids who were bored beyond description. They were trading jokes while the teachers tried to speak. They were literally falling asleep at their desks. One boy who had no interest in the subject matter—it was American history, by the way—was allowed to get up and leave. Another sat in his seat, strumming his finger across his lips, making baby noises.

Dealing with apathy as deep as this is challenge enough for anyone. It requires more teachers, more money, inspiration, real change—all of which are hard to come by. Throw that in with the other problems in our high schools, and the task becomes monumental.

I'm not saying that administrators aren't trying to cope with that task. I know they are. But frequently they waste time and distance themselves from students by exerting their authority in other ways. Make sure the kids don't wear shorts. See to it they put away their lunch trays. Bring in the dogs every once in a while and let them sniff around the lockers. In the face of everything else, keep the school quiet. It's a way the adults tell themselves they're in charge. It's a way they tell themselves they're making a difference.

In the meantime, the ideas that our high schools should promote— freedom of thought and expression, for one—get shoved aside. And the students whom we should be encouraging—the ones who have the brains and spirit to start their own magazine, to protest silly rules, to ask what the color of one's hair has to do with an education—are lectured, suspended and told to get back in line.

Kids know it stinks. Once in a while, they find the guts to step forward and say so, even if it means getting in trouble. I think they should do it more often. Because if there's anything I regret about my own days in high school, it's that more of us didn't fight against the absurdity with every ounce of adolescent ingenuity and irreverence we had.

We should have commandeered the p.a. system one morning and read aloud from Thoreau's *Civil Disobedience*. We should have boycotted the food in the cafeteria for a solid week. We should have sent a note home to the principal's parents informing them he was suspended until he grew up. We should have boned up on our rights in a law library and published what we found in the school paper. And every time an adult said "imma-tour," we should have pulled kazoos out of our pockets and blown on them to our heart's content.

PARAGRAPHING ACTIVITY 3.11

Review the opening and concluding paragraphs of your latest draft, and make any revisions that will add to their interest and effectiveness.

SENTENCE REVISION

In the first two units, you worked on improving first-draft sentences by eliminating unnecessary words, smoothing out awkward phrasing, replacing questionable word choices, and using concrete, visual language. Another consideration in sentence revision is *sentence variety:* using a variety of sentence structures and joining words to express your thoughts most effectively. In this section you begin working with a number of different sentence structures.

Guidelines for Improving Sentence Variety

By using a variety of sentence structures and joining words, you make your writing interesting for readers and express yourself most effectively. Some of the most common sentence problems are described here, with suggestions for solving them.

1. *Overreliance on a particular sentence structure:* You may find that you are using simple sentences (one subject, one verb) to the exclusion of other types.

    EXAMPLE   At 7:00 A.M. it was cool and breezy in Turlock. However, by 10:00 A.M. the breeze had stopped. The temperature began rising slowly. By 3:00 P.M. the temperature had reached 100 degrees. Then the breeze came up again at about 7:00 P.M. By 10:00 P.M. it was cool and windy. There was a 40-degree difference between the high and low for the day.

   Check your sentences to see if you have relied on a particular sentence structure to the exclusion of others: simple (one subject, one verb); compound (two sentences joined by *and, but, so, or, yet, for*); or complex (sentences joined or beginning with *because, if, while, unless, although, before, after*). Revise sentences to include a variety of simple, compound, and complex sentences.

2. *Overreliance on one or two joining words:* You may be using *and* to the exclusion of other options.

    EXAMPLE   A blue jay built her nest in a hanging plant on our apartment patio, and we inspected it occasionally, and a couple neighborhood cats also kept watch. The nest was about six feet above the ground, and we didn't worry about the cats. The blue jay would return regularly, and she would dive-bomb the cats and scare them away. One day the blue jay didn't return to the nest, and we never saw her again after that. After a couple months we took down the nest and threw the unhatched eggs away.

Check your sentences to see if you have relied on one or two joining words exclusively, such as *and, so,* or *because.* If you have, replace the overused word with other appropriate word choices.

3. *Overreliance on short or long sentences:* You may be using too many long sentences (as in the following sample paragraph) or too many short sentences (as in the paragraph example from number 1 about the weather).

EXAMPLE   I feel very uncomfortable in my Psychology II class this semester because it is a small class, and everyone is expected to participate in discussions. There are a number of older students in the class, some of whom have obviously taken a few psychology courses, and they frequently talk in jargon that I can't understand and make references to books I haven't read and psychological experiments that I've never heard of. When I do speak up in class, my observations and opinions sound pretty weak to me, and I'm sure these older students feel the same way although they don't reveal it and are always very considerate of the other students like myself, which is the one thing that makes the class tolerable.

Check the lengths of your sentences to see if you have too many short sentences (which hurts the flow of your paper) or overly long sentences (which readers can get lost in or bored with). Revise groups of short sentences by combining them with joining words or developing their content. Revise overly long sentences by dividing them into two or more complete sentences (which may involve deleting some joining words).

SENTENCE REVISION ACTIVITY 3.12

Revise the following first-draft paragraphs by varying sentence structures, replacing overused joining words, combining very short sentences, and dividing overly long sentences. Add, delete, and move words around any way you wish. Possible wording options include coordinate conjunctions (and, but, so, for, or, yet) or subordinate conjunctions (although, because, since, if, unless, until, when, before, after, while, who, which, that).

Gretchen wanted to move out of the dorms, but she didn't know anyone to share an apartment with. She decided to look in the paper for "roommates wanted" ads, but she was leery about living with strangers. She finally decided to check out one ad because the apartment was in walking distance to the school, and because there were three girls who needed one roommate, and that would mean dividing the rent four ways, which was the cheapest way to go.

Gretchen went to the apartment and met the girls. They were a year older than she was and seemed nice. Their apartment looked clean and was nicely furnished. Her rent would be $150 a month and her share of the utility bill $50. Although she knew little about the girls, Gretchen decided to move in with them although she would have to buy a bicycle to go to and from classes. Although her mother was concerned about the move, Gretchen felt she had made the right decision. She moved her belongings from the dorm. She got her cleaning deposit back. She said farewell to her dormitory friends. She said good-bye to her floor supervisor.

SENTENCE REVISION ACTIVITY 3.13

Review the sentences in your latest draft and, if necessary, make revisions to include more sentence variety, replace overused joining words, combine pairs or groups of short sentences, and divide overly long sentences.

Combining Sentences

Practice in combining sentences has proven successful in helping students develop their sentence-writing skills. The Appendix includes a number of combining activities for students who could benefit from working with a variety of simple, compound, and complex sentence structures. Your instructor may assign these activities throughout the course to give you regular sentence-combining practice.

WORDING PROBLEM REVIEW

Here is a review from Unit 1 of some common first-draft wording problems.

1. *Wordiness:* using more words than necessary to express a thought.

    EXAMPLE   The hailstones that had collected on the lawn in front of the house gave the appearance of snow to anyone who saw them on the lawn.

    REVISED   The hailstones on the front lawn of the house looked like snow.

2. *Awkward phrasing:* using words and phrases that don't fit together smoothly or logically.

    EXAMPLE   Because we've lived in weather where the temperature is cold all our lives, so we are used to dressing the proper way.

    REVISED   Because we've lived with cold weather all our lives, we're used to dressing warmly.

3. *Poor word choice:* using an incorrect or questionable word to express a thought.

EXAMPLE   Your speech on positive thinking transpired all of us.

REVISED   Your speech on positive thinking inspired all of us.

REVISION ACTIVITY 3.14

The following first-draft sentences need revising because of problems with wordiness, awkward phrasing, and poor word choices. Revise each sentence to make it smoother and clearer. Then evaluate your first- (or second-) draft sentences a final time.

EXAMPLE   John had a bald spot that parted his hair in the middle that was black. *(wordy, awkward, poor word choice)*

REVISED   John had a bald spot in the middle of his black hair.

1. The first thing is to let the oil settle down on the oil pan and let the oil cool down right there.

2. In football you don't have to have that good of an endurance to play it.

3. We went to a good show, and we saw it last weekend together.

4. Even though I am his cousin, but he doesn't let me borrow his notes.

5. From all of the dish washing, your hands are pruning and aging with rapidity.

6. It's hot outside tonight with very few breezes.

7. The doctor told my dad I was on time to stop the infection from spreading.

8. By looking at their patio from north to south, it is 12 feet by 12 feet.

9. The accident almost cost me to lose my life.

10. I was curious to see what a group of cat's behaviors were together, so I followed that group of cats.

FINAL EDITING

The last step in the writing process is to proofread your paper for any remaining errors. By this time in the course you are probably aware of your error tendencies, so pay particular attention to those areas.

This section introduces two new considerations that give some writers problems: sentence fragments and subject-verb agreement. You may want to cover these topics before proofreading your latest draft.

PROOFREADING GUIDELINES

1. Make sure you have a period at the end of each complete sentence. Check in particular for run-on sentences and for sentence fragments that need correcting. (See the section on "Fragments" in this unit.)

2. Check your word endings to make sure you haven't inadvertently left off an *s* on a plural word, an *ed* on a past tense verb, or an *ly* on an adverb. Also make sure that your present tense verb endings agree with their subjects. (See the section on "Subjects and Verbs" in this unit.)

3. Check your spelling carefully, and look up any words you are uncertain of. Also make sure you have made the correct homonym choices among words such as there/their/they're, your/you're, no/know, its/it's, and through/threw. (Check the sections on these confusing homonyms under "Spelling" in the Appendix.) Also be sure to use the spelling check in your word processing program.

4. Check your internal punctuation, including comma usage in series of words, compound sentences, and after introductory groups of words; apostrophes in contractions and possessives; and quotation marks with dialogue. (If you have any problems with contractions, see the "Spelling" section in the Appendix.)

5. Check your use of pronouns in compound subjects (Marsha and I, Ross and she, my mother and I, he and I, the Williamses and they).

EDITING ACTIVITY 3.15

In small groups, proofread the following student draft for errors and make the necessary corrections.

Then, following the guidelines presented, proofread your latest draft for errors, and make the necessary corrections. (Your instructor may have you cover the upcoming sections on "Fragments" and "Subjects and Verbs" before you proofread.)

Finally, write or print out the final error-free draft of your paper, to share with your instructor and classmates.

The Best Holiday

Christmas has to be the best holiday of the year. I can remember when I was ten years old. It was Christmas Eve and everyone was asleep but me. I had snuck out of my room to look at the gifts, I had crawled under the tree and started grabbing my gifts.

I thought that I was so smart I had planed to put all my gifts in one spot so that the next day I would go strate to them and not have to go under the tree. But I did not count on my dad being up that late and he caught me he made me put them back and sent me to bed. However, I could not sleep I could only think of the next day when all my famile would come over for dinner.

The way we did it was half of the family you know the ones you really like would come over for breakfast, and we would eat. After that we would open the gifts from them. After they would go home and my mom would get all the stuff ready for dinner. All my other relatives would show up to eat then we would open there gifts, talk, and play.

The reason that Christmas stands out is that year started a bad tradition that I just broke last year. That is the Christmas tree falling on me. It started when I went under the tree to get the cat out it jump into the tree and throw the tree off balance, and it fell. The next year a bulb fell off, so I turned it back on, and as I turned to leave, the tree fell on me and kept doing so every year until last. So I'm looking forward to next year and hoping the tree doesn't hit me again.

JOURNAL ENTRY ELEVEN

Under Journal Entry Eleven, record the kinds of recurring errors you still have to watch out for in your writing. In addition, relate how much error correction you do during the drafting process. How much do you do during the final proofreading?

SENTENCE PROBLEMS

In the first units, you worked on identifying and correcting run-on sentences in your writing. A less frequent but equally troublesome problem is the *sentence fragment,* which is covered in this section.

Fragments

Here are some common features of sentence fragments.

1. A fragment is an incomplete sentence. While a sentence expresses a complete idea and makes sense by itself, a fragment does not.

   EXAMPLES   The man walking down the freeway.

   Because it has been snowing all weekend.

   Driving to school in an old Volkswagen bus.

2. A fragment often leaves the reader with an unanswered question.

   EXAMPLES   The girl standing in the fountain. *(What happened to her?)*

   If you do all your homework tonight. *(What will happen?)*

   Whenever I start to apologize to you. *(What happens?)*

3. Fragments are often separate thoughts that belong in one sentence.

EXAMPLES   (FRAGMENTS UNDERLINED)

If you want a ride to school tomorrow. You can give me a call.

I hope the game is over. Before it starts raining hard.

4. Since fragments are incorrect sentence structures that confuse readers, they need to be revised to form complete sentences. To correct a sentence fragment, either add words to the fragment to make it a sentence, or connect it to the sentence that it belongs with.

EXAMPLE   The girl standing in the fountain.

REVISED   The girl standing in the fountain is cooling her feet.

EXAMPLE   After we pay this month's bills. We'll have little money left for entertainment.

REVISED   After we pay this month's bills, we'll have little money left for entertainment.

EXAMPLE   You can always take the bus to the downtown library. If you can't get a ride from your sister.

REVISED   You can always take the bus to the downtown library if you can't get a ride from your sister.

FRAGMENT ACTIVITY 3.16

The following paragraph contains a number of fragments. Some are the result of a sentence being incorrectly split into a sentence and a fragment, and others are missing the words to form a complete sentence. Rewrite the paragraph and correct all fragments by uniting split sentences and by adding words to fragments that are incomplete. When you finish, check your latest draft for fragments and make the necessary corrections.

EXAMPLE   Patricia was interested in fashion merchandising. Because she loved to buy clothes. Expensive clothes in particular.

REVISED   Patricia was interested in fashion merchandising because she loved to buy clothes. She liked expensive clothes in particular.

It was a bad time to be looking for apartments. Because they were scarce and rent was high. A one-bedroom apartment $300 a month. Maria and Henry were hoping to find a two-bedroom apartment. Since she was expecting a baby in April. They needed to live closer to the campus. Because Henry didn't own a car. The only two-bedroom place they found was renting for $350. They decided to take it. Although the payments would be difficult. Could survive until Henry graduated in June. They moved their belongings into the apartment. They felt everything would work out. Unless Henry's grant application was not accepted.

CORRECT USAGE

Writers sometimes make grammatical errors within a sentence that distract readers. Knowledge of the basic rules of grammar help writers eliminate such errors. This section introduces the basic rules for subject-verb identification that every writer should know.

Subjects and Verbs

As a general rule, every sentence you write contains a subject and a verb. The *subject* is who or what the sentence is about, and the *verb* tells what the subject is doing or joins the subject with words that describe it. To understand subject-verb agreement, you need to be able to identify these main sentence parts.

Subject-Verb Identification

The following sentences have their subjects underlined once and the verbs twice. Notice that in each sentence, the *subject* is who or what the sentence is about, and the *verb* tells what the subject is doing.

EXAMPLES   The <u>dolphin</u> <u>leaped</u> through the air. (*The sentence is about a* dolphin. Leaped *tells what the dolphin did.*)

The <u>doctor</u> <u>made</u> house calls. (*The sentence is about a* doctor. Made *house calls tells what he did.*)

The <u>boulders</u> <u>tumbled</u> down the mountain. (*The sentence is about* boulders. Tumbled *tells what they did.*)

A second way of finding the subject and verb is to locate the verb first and then the subject. To find the verb, look for the *action* in the sentence: running, thinking, talking, looking, touching, and so on. To find the subject, ask, "Who or what is doing the action?" Here are more examples.

EXAMPLES   The <u>raisins</u> <u>shrivel</u> in the sun. (*The action is* shrivel. *What is shriveling? The* raisins.)

<u>Jogging</u> <u>builds</u> Jolene's stamina. (*The action is* builds. *What builds?* Jogging.)

<u>Clyde</u> <u>hates</u> sardines and anchovies. (*The action is* hates. *Who hates?* Clyde.)

SUBJECT-VERB ACTIVITY 3.17

Underline the subject once and the verb twice in the following sentences. Either find out what the sentence is about (the subject) and what the subject is doing (the verb), or look for the action in the sentence (the verb) and find who or what is doing it (the subject).

EXAMPLES   The <u>noose</u> <u>tightened</u> around his neck.

The <u>skier</u> <u>fell</u> off the ski lift.

1. Juanita's ankle aches from roller skating.

2. The tarantula crawled inside Felix's sleeping bag.

3. Aunt Lottie from Toledo cracks walnuts on her head.

4. Ashes from the volcano covered the city.

5. Knitting relaxes Jose.

6. Today the stock market dropped to a record low.

7. Sal often thinks about joining the circus.

8. A fire spreading from a tool shed destroyed the family's belongings.

9. The countries in the Middle East negotiated a new peace treaty.

10. The rats chewed through the pantry wall.

11. High interest rates in March and April killed Fred's chances for a loan.

12. The hockey team from Calgary practices at 4:00 A.M. every day.

13. The opportunity for fame escaped Alice.

14. The poetry competition between classes ends today.

15. Ink blots from his fountain pen stained Rasheed's shirt pocket.

Subject-Verb Agreement

The following rules for subject-verb agreement will help you use the correct present tense verb forms.

1. The subject of a sentence can be *singular* (one of anything) or *plural* (more than one of anything). The plural of most words is formed by adding *s* or *es:* cats, dogs, dresses, boxes.

2. There are two forms of present tense verbs: one ends in *s* and one does not (ride/rides, fight/fights, sing/sings).

3. When you use a present tense verb, you must select the correct form of the verb to agree with the subject. If the subject of the sentence is

singular, use the form that ends in *s.* If the subject is *plural,* use the form that does *not* end in *s.*

a. *Singular subject:* present tense verb ends in *s.*

b. *Plural subject:* present tense verb does not end in *s.*

EXAMPLES   (SUBJECT UNDERLINED ONCE, VERB UNDERLINED TWICE)

SINGULAR
SUBJECT   The <u>elm tree</u> <u>sheds</u> its leaves in early December.

PLURAL
SUBJECT   The <u>elm trees</u> <u>shed</u> their leaves in early December.

SINGULAR
SUBJECT   Your <u>aunt</u> <u>believes</u> in reincarnation.

PLURAL
SUBJECT   Your <u>aunts</u> <u>believe</u> in reincarnation.

4. There are a few exceptions to the basic subject-verb agreement rules. With the singular subject pronouns *I* and *you,* the verb does *not* end in *s:* I enjoy roller-skating; you prefer skateboarding. Verbs such as *dress, press, regress,* and *impress* end in *s* with a plural subject—The Johnson girls dress alike—and in *es* with a singular subject—Sarah dresses very differently from her twin sister.

SUBJECT-VERB AGREEMENT ACTIVITY 3.18

Circle the correct form of the present tense verb in parentheses that agrees with the subject of the sentence.

EXAMPLES   Your uncle (build, builds) huge sand castles.

Your uncles (build, builds) huge sand castles.

1. Juanita often (practice, practices) her baton twirling three nights a week.

2. The girls (practice, practices) karate in the school's gymnastics room.

3. My nephew from New Orleans (believe, believes) in extraterrestrial beings.

4. My nieces (believe, believes) that my nephew is crazy.

5. The pole-vaulters from Central College (warm, warms) up for their event by using a trampoline.

6. The high jumper from Drake University (warm, warms) up for her event by doing stretching exercises.

7. The city newspapers that I subscribe to (do, does) a lousy job of covering campus activities.

8. The college newspaper (do, does) a great job of covering city events.

9. That pickle on your hamburger (look, looks) like it's been nibbled on by a rat.

10. Those olives (look, looks) like they've been dehydrated.

11. Your dentist (need, needs) braces on his lower teeth.

12. Most physicians that I know (need, needs) to take better care of their own health.

13. Your success (prove, proves) that hard work sometimes pays off.

14. My recent failures in math (prove, proves) that hard work isn't always enough.

15. A savings account (are, is) one thing I need to open immediately.

16. Savings accounts (are, is) great if you have anything to put into them.

Subject-Verb Variations

Here are some variations in the subject-verb pattern that often create agreement problems for writers.

1. Separated subject and verb: The subject and verb are separated by a group of words, most often a *prepositional phrase*, that confuses the agreement situation. *Solution:* Ignore any words between a subject and verb when making decisions about agreement.

   PREPOSITIONAL PHRASES *(PREPOSITIONS ITALICIZED)*

after the game	*from* his room
against his will	*in* the boat
among the roses	*into* the water
around the house	*of* the three churches
before the test	*on* the table
behind the batter	*to* the ground
between the lines	*through* the mail
for good mileage	*with* her friends

   EXAMPLES   *(SUBJECT AND VERB UNDERLINED, PREPOSITIONAL PHRASES CROSSED OUT)*

   One ~~of the women teachers~~ smokes a pipe in the lounge.

   The aroma ~~of barbecuing steaks~~ nauseates Herman.

   Men ~~in the back of the room by the pencil sharpener~~ look threatening.

   Each ~~of the sixteen yellow raincoats~~ has a flaw in it.

2. Sentences beginning with there plus a form of to be: Sentences beginning with *there is, there are, there was,* and *there were* cause writers problems because the subject comes *after* the verb. *Solution:* Because *there* is never the subject in a *there + to be* sentence, find the subject after the verb and use *is* or *was* with singular subjects and *are* or *were* with plural subjects.

EXAMPLES   *(SUBJECTS AND VERBS UNDERLINED)*

There <u>is</u> a <u>snake</u> in the basement.

There <u>are</u> sixteen <u>ways</u> to cook potatoes.

There <u>was</u> <u>no one</u> home at the Garcias'.

There <u>were</u> no Christmas <u>trees</u> left in the lot when I went shopping.

3. *Compound verbs:* If a sentence has a single subject and two or more main verbs (compound verb), each main verb must agree with the subject.

EXAMPLES   *(SUBJECTS AND VERBS UNDERLINED)*

<u>Mavis</u> <u>jogs</u> to work, <u>does</u> aerobics on her lunch hour, and <u>lifts</u> weights at night.

My <u>uncles</u> <u>make</u> great chili and <u>serve</u> it in old tin cans.

<u>G Street</u> <u>winds</u> around our suburb and then <u>dead-ends</u> by the canal.

<u>Sarah and Clyde</u> <u>love</u> to fight and <u>love</u> to make up even more.

SUBJECT-VERB AGREEMENT ACTIVITY 3.19

Underline the subject in each of the following sentences, and then circle the verb in parentheses that *agrees* with the subject. When you finish, proofread your latest draft for any subject-verb agreement problems.

EXAMPLE   <u>One</u> of my goldfish (look, looks) ill.

1. Sarah and Jesus (dances, dance) smoothly together.

2. No one in the audience (understand, understands) the plot of the Fellini movie.

3. The huge planes (circles, circle) the runway in the fog.

4. The french fries from the Happy Hamburger (is, are) greasy.

5. The children from Grant School (appears, appear) bored after Act One of *The Great Anchovy.*

6. There (is, are) something about you that I like.

7. Before the election, the mayor (hires, hire) his campaign manager and (prepares, prepare) his speech.

8. Tryouts for the philharmonic orchestra (begins, begin) on Monday.

9. Julia and Fred (seems, seem) surprised by the attention from the press.

10. The students from Sweden and Israel (speaks, speak) and (writes, write) excellent English.

11. In the back of your locker (lies, lie) a pair of stinky sweat socks.

12. The view across the bay from the middle of the bridge (was, were) magnificent.

13. There (is, are) one of the Daffney twins, but I (don't, doesn't) know the whereabouts of her sister.

14. There (is, are) no good reason for you to miss the farewell party for Gonzo.

15. From the looks of your car, it (needs, need) a good wash and wax job.

JOURNAL ENTRY TWELVE

Under Journal Entry Twelve in your notebook, relate what you learned through the writing process and activities in this unit that may help you for future writing that you do.

WRITING REVIEW

In the "Writing Review" section at the end of each unit, you work more independently on a paper and apply what you have learned during the unit. Write a second thesis-centered paper following the writing process provided.

WRITING PROCESS

1. Select a writing topic and generate a thesis following these suggestions:

   a. Choose a topic that you are interested in, have a definite opinion on, and are knowledgeable about. Spend some time thinking about a topic you would really like to write on.

   b. Write a tentative thesis statement: a sentence expressing your opinion on the topic that you will support throughout your paper.

c. Your audience for the paper is your classmates. What purpose might you have in writing to them about this particular topic? What might they get out of the paper?

STUDENT SAMPLE IDEAS I'd like to write about selecting a major in college because it was something I had a problem with. I'd never rush into it again. That was a mistake, and I think I got some bad advice. My purpose would be to help classmates learn from my mistake.

TOPIC Choosing a college major

THESIS STATEMENT Choosing a major before you are ready is a big mistake.

2. To generate ideas for your paper, use the listing process:

a. List four or five supporting points for your thesis: the main reasons that you feel or think the way you do about the topic.

b. Order your points as you want to present them in your draft. You might order them from the most to least important point, present your strongest points first and last, or present related or similar points in succession.

c. For each supporting point, think of an example or two you could use to clarify the point for readers.

d. Consider how you might begin your first draft: how you will introduce your topic, create reader interest, and present your thesis statement.

_____

_____

_____

_____

STUDENT SAMPLE Thesis: Choosing a major before you are ready is a big mistake.

a. May take unnecessary courses (provide personal examples)

b. Will probably change mind later (provide personal example)

c. Waste time and money (provide personal examples)

d. Don't need major (take basic general ed classes first)

Reorder points for first draft—a c b d—to present similar points in succession.

3. When you have completed your prewriting work, write the first draft of your paper following these guidelines:

   a. Include a beginning, middle, and ending to your paper. Apply what you have learned about effective openings and conclusions, and develop your supporting points in the middle paragraphs.

   b. Follow your prewriting plan from the listing activity, but feel free to add points, examples, or explanations you hadn't thought of, or to revise your plan as you write the draft.

   c. Keep your thesis (your opinion on the topic) in mind to provide focus throughout the paper.

   d. Keep your audience (classmates) in mind as you write, and your purpose: what you want them to get out of the paper.

   e. Don't worry about perfect wording or making an occasional error. Revision and editing lie ahead.

Selecting a Major

Everyone tells you to get a major in college as soon as possible: counselors, advisors, parents. That way you'll have direction throughout your college career, and you won't waste time taking classes you don't need.

Like a good freshman, I listened to people and selected a major as soon as I got to college: pre-optometry. My girlfriend's father recommended it. I liked the idea of being called "doctor," and I wouldn't have to go to school nearly as long as an MD. Did I have any idea what optometrists really did? Not actually. Choosing a major before I was really ready was a big mistake.

As I progressed through my first two years, I dutifully took every math and chemistry class required and ignored most of the general ed requirements since I wouldn't need them for a BS degree to transfer to the optometry school I wanted to go to. I stuck to my pre-optometry schedule, happy to have a major and the "direction" that many of my friends still lacked.

However, something happened near the end of my sophomore year. I started thinking for myself a little. I began wondering what optometrists really did, and I arranged to meet an optometrist friend and spend a day with him at an eye clinic. I'd never been so bored in my life. The work was very routine, and there appeared to be no challenge or excitement to the job. I began to have real doubts about my major, and I felt guilty about that.

During this same time, I was taking a biology class that had me excited. I was learning a lot about DNA, genetic research, and the career opportunities for doing really meaningful work in medical research. I was getting excited about genetics from the work I was doing in the lab and from talking to researchers rather than from some vague career notion that I had had as a seventeen-year-old. For the first time, I was ready to declare a major.

How did a change in major affect me? First, it cost me an extra undergraduate year and an extra year of expense. I have to take two semesters of general ed requirements I'll need to graduate, and then in my fifth year, I'll take biology major courses exclusively. I was also made to feel guilty by my dad, who tried to talk me out of changing majors, and my counselor, who told me, "Most students have doubts about their major from time to time. Hang in there!" I felt that was bad advice, and I didn't take it.

From this experience, I'd say the worst thing a person can do is declare a major because he or she feels pressured to do it. Many seventeen and eighteen-year-old college freshmen aren't ready to make this decision, and counselors and parents need to accept that. It makes a lot more sense for undecided students to get their general ed requirements out of the way and take the time to find out more about what interests them. Sometimes taking courses from different disciplines is the best way to discover a major that interests you.

The one positive thing from my experience is that I did change majors to something I liked rather than stick with my original choice. I really feel good about my schooling and my future for the first time in college. So if someone does feel stuck in a major they don't like, my advice is that it's better to change majors and spend more time in school than to stay with a major that isn't for you.

In the end, I was the only person who could ultimately decide what I wanted in a major and a career, and I was the only one who had to live with my decision. So don't let anyone pressure you into selecting a major before you're ready, and if you feel at some point like changing majors, don't feel guilty about it. It may be the best decision you ever make.

4. When you finish your first draft, set it aside for a while before evaluating it. Then read the draft carefully for possible revisions, following these guidelines.

   a. Is your opening a strong part of your paper? Do you introduce your topic in an interesting way and clearly state your thesis? How might you improve the opening?

   b. Do you support your thesis well in the middle paragraphs? Is each supporting point developed through appropriate details, explanations, and examples? What might you add to improve any of your middle paragraphs?

c. Is your paper paragraphed effectively? Are the opening, middle, and endings paragraphed separately? Do you develop each supporting point in a separate paragraph? Are the sentences within each paragraph related? Do you have any overly long paragraphs that need dividing or short paragraphs that need combining or developing further?

d. Is your paper organized effectively? Have you presented your supporting points in the best possible order? Are there any sentences or paragraphs that would fit more logically in a different location?

e. Revise the wording of individual sentences to make them clearer, smoother, more concise, and more concrete (visual). Check your sentences to see if you can improve their structural variety, replace overused joining words, combine pairs or groups of short sentences, or divide overly long sentences.

f. Do you have a strong conclusion to your paper? Does it leave readers with a sense of completion and help you accomplish your purpose?

g. Evaluate the overall impact of your paper on your reading audience. What can you do to make it more interesting, more informative, or more convincing?

5. Following the proofreading guidelines on page 93, proofread your draft carefully for errors and make the necessary corrections.

6. Write or print out the final draft of your paper, and share it with your instructor and classmates.

WRITING TO COMPARE

The writing assignments in the text require you to use different thought processes that help you develop both your thinking and writing skills. Good thinking leads to good writing, and good writing requires a lot of thought: What am I going to write about? What will my approach be? How will I best support it? How can I capture and maintain my readers' interest? How shall I conclude my paper? What can I do to make my paper better? No act of communication requires more thinking and decision making than writing, and that is why writing is so valuable to a person's intellectual growth.

As you write papers for this course, you draw upon and expand your ability to recollect, to analyze, to compare, to evaluate, to organize, to draw conclusions, to persuade, and to create. In short, you are developing thinking skills that will help you in other college courses, in your future career, and in everyday life.

In the writing for this unit, you compare similar subjects to evaluate their relative worth or merit and decide which one you would recommend to readers. The purposes for writing a comparative paper are to learn to identify the most important factors for comparing subjects, to evaluate these factors for each subject, to weigh the relative value of each factor, and to make decisions based on your evaluation. During the planning and writing process, you will use different thinking skills—comparing, evaluating, classifying, and drawing conclusions—that are beneficial for most decision making you will do.

Comparing subjects and making decisions are familiar acts to all of us. We decide where to live, what to eat, where to shop, where to go to school, what team to root for, what to wear, and whom to vote for based on comparing and evaluating similar choices. Sometimes the process is quite simple—such as choosing chocolate swirl ice cream over strawberry or vanilla—and sometimes it can be complicated—such as deciding which college to attend or what apartment complex to live in. For your upcoming writing assignment, you will compare subjects to provide readers with the best information and advice for making their own decisions.

PREWRITING

For most people, writing a comparative paper requires some planning. You decide what subjects you want to compare, the factors you want to compare them by, what you might need to find out to provide the best comparison, and how best to organize your paper to make your comparison.

While some writers prefer making a detailed outline before writing, others prefer beginning with a general idea and using the drafting process to help discover their direction. People who tend to plan and organize in detail in other aspects of their lives often do the same with their writing. People who are less organized and more spontaneous tend to do less detailed planning. In the end, there is no one "best way" to prepare for writing a paper. Most writers ultimately settle on an approach that works well for them and that is true to their nature.

For your prewriting work for the upcoming writing assignment, you will do some tasks that are particularly important for making comparisons—such as deciding on factors to compare and weighing the value of those factors—and others that are useful for any writing—such as generating material for your first draft. The purpose of all prewriting work is to prepare you for writing your first draft, and anything you do to help you get started is valuable.

TOPIC SELECTION

To select your writing topic for the unit, consider these suggestions:

1. What topic areas am I most knowledgeable in? Cars? Sports? Musical equipment? Computers? Politics? Religion? Fashion? Cooking?

2. What subjects could I compare that might help readers make a decision or choice? Different majors? Different teachers teaching the same course? Different stereo systems? Different colleges? Different college football programs? Different cars? Different clothing stores? Different living situations? Different candidates running for political office?

3. What specific subjects would I compare? What two or three restaurants? What brands of jogging shoes? What specific colleges? What specific instructors? What specific stores? What brands of stereos? What specific word processing programs? What specific economy cars? What specific ways of cooking pork ribs?

4. What would my purpose be in making this particular comparison? To help readers decide what to buy? where to shop? where to enroll? where to work? what teacher or course to take? what to believe? what course of action to take? where to eat?

5. What reading audience would be most interested in the subjects I am comparing? Sports enthusiasts? Model car collectors? Women who love to shop for clothes? Classmates who are transferring to another college? Consider the best reading audience for your topic.

TOPIC SELECTION ACTIVITY 4.1

In small groups, discuss possible topics for comparison that different group members are interested in. In particular, come up with topics that classmates would like to have more information on.

TOPIC SELECTION ACTIVITY 4.2

Applying the topic selection suggestions presented, do the following:

1. Select a topic for your comparison paper. Take your time and decide on a topic that interests you, that you are knowledgeable about, and that would interest some of your classmates. Select a topic that you may know more about than some of your classmates so that they will learn from your comparison.

2. Decide what similar subjects you want to compare within your topic, selecting two to four subjects. (For example, comparing living in the dormitories to living in an apartment while attending college is a useful two-subject comparison, while comparing three or four different kinds of car stereo systems may be more valuable than just comparing two.)

3. Make sure that you are comparing "apples to apples." Comparing sports utility vehicles (SUVs) to sports cars is not a similar comparison. Instead, you would compare different makes and models of SUVs in a paper, or you would compare different makes and models of sports cars in a different paper.

4. Depending on your topic, you may write this paper primarily for a particular group of classmates: those interested in shopping for clothes, or those who may be interested in space shuttles. Decide what group of classmates in particular you may direct your paper towards.

STUDENT SAMPLE DRAFT

What shall I compare? I know a lot about car stereos. I've owned enough of them, and I could compare three or four different brands that people might consider buying. This might interest classmates who own cars and are into music. I've taken three different math teachers at the college, and they are very different. I could compare them for other students so they would know what to expect when they had them. This might interest classmates who still have some math ahead of them.

I could compare college to high school because they are very different, but I'm not sure what my purpose would be. And my classmates have also gone through both experiences. That's not an "apples to apples" comparison anyway, is it? I could compare some movies that I've seen recently and recommend them to people who haven't seen them, but that sounds boring.

I keep going back to my first topic: comparing car stereos. That topic interests me, and I know there are always people who are shopping for car stereo systems.

TOPIC   Comparing car stereo systems

SUBJECTS FOR COMPARISON   Alpine, Pioneer, Sanyo

AUDIENCE   Classmates who own cars and like music

PURPOSE   To recommend the best car stereo system for their money

FACTORS TO COMPARE

When you make comparisons and draw conclusions, you consider different factors, some of which may be more important than others. Then you draw your conclusions based on how your subjects compare on each factor.

For example, if you are looking for an apartment to rent, you might consider the following factors:

rent	tenants
size	condition
location	

The apartment you ultimately select would probably meet your expectations in these five areas better than the apartments you compared it to. And some factors may have figured more prominently in your decision than others. For example, if the rent was good and the apartment was in walking distance to campus, you might settle for something a little smaller or older than you would have preferred. Some factors may be more important than others.

To decide on the factors to compare your subjects on, follow these guidelines.

1. Your factors are the critical areas of comparison that readers should consider. For example, in comparing used guitars, your factors might include price, brand, condition, and looks. In comparing breeds of dogs, your factors might include price, looks, temperament, size, and gender. In comparing professional football teams, your factors might include team records, prominent players, coaches, relative age of players, and effects of free agency.

2. For your factors, select three to five important areas of comparison that you can cover thoroughly in a paper. For example, in buying a house, there might be thirty different factors you could compare, but in a paper, you would deal only with the most critical factors. Focus on those factors that would be most important to readers in making a decision.

PREWRITING ACTIVITY 4.3

In small groups, list four our five factors that you would compare for each of the following topics. Select those factors that would seem most important in deciding which subject is best.

1. comparing colleges to attend

2. comparing brands of tennis shoes to buy

3. comparing instructors who teach the same course

4. comparing malls to shop at

PREWRITING ACTIVITY 4.4

Applying the suggestions presented, decide on the factors you will compare your subjects on. Select three to five important areas of comparison from which you will draw your conclusions. Next, decide on the relative value of each factor. Are some more important than others? Should they receive more attention as you decide on your recommendation?

When you have decided on your factors, spend some time evaluating your different subjects for each factor. For example, let's say your topic is jogging shoes, and your subjects are Nike, Adidas, and Reebok shoes. If your factors include looks, comfort, durability, and price, evaluate Nike, Adidas, and Reebok on each factor. Which brand looks the best? Which is most comfortable? Which lasts the longest? This will help prepare you to write your first draft.

TOPIC   Car stereo systems

SUBJECTS TO COMPARE   Alpine, Pioneer, Sanyo

FACTORS TO COMPARE   Quality of sound
Price
Features
Warranty

JOURNAL ENTRY THIRTEEN

Now that you have completed the prewriting activities, how well prepared do you feel to write your first draft? Of the prewriting work you did, record in your journal what seemed most useful to you. What, if anything, could you have done without?

FIRST DRAFTS

After selecting your topic, deciding on the subjects to compare and the areas of comparison (factors), and spending some time comparing your subjects on each factor, you are ready to write your first draft. Keep the following suggestions in mind.

DRAFTING GUIDELINES

1. Include an opening, middle, and ending as you did in the previous unit's paper. In the opening, introduce your topic in a way that helps readers understand your purpose: to help them make a particular decision or judgment regarding the topic. In the middle, compare your subjects on the factors you have selected for comparison. In the ending, draw your conclusion for readers: what you would recommend based on the comparative information.

2. Organize your comparison in some manner: by comparing your subjects one factor at a time (how Alpine, Pioneer, and Sanyo stereos compare in sound; how they compare in price; how they compare in features, and so on), or by evaluating one subject at a time on all fac-

tors (how Alpine fares regarding sound, price, features, warranty; how Pioneer fares regarding sound, price, features, warranty; how Sanyo fares regarding sound, price, features, warranty).

If you compare all subjects on one factor at a time, change paragraphs as you change factors. If you evaluate one subject at a time on all factors, change paragraphs as you change subjects.

3. Draw your conclusion (make your recommendation) for readers based on the comparative information you provide in the middle paragraphs.

You might draw an *unqualified* conclusion—meaning you would recommend the same choice to all readers:

- No one can go wrong in taking Mr. Allen for Calculus I at Kings College.

- The best place to buy boots in Clovis is Western Wear.

- You might draw a *qualified* conclusion—giving readers choices based on their needs and financial situation:

If you are a math major, take Mr. Allen's Calculus I class, but if you are a nonmajor filling a requirement, take Dr. Fillmore's.

- If money is no object, buy your boots at Western Wear. If you are on a tight budget, go across the street to Boot World.

Keep your readers (classmates) in mind as you draw your conclusion and make recommendations, taking into account the differences among individuals.

4. Keep your purpose in mind as you write: to present the best comparative information and to draw the most reasonable conclusion for readers so they can make a wise decision or choice.

ON-LINE ACTIVITY: PARTS OF A COMPOSITION

If you had a difficult time writing a particular part of your paper—the introduction, thesis statement, or conclusion, there is help on-line. Go once again to http://leo.stcloud.edu/. When you arrive, scroll down and click on the topic "I have problems with particular parts of a paper—introductions, thesis statements, conclusions." Then you will have a choice of three topics: "I'd like some help with introductions, thesis statement, or conclusions." Click on the particular topic you need help with, or take a look at all three. Apply what you learn to your upcoming draft. You may also want to refer to this site from time to time as you work on other papers.

DRAFTING ACTIVITY 4.5

Read the following student sample draft "Car Stereo Systems" and the subsequent essay "Why Johnny Can't Read, but Yoshio Can" by Richard Lynn. In small groups, discuss the following:

1. How does each writer introduce his or her topic?

2. What comparisons does each writer make in the middle paragraphs among or between subjects?

3. What conclusion does each writer draw at the end?

4. What was the purpose of each paper, and what reading audience do you think each was intended for?

5. Then write the first draft of your paper with the suggestions presented in mind.

Car Stereo Systems

STUDENT SAMPLE
DRAFT

If you are in the market for a car stereo, there are a lot of options available. I've put in a few systems myself over the years, and basically you get what you pay for. However, there are some good buys out there, depending on what your particular needs are.

Three car stereo brands that represent the high-price to low-price range are Alpine, Pioneer, and Sanyo. Nakamichi ranks with Alpine in the high range; Kenwood, Panasonic, and Sony are in the medium range with Pioneer; and Kraco, Craig, and Realistic join Sanyo in the lower-priced range.

In sound quality, there's not much difference between Alpine and Pioneer. Their frequency response, sound/noise ratio, and dynamic range are similar. If I listened to one and then the other using the same speakers, I couldn't tell which was which. The Sanyo, however, and its lower-priced cousins, don't sound as good. You get more noise with them as the volume increases, and their sound range isn't as great as the others.

In terms of features, all of the stereos offer cassette decks and CD players. Digital display and programming are standard on the Alpine and Pioneer, but not on the Sanyo. Alpine and Pioneer also offer pull-out models, remote control, and channel memory, not available with Sanyo and other cheaper brands.

The warranty on the different brands has to do with the quality of components and construction. As might be expected, the Alpine has the longest warranty of three years on parts and service while the Pioneer has a one-year parts-and-service warranty and Sanyo a 90-day to one-year parts-only warranty. Clearly, the Alpine is better constructed, whereas the Pioneer and Sanyo are not going to hold up as well for as long a time.

The prices on the three models differ considerably. The Alpine models are priced from $500 to $1,500, Pioneer from $200 to $500, and Sanyo from $50 to $200. The range of prices within each brand reflects the different quality of models each offers. A $1,500 Alpine model would represent a state-of-the-art stereo of the finest craftsmanship, highest quality components, and the optimal number of features.

If I had money to burn, it would be great to have the $1,500 Alpine, knowing I've got about the best car stereo money can buy. However, not many people I know can afford one. For the money, I believe the best buy would be a mid-priced brand like the Pioneer pull-out model with cassette and CD player, which you could get for under $300. You'd have good quality sound, the option to use tapes or CDs, and the security of being able to remove your stereo when you're parked. You could get the Pioneer even cheaper if you went with just a cassette or CD player and without the pull-out feature, if security isn't a problem.

Personally, I wouldn't recommend one of the lower-priced stereos like the Sanyo unless you aren't going to be in your car much or you really don't care about the quality of sound. Given the short warranty and lack of quality construction, you probably aren't going to be better off financially in the long run than if you'd bought a mid-priced stereo.

Finally, whatever you decide on, I'd recommend shopping around and looking for a good sale. Sale prices are more common on the mid-priced stereos since people who buy the more expensive ones aren't that price conscious and the cheaper stereos don't have much of a profit margin to discount. The only other consideration is whether you buy an American or foreign brand stereo—both are available at every price range—and that's an individual choice.

Why Johnny Can't Read, but Yoshio Can
by Richard Lynn

There can be no doubt that American schools compare poorly with Japanese schools. In the latter, there are no serious problems with poor discipline, violence, or truancy; Japanese children take school seriously and work hard. Japanese educational standards are high, and illiteracy is virtually unknown.

The evidence of Japan's high educational standards began to appear as long ago as the 1960s. In 1967 there was published the first of a series of studies of educational standards in a dozen or so economically developed nations, based on tests of carefully drawn representative samples of children. The first study was concerned with achievement in math on the part of 13- and 18-year-olds. In both age groups the Japanese children came out well ahead of their coevals in other countries. The American 13-year-olds came out second to last for their age group; the American 18-year-olds, last. In both age groups, European children scored about halfway between the Japanese and the Americans.

Since then, further studies have appeared, covering science as well as math. The pattern of results has always been the same: the Japanese have generally scored first, the Americans last or nearly last, and the Europeans have fallen somewhere in between. In early adolescence, when the first tests are taken, Japanese children are two or three years ahead of American children; by age 18, approximately 98 percent of Japanese children surpass their American counterparts.

Meanwhile, under the Reagan Administration, the United States at least started to take notice of the problem. In 1983 the President's report, *A Nation at Risk,* described the state of American schools as a national disaster. A follow-up report issued by the then-secretary of education, Mr. William Bennett, earlier this year claims that although some improvements have been made, these have been "disappointingly slow."

An examination of Japan's school system suggests that there are three factors responsible for its success, which might be emulated by other countries: a strong national curriculum, stipulated by the government; strong incentives for students; and the stimulating effects of competition between schools.

The national curriculum in Japan is drawn up by the Department of Education. It covers Japanese language and literature, math, science, social science, music, moral education, and physical education. From time to time, the Department of Education requests advice on the content of the curriculum from representatives of the teaching profession, industry, and the trade unions. Syllabi are then drawn up, setting out in detail the subject matter that has to be taught at each grade. These syllabi are issued to school principals, who are responsible for ensuring that the stipulated curriculum is taught in their schools. Inspectors periodically check that this is being done.

The Japanese national curriculum ensures such uniformly high standards of teaching that almost all parents are happy to send their children to the local public school. There is no flight into private schools of the kind that has been taking place in America in recent years. Private schools do exist in Japan, but they are attended by less than 1 percent of children in the age range of compulsory schooling (six to 15 years).

This tightly stipulated national curriculum provides a striking contrast with the decentralized curriculum of schools in America. Officially, the curriculum in America is the responsibility of school principals with guidelines from state education officials. In practice, even school principals often have little idea of what is actually being taught in the classroom.

America and Britain have been unusual in leaving the curriculum so largely in the hands of teachers. Some form of national curriculum is used throughout Continental Europe, although the syllabus is typically not specified in as much detail as in Japan. And now Britain is changing course: legislation currently going through Parliament will introduce a national curriculum for England and Wales, with the principal subjects being English, math, science, technology, a foreign language, history and geography, and art, music, and design. It is envisioned that the new curriculum will take up approximately 70 percent of teaching time, leaving the remainder free for optional subjects such as a second foreign language, or extra science.

Under the terms of the new legislation, schoolchildren are going to be given national tests at the ages of 7, 11, 14, and 16 to ensure that the curriculum has been taught and that children have learned it to a satisfactory standard. When the British national curriculum comes into effect, America will be left as the only major economically developed country without one.

To achieve high educational standards in schools it is necessary to have motivated students as well as good teachers. A national curriculum acts as a discipline on teachers, causing them to teach efficiently, but it does nothing to provide incentives for students, an area in which American education is particularly weak.

One of the key factors in the Japanese education system is that secondary schooling is split into two stages. At the age of 11 or 12, Japanese children enter junior high school. After three years there, they take competitive entrance examinations for senior high schools. In each locality there is a hierarchy of public esteem for these senior high schools, from the two or three that are regarded as the best in the area, through those considered to be good or average, down to those that (at least by Japanese standards) are considered to be poor.

The top schools enjoy national reputations, somewhat akin to the famous English schools such as Eton and Harrow. But in England the high fees exacted by these schools mean that very few parents can afford them. Consequently there are few candidates for entry, and the entrance examinations offer little incentive to work for the great mass of children. By contrast, in Japan the elite senior high schools are open to everyone. While a good number of these schools are private (approximately 30 percent nationwide, though in some major cities the figure is as high as 50 percent), even these schools are enabled, by government subsidies, to keep their fees within the means of a large proportion of parents. The public schools also charge fees, but these are nominal, amounting to only a few hundred dollars a year, and loans are available to cover both fees and living expenses.

Thus children have every expectation of being able to attend the best school they can qualify for; and, hence, the hierarchical rankings of senior high schools act as a powerful incentive for children preparing for the entrance examinations. There is no doubt that Japanese children work hard in response to these incentives. Starting as early as age 10, approximately half of them take extra tutoring on weekends, in the evenings, and in the school holidays at supplementary coaching establishments known as *juku*, and even at that early age they do far more homework than American children. At about the age of 12, Japanese children enter the period of their lives known as *examination hell:* during this time, which lasts fully two years, it is said that those who sleep more than five hours a night have no hope of success, either in school or in life. For, in addition to conferring great social and intellectual status on their students, the elite senior high schools provide a first-rate academic education, which, in turn, normally enables the students to get into one of the elite universities and, eventually, to move into a good job in industry or government.

Although Japanese children are permitted to leave school at the age of 15, 94 percent of them proceed voluntarily to the senior high schools. Thus virtually all Japanese are exposed in early adolescence to the powerful incentive for academic work represented by the senior-high-school entrance examinations. There is nothing in the school systems of any of the Western countries resembling this powerful incentive.

The prestige of the elite senior high schools is sustained by the extensive publicity they receive from the media. Each year the top hundred or so schools in Japan are ranked on the basis of the percentage of their pupils who obtain entry to the University of Tokyo, Japan's most prestigious university. These rankings are widely reported in the print media, and the positions of the top twenty schools are announced on TV news programs, rather like the scores made by leading sports teams in the United States and Europe. At a local level, more detailed media coverage is devoted to the academic achievements of all the schools in the various localities, this time analyzed in terms of their pupils' success in obtaining entry to the lesser, but still highly regarded, local universities.

Thus, once Japanese 15-year-olds have been admitted to their senior high schools, they are confronted with a fresh set of incentives in the form of entrance examinations to universities and colleges, which are likewise hierarchically ordered in public esteem. After the University of Tokyo, which stands at the apex of the status heirarchy, come the University of Kyoto and ten or so other highly prestigious universities, including the former Imperial Universities in the major provincial cities and the technological university of Hitosubashi, whose standing and reputation in Japan resembles that of the Massachusetts Institute of Technology in the United States.

Below these top dozen institutions stand some forty or so less prestigious but still well-regarded universities. And after these come numerous smaller universities and colleges of varying degrees of standing and reputation.

To some extent the situation in Japan has parallels in the United States and Europe, but there are two factors that make the importance of securing admission to an elite university substantially greater in Japan than in the West. In the first place, the entire Japanese system is geared toward providing lifelong employment, both in the private sector and in the civil service. It is practically unheard of for executives to switch from one corporation to another, or into public service and then back into the private sector, as in the United States and Europe. Employees are recruited directly out of college, and, needless to say, the major corporations and the civil service recruit virtually entirely from the top dozen universities. The smaller Japanese corporations operate along the same lines, although they widen their recruitment net to cover the next forty or so universities in the prestige hierarchy. Thus, obtaining entry to a prestigious university is a far more vital step for a successful career in Japan than it is in the United States or Europe.

Secondly, like the elite senior high schools, the elite universities are meritocratic. The great majority of universities are public institutions, receiving substantial government subsidies. Again, as with the senior high schools, fees are quite low, and loans are available to defray expenses. In principle and to a considerable extent in practice, any young Japanese can get into the University of Tokyo, or one of the other elite universities, provided only that he or she is talented enough and is prepared to do the work necessary to pass the entrance examinations. Knowing this, the public believes that *all* the most talented young Japanese go to one of these universities—and, conversely, that anyone who fails to get into one of these schools is necessarily less bright. Avoiding this stigma is, of course, a further incentive for the student to work hard to get in.

The third significant factor responsible for the high educational standards in Japan is competition among schools. This operates principally among the senior high schools, and what they are competing for is academic reputation. The most prestigious senior high school in Japan is Kansei in Tokyo, and being a teacher at Kansei is something like being a professor at Harvard. The teachers' self-esteem is bound up with the academic reputation of their schools—a powerful motivator for teachers to teach well.

In addition to this important factor of self-esteem, there is practical necessity. Since students are free to attend any school they can get into, if a school failed to provide good-quality teaching, it would no longer attract students. In business terms, its customers would fade away, and it would be forced to close. Thus the essential feature of the competition among the Japanese senior high schools is that it exposes the teachers to the discipline of the free-enterprise system. In the case of the public senior high schools, the system can be regarded as a form of market socialism in which the competing institutions are state-owned but nevertheless compete against each other for their customers. Here the Japanese have been successfully operating the kind of system that Mikhail Gorbachev may be feeling his way toward introducing in the Soviet Union. The Japanese private senior high schools add a further capitalist element to the system insofar as they offer their educational services more or less like firms operating in a conventional market.

The problem of how market disciplines can be brought to bear on schools has been widely discussed in America and also in Britain ever since Milton Friedman raised it a quarter of a century or so ago, but solutions such as Friedman's voucher proposal seem as distant today as they did then. Although the proposal has been looked at sympathetically by Republicans in the United States and by Conservatives in Britain, politicians in both countries have fought shy of introducing it. Probably they have concluded that the problems of getting vouchers into the hands of all parents, and dealing with losses, fraud, counterfeits, and so forth, are likely to be too great for the scheme to be feasible.

The Japanese have evolved a different method of exposing schools to market forces. Subsidies are paid directly to the schools on a per-capita basis in accordance with the number of students they have. If a school's rolls decline, so do its incomes, both from subsidies and from fees. This applies to both the public and private senior high schools, although the public schools obviously receive a much greater proportion of their income as subsidies and a smaller portion from fees.

A similar scheme is being introduced in Britain. The Thatcher government is currently bringing in legislation that will permit public schools to opt out of local-authority control. Those that opt out will receive subsidies from the central government on the basis of the number of students they have. They will then be on their own, to sink or swim.

There is little doubt that this is the route that should be followed in America. The exposure of American schools to the invigorating stimulus of competition, combined with the introduction of a national curriculum and the provision of stronger incentives for students, would work wonders. Rather than complaining about Japanese aggressiveness and instituting counterproductive protectionist measures, Americans ought to be looking to the source of Japan's power.

REVISIONS

During the revision process, you look at your draft through fresh eyes to evaluate what you've done well and what you might do better. Though you may write your first draft with little thought for readers, you evaluate and revise the draft with your readers clearly in mind. The effectiveness of your writing is based on how well they understand your thoughts and respond to them. The shift in emphasis from first to second draft is from getting your ideas on paper to presenting them most effectively to your readers.

REVISION GUIDELINES

As you read and evaluate your draft, consider these suggestions.

1. Evaluate the strength of your opening. Have you introduced your topic in an interesting way? Do readers know you are going to make a comparison that may eventually help them make a decision?

2. Evaluate the effectiveness of your comparisons. Can readers clearly see the differences (and similarities) among subjects in the important areas of comparison? Have you evaluated each subject in each area? Have you covered all of the most important factors that readers should consider?

3. Evaluate your ending. Do you draw a clear conclusion for readers based on your comparative information and on what you think is the best advice? Have you drawn an unqualified conclusion (one recommendation for everyone) or a qualified conclusion (different recommendations based on readers' needs), and does it make the most sense for your topic and readers?

4. Have you paragraphed your paper so that your opening, your areas of comparison, and your conclusion stand out for readers? Have you changed paragraphs as you compared different factors? Have you avoided extremely long or short paragraphs? Have you used *transitions* to tie your sentences and paragraphs together? (See the upcoming section "Paragraph Transitions.")

5. Read each sentence carefully to see how you might make it clearer, more concise, smoother, or more concrete (visual). Check to see if you have varied your sentence structures, joining words, and sentence lengths. (See the review section on "Sentence Revision" later in the unit.)

REVISION ACTIVITY 4.6

In small groups, read and evaluate the following student first draft by applying the revision guidelines presented and noting suggestions for improvement.

Next, read and evaluate each classmate's draft—with group members providing copies of their drafts—and make suggestions for possible revisions.

Living Options

STUDENT SAMPLE DRAFT

Living in an apartment or living in a dorm provides almost the same living style, except for a few differences. I have had the experience of living in an apartment and a dorm. From what I can see, they have very little difference. It would not make a difference as to where I lived as long as I had a place.

Having an apartment has some good qualities. In an apartment you have your own bathroom and don't have to share with anyone besides a roommate. Living in an apartment makes it easier to take a shower because you don't have to wait in line. Another thing is no waiting in line for the bathroom. You would always have to bring your shampoo and soap back and forth if living in a dorm. If you live in an apartment, you keep all your necessities in your bathroom. You also have more privacy. You don't have to hear the other college students doing other things besides homework. Lastly, you choose a person to live with as in a dorm, you get stuck with whoever it may be.

Living in a dorm is not too bad. You might not like your roommate, but you have many other students in the same building you get along with. It makes it easier when you need help with your homework, the reason being there are many other people who could help. If you live in an apartment, the only person to help is your roommate. Another good thing about living in a dorm is not having to clean the bathroom or the kitchen. Having an apartment means a lot more cleaning. In a dorm all you have to clean is your room. The best thing of all is you don't have to cook. You are able to eat at the cafeteria.

Based on what I have experienced, I would recommend an apartment for more quiet and reserved people. A dorm would be for someone who liked to socialize more. I would feel more comfortable living in an apartment. That is for the fact of more privacy. I would not mind cleaning and cooking for myself. The last reason would be because I am very strict as to whom I live with.

REVISION ACTIVITY 4.7

Evaluate your draft a final time, noting revisions you may want to make to improve your paper. (Your instructor may have you cover the upcoming sections on "Paragraph Transitions" and "Sentence Revision" before evaluating your draft.)

When you are ready, write your second draft, including all revisions you have noted for improving its content, organization, and wording.

JOURNAL ENTRY FOURTEEN

If you wrote your first draft on a computer, relate in your journal how much revising you did as you wrote. Did you write the entire first draft with little or no sentence revision, or did you do some sentence revision as you wrote the draft? What kinds of revisions did you make in the second draft to improve your paper?

PARAGRAPH TRANSITIONS

Writers use a variety of words called *transitions* to tie their sentences and paragraphs together effectively. The purpose of transitional wording is to help readers understand the relationship between different thoughts and also the relationship between different paragraphs.

You undoubtedly use some transitions in your writing already. The purpose of this section is to make you more aware of their value, to present the range of transitional wording available, and to help you use transitions more effectively in your writing.

Useful Transitions

The following transitional words and phrases are useful for most writing you do.

1. Transitions that show movement in time, place, or sequence: first, second, next, also, then, after, before, while, now, in the meantime, in conclusion, as you can see, finally, last, in summary.

2. Transitions that connect supporting points, ideas, or examples: first, second, also, another, in addition, additionally, furthermore, moreover, whereas, on top of that, beyond that, for example, for instance, such as, like.

3. Transitions that show relationships between thoughts: however, therefore, nevertheless, thus, despite, in spite of, on the contrary, on the other hand, consequently, moreover, frankly, honestly, between you and me, confidentially, actually, truthfully, in fact, of course, in reality.

The following groupings of transitions by meaning or function will help you use them correctly and be aware of the options available.

Contrasting transitions	Cause-effect transitions	Comparative transitions
on the other hand	therefore	while
however	thus	whereas
nevertheless	consequently	on the other hand
on the contrary		however
despite		whether
in spite of		

"Adding" transitions	"Example" transitions	Concluding transitions
furthermore	for example	in conclusion
moreover	for instance	as you can see
on top of that	like	last
in addition	such as	in summary
beyond that	finally	
additionally	last but not least	

"Straight talk" transitions

frankly

honestly

to be frank

between you and me

confidentially

actually

in fact

truthfully

of course

in reality

Transitions such as *however, therefore, furthermore,* and *nevertheless* are often preceded by a semicolon (;). The semicolon indicates the beginning of a new sentence closely related to the sentence preceding it. When you use a semicolon to separate two sentences, you do *not* capitalize the first letter of the second sentence.

EXAMPLES   I need to go Christmas shopping; however, I don't know when I will find time.

Louise is living at home this semester; therefore, she'll save the cost of renting an apartment.

Alicia got an A on her English final; furthermore, she passed biology after two previous attempts.

Felix bowled a score of 23 his first game; nevertheless, he had a good time.

TRANSITION ACTIVITY 4.8

In small groups, read the following paragraphs with their transitions underlined. For each underlined transition, come up with one or two optional transitions that could also be used effectively in place of the underlined transitions.

Getting across town from east to west can take time; <u>therefore</u>, you need to plan the best route and time to reach your destination. Herndon is probably the best east-west street to take at most times. <u>However</u>, at 5:00 rush hour, it gets very congested. <u>Consequently</u>, you may want to take Bullard Avenue at rush hour because it is less conjested. <u>Furthermore</u>, Bullard has been worked on in the last year, so the road is very smooth.

<u>On the other hand</u>, there are a couple of routes, <u>like</u> Highway 168 and Highway 41, that may seem out of the way because they run more north-south. <u>Despite</u> their direction, they can ultimately deliver you to a westerly destination in a reasonable time because you can drive 70–75 miles per hour rather than 40–45 on Herndon or Bullard. <u>Moreover</u>, they are wide, beautiful new freeways that are easy and relaxing to drive on. <u>Therefore</u>, while you are taking a more roundabout route and driving more miles on the freeways, you'll get there at about the same time and in a better mood.

<u>As you can see</u>, there are different options for getting from the west to the east side of town, <u>such as</u> Herndon, Bullard, Highway 168, or Highway 41. Herndon and Bullard are more direct routes <u>whereas</u> on the freeways, you drive faster and more relaxed. I've taken different routes, and the one I choose depends on my mood, the time of day, and how rushed I am. <u>Frankly</u>, there's no really good way to drive east to west in town, and until the county builds an east-to-west running freeway, people who commute in that direction are going to be frustrated.

TRANSITION ACTIVITY 4.9

In small groups, read the following essay "Through the One-Way Mirror" by Margaret Atwood. Identify the transitions that she uses in each paragraph, and the purpose for each transition. Then discuss the questions at the end of the essay.

Then check your latest draft for transitional wording, and insert transitions wherever you think they would help connect ideas, sentences, or paragraphs.

Through the One-Way Mirror
by Margaret Atwood

The noses of a great many Canadians resemble Porky Pig's. This comes from spending so much time pressing them against the longest undefended one-way mirror in the world. The Canadians looking through this mirror behave the way people on the hidden side of such mirrors usually do: they observe, analyze, ponder, snoop and wonder what all the activity on the other side means in decipherable human terms.

The Americans, bless their innocent little hearts, are rarely aware that they are even being watched, much less by the Canadians. They just go on doing body language, playing in the sandbox of the world, bashing one another on the head and planning how to blow things up, same as always. If they think about Canada at all, it's only when things get a bit snowy or the water goes off or the Canadians start fussing over some piddly detail, such as fish. Then they regard them as unpatriotic; for Americans don't really see Canadians as foreigners, not like the Mexicans, unless they do something weird like speak French or beat the New York Yankees at baseball. Actually, think the Americans, the Canadians are just like us, or would be if they could.

On the other hand, we could switch metaphors and call the border the longest undefended backyard fence in the world. The Canadians are the folks in the neat little bungalow, with the tidy little garden and the duck pond. The Americans are the other folks, the ones in the sprawly mansion with the bad-taste statues on the lawn. There's a perpetual party, or something, going on there, such as loud music, raucous laughter, smoke billowing from the barbecue. Beer bottles and Coke cans land among the peonies. The Canadians have their own beer bottles and barbecue smoke, but they tend to overlook it. Frankly, your own mess is always more forgivable than the mess someone else makes on your patio.

However, the Canadians can't exactly call the police—they suspect that the Americans are the police—and part of their distress, which seems permanent, comes from their uncertainty as to whether or not they've been invited. Sometimes they do drop by next door, and find it exciting but scary. Sometimes the Americans drop by their house and find it clean. This worries the Canadians. In fact, they worry a lot. Maybe those Americans will want to buy up their duck pond, with all the money they seem to have, and turn it into a cesspool or a water-skiing emporium.

Moreover, it worries them that the Americans don't seem to know who the Canadians are, or even where, exactly, they are. Sometimes the Americans call Canada their backyard, sometimes their front yard, both of which imply ownership. Sometimes they say they are the Mounties and the Canadians are Rose Marie. (All these things have, in fact, been said by American politicians.) Then they accuse the Canadians of being paranoid and having an identity crisis. Heck, there is no call for the Canadians to fret about their identity, because everyone knows they're Americans, really. If the Canadians disagree with that, they're told not to be so insecure.

One of the problems is that Canadians and Americans are educated backward from one another. The Canadians—except for the Quebecois, one keeps saying—are taught about the rest of the world first and Canada second. The Americans are taught about the United States first, and maybe later about other places, if they're of strategic importance. The Vietnam

War draft dodgers got more culture shock in Canada than they did in Sweden. It's not the clothing that is different, it's those mental noises.

Of course, none of this holds true when you get close enough, where concepts like "Americans" and "Canadians" dissolve and people are just people, or anyway some of them are, the ones you happen to approve of. I, for instance, have never met any Americans I didn't like, but I only get to meet the nice ones. That's what the businessmen think too, though they have other individuals in mind. But big-scale national mythologies have a way of showing up in things like foreign policy, and at events like international writers' congresses, where the Canadians often find they have more to talk about with the Australians, the West Indians, the New Zealanders and even the once-loathed snooty Brits, now declining into humanity with the dissolution of empire, than they do with the impenetrable and mysterious Yanks.

But only sometimes. Because surely the Canadians understand the Yanks. Shoot, don't they see Yank movies, read Yank mags, bobble round to Yank music and watch Yank telly, as well as their own, when there is any?

Sometimes the Canadians think it's their job to interpret the Yanks to the rest of the world; explain them, sort of. This is an illusion: they don't understand the Yanks as much as they think they do, and it isn't their job.

But, as we say up here among God's frozen people, when Washington catches a cold, Ottawa sneezes. Some Canadians even refer to their capital city as Washington North and wonder why we're paying those guys in Ottawa when a telephone order service would be cheaper. Canadians make jokes about the relationship with Washington which the Americans, in their thin-skinned, bunion-toed way, construe as anti-American (they tend to see any nonworshipful comment coming from that gray, protoplasmic fuzz outside their borders as anti-American). They are no more anti-American than the jokes Canadians make about the weather: it's there, it's big, it's hard to influence, and it affects your life.

Of course, in any conflict with the Dreaded Menace, whatever it might be, the Canadians would line up with the Yanks, probably, if they thought it was a real menace, or if the Yanks twisted their arms or other bodily parts enough or threatened a "scorched-earth policy" (another real quote). Note the qualifiers. The Canadian idea of a menace is not the same as the U.S. one. Canada, for instance, never broke off diplomatic relations with Cuba, and it was quick to recognize China. Contemplating the U.S.–Soviet growling match, Canadians are apt to recall a line from Blake: "They became what they beheld." Certainly both superpowers suffer from the imperial diseases once so noteworthy among the Romans, the British and the French: arrogance and myopia. But the bodily-parts threat is real enough, and accounts for the observable wimpiness and flunkiness of some Ottawa politicians. Nobody, except at welcoming-committee time, pretends this is an equal relationship.

In reality, Americans don't have Porky Pig noses. Instead they have Mr. Magoo eyes, with which they see the rest of the world. That would not be a problem if the United States were not so powerful. But it is, so it is.

QUESTIONS FOR DISCUSSION

1. What are the main points of comparison between Canadians and Americans in the essay? Why do you think Atwood selected these particular points?

2. Based on the points of comparison, how do Canadians and Americans differ, and how are they similar? What evidence does Atwood use to support her contentions?

3. How is the comparison organized?

4. What audience do you think the essay is intended for? What is Atwood's purpose for writing the essay? How well do you feel the purpose is accomplished?

5. How does your viewpoint of Canada and Canadians compare to how Atwood feels Americans view them? How accurately do you think Atwood captures America's world view (Americans have "Mr. Magoo eyes")?

TRANSITION ACTIVITY 4.10

Fill in the following paragraphs with transitional words to tie sentences and paragraphs together. Fill each blank with a word or phrase from the list of transitions that makes the most appropriate connection. Then reread your latest draft and see where you might add a transitional word or phrase to show a relationship between thoughts or different paragraphs, or to begin your concluding paragraph.

EXAMPLES <u>Before</u> buying a new typewriter, shop around for a used one.

<u>Then</u> look for reasonably priced typing paper.

Buying a used car is a complicated business. _____, decide the make and year of car you're interested in. _____ look through the newspaper to see what's available. You will find the largest number of cars in the ads for used car lots. _____, you may find your best buy under the private owner ads since these cars aren't marked up for profits as much as lot cars are.

_____, pick out a few cars that look interesting and spend a day looking at them. Take along pen and paper so you can take notes on each car and make comparisons.

_____ you look at a car, check the odometer for mileage, and confirm that the reading is accurate. The fewer miles on the car, the longer life it will have. _____ check the tires for wear and the body for dents or indications of body work done for accident repair. If the body looks good, the miles are reasonably low, and the tires are safe, take the car for a test drive._____, test the brakes. _____ see how the car handles. Does it veer to the right or left when you release the wheel? Does it vibrate as you increase speed? Does the engine make any suspicious noises? Are there bothersome rattles inside the car? Does everything work: lights, radio, windshield wipers, heater, turn signals? Any combination of negative signs could indicate serious problems for the future. _____, some problems are easily curable, and if you like the car except for a problem or two, don't completely write it off.

_____ you finish with one car, check out the other cars similarly. _____ compare all the cars to see which one you prefer. You may not like any of them; _____, you should wait for new cars to surface in the paper and try again instead of settling for a car you don't want.

_____, if there is a car you are interested in, take one last step. Take the car to a professional mechanic to give it a thorough inspection. For about $30, a mechanic can check it over carefully and test drive it to give you an expert's viewpoint. _____ you have done all you can to ensure you're getting a good car. _____ all your precautions, you may still have some trouble, but you've gone a long way toward buying a reliable used car.

SENTENCE REVISION

For most writers, sentence revision is an important part of the writing process. You revise sentences to help readers understand your ideas better and to find the best wording possible. To accomplish this, you might change a word or two in one sentence, move a phrase in another, and completely reword a third.

In this section, you continue to hone your skills by revising typical first-draft sentences. Then you apply what you learn to revising the latest draft of your comparison paper.

Wording Problems Review

An important part of draft revision is improving the wording of individual sentences. Not only are you making your sentences more readable, you are also clarifying your thoughts for your readers and yourself.

REVISION REVIEW ACTIVITY 4.11

The following first-draft sentences have problems with wordiness, awkward phrasing, weak word choices, and vagueness. Rewrite each sentence to make it smoother, clearer, and more concise. Then read the latest draft of your comparison paper for possible sentence revisions.

EXAMPLE	When I work this summer at a job, I'm going to save my money for a car that is used.
REVISED	When I work this summer, I'm going to save my money for a used car.

1. One person I'll always remember and never forget is a girl named Cloretta.

2. It takes a special person who can deal with the many problems faced daily by an automotive mechanic to be one.

3. I have been learning my boys, two of them, to swim, but they haven't learned yet.

4. My best friend I ever had was not a person that I even liked to begin with.

5. The trees are easy to see if you go through the sidewalk.

6. The tree is full of golden leaves, and there are some leaves that are about to fall and about to announce that fall is almost upon us.

7. When buying a used car, the first thing you do is to find a lot of used cars to look at.

8. The game of golf can be conducted with the whole family in assemblage.

9. She is the type of person whom you can tell secrets to and not worry about spreading of those secrets.

10. In the profession of boxing, the price of successfulness is often physical damage that could last a lifetime or even less.

11. The taillights and turn signals are together, red being the taillights and yellow the turn signals, the taillight above the turn signal.

12. The Volkswagen was a vast growth in Germany in the 1940s.

13. The next step is for you to go over every one of your sentences and try to find different ways that you can improve each one to make better sentences.

14. It was with immense difficulty that we affirmatively located the establishment selling foods of a fried nature.

15. Lonette couldn't find a way that was best for her to study for the biology test that covered over four chapters and over a hundred pages of material.

Sentence Variety

Writers who use a variety of sentence structures express themselves most effectively and produce the most readable writing. The more structural options you use, the better equipped you are to express yourself, and the more readers can appreciate your writing.

Relative Clauses

A sentence structure that many writers find useful is the complex sentence with a *relative clause*. A relative clause begins with a relative pronoun—*who, whom, whose, which,* or *that*—that modifies the word preceding it.

EXAMPLES   The man <u>who borrowed your lawn mower</u> moved to Alaska.

Here on the table are the books <u>that you left at my house</u>.

The math problem <u>that Joan had trouble with</u> is puzzling everyone.

The men <u>who own the fruit stand</u> are selling some beautiful nectarines.

That blue Mazda is the car <u>that I'd like to own someday</u>.

Ralph picked the watermelon <u>that was the largest and ripest</u>.

The woman <u>whose money you found</u> lives in Paris.

Hanna's umbrella, <u>which she bought for $30</u>, has a hole in it.

The students <u>who did well on the geology final</u> all studied together.

As you can see, the underlined clauses beginning with *who, which, that,* and *whose* describe or identify the word directly before them. Here is how the relative pronouns are used.

WHO   used with *people* The child <u>who</u> ate the gooseberries got sick.

WHOM   used with *people* The plumber <u>whom</u> you sent to my house was expensive.

WHOSE   used with *people* The girl <u>whose</u> book was lost is in the library.

WHOSE   used with *things* The textbook <u>whose</u> cover is torn was sold at half price.

THAT   used with *people* The family <u>that</u> lives next door moved.

used with *things* The magazine <u>that</u> you subscribe to is terrific.

WHICH   used with *things* The "L" Street route, <u>which</u> is lined with trees, is very direct.

RELATIVE CLAUSE ACTIVITY 4.12

Complete the following complex sentences with your own words.

EXAMPLE   The man who lives behind us <u>*mows his lawn at night*</u>

The alligator that _____

She was the actress who _____

The only students who _____

Your new toaster, which _____

That new teacher whom you _____

The rock group that _____

I like a hamburger that _____

Please return my stamp collection, which_____

The kind of dog that _____

The movie star whose _____

I really prefer a doctor who _____

RELATIVE CLAUSE ACTIVITY 4.13

Combine each of the following pairs of sentences to form a single sentence with a relative clause beginning with *who, whom, whose, which,* or *that*. Delete unnecessary words when you combine sentences. Separate the relative clause in the new sentence with commas when the person or thing it modifies is *named:* John Brown, who is a golfing instructor, attends college at night. The Barkley Tower, which stands in the middle of Heathcliff College, is three hundred feet tall. The man who is a golfing instructor attends college at night. The tower that stands in the middle of Heathcliff College is three hundred feet tall. Never use commas with relative clauses beginning with *that*.

EXAMPLE   Maria Gomez works at Bank of America. She lives down the street from me.

EXAMPLE   Maria Gomez, who works at Bank of America, lives down
                 the street from me.

REVISED (OPTION) Maria Gomez, who lives down the street from me, works
                  at Bank of America.

1. The boy sat behind me in Algebra. He dropped the class after two weeks.

2. You took the woman's seat on the bus. She is very mad.

3. The Kings River flooded its banks yesterday. It is often dry this time of year.

4. The foreign students are from Laos and Cambodia. I met them at the student union yesterday.

5. Glen and Elvira are good students. They will do very well in graduate school.

6. *The Congo* by Michael Crichton was an intriguing book. I couldn't put it down.

7. I found a man's wallet at the supermarket yesterday. He gave me a $25 reward.

8. I tried to buy concert tickets from a scalper. They would have cost me $100 apiece.

9. Melissa Guthridge contributes to numerous charities for children. She is very generous with her money.

10. The Bay Bridge is over five miles long. It is the longest bridge in the western United States.

REVISION ACTIVITY 4.14

Read the latest draft of your comparison paper and revise sentences to vary your sentence structures, to replace any overused joining words (such as *and, but, so,* or *because*), to combine short sentences or divide overly long ones, or to combine pairs of sentences by inserting relative clauses.

FINAL EDITING

The last step in the writing process is to give your latest draft a final proofreading for errors. If you are using a computer, print out the draft rather than reading it on the screen. You will often find errors on the printed page that you would overlook otherwise.

PROOFREADING GUIDELINES

When you proofread your latest draft, make sure to cover the following areas, and pay particular attention to your personal error tendencies.

1. Make sure you have a period at the end of each sentence. Check for run-on sentences that need periods (or joining words) and for sentence fragments that should be attached to the sentences they belong with. (See the upcoming review sections on run-on sentences and fragments.)

2. Check word endings to make sure you have an *s* on plural words and an *ed* on regular past tense verbs and that your subjects and verbs agree. (See the review section on subject-verb agreement later in the unit.)

3. Check your spelling carefully, including homonyms such as there/their/they're, know/no, its/it's, your/you're, and threw/through.

4. Check your internal punctuation, including comma usage in words in series, in compound sentences, after introductory groups of words, and to set off relative clauses, "interrupters," and ending phrases. (See the section on "Comma Usage" with relative clauses, interrupters, and ending phrases.) Make sure you have apostrophes in contractions and possessive words (John's dog, the pencil's eraser, the legislature's schedule) and quotation marks around direct quotations. (See the section on "Possessives" under "Spelling" in the Appendix.)

5. Check your use of subject pronouns (Martha and I; my mother, father, and I; Gretchen and she; the Joneses and they), and make sure all pronouns agree with their antecedents. (See the "Correct Usage" section later in the unit.)

PROOFREADING ACTIVITY 4.15

In small groups, proofread the following student draft for errors and make the necessary corrections. Next, proofread your latest draft for errors following the revision guidelines presented, and make corrections. (Your instructor may have you cover the upcoming sections on punctuation and grammar before proofreading.) Finally, write or print out your final draft to share with classmates and your instructor.

Space Vessels

Student Sample Draft There is only one type of space vessel that we as a planet use that is the space shuttle. That is the one everyone knows about and has seen. Rite now they are working on a new one that they call the X-33. Which looks a lot like a plane rather than a space shuttle.

The old shuttle was more of a bullet shape with wings; its engines made a lot of unwanted pollution as a by-product of its engines working. However, the X-33's engines instead of polluting the air, make water, which gives the astronauts plenty of water. Which is a big help because they don't have to put any water on bored, making the ship lighter.

The old shuttle only had one way to take off and that was strait up, but the X-33 does not it can take off just like a plane making it much more practical than having to build a launch pad, not to mention those one-time usable booster rockets that costs about $400,000,000 to build.

The X-33 can also go faster and farther than the old shuttle could go. It also has a fully automatic venting system, which the shuttle does not the system will automatically suck any smoke or tocsin out into space it also reuses the air in the shuttle.

The X-33 also has new thermal plates that are able to stand reentry at least two time instead of one. So overall, the X-33 is a better ship for us all together. Which makes me think that we will see a lot more of space after it is finished in 2010.

JOURNAL ENTRY FIFTEEN

In your journal, relate one particular error tendency that you still have, the progress you have made in correcting it, and what you still need to do to eliminate the error in future writing.

SENTENCE PROBLEMS

The most common sentence problems—run-on sentences and fragments—have been introduced in earlier units. However, for students who have recurring problems, they will be reviewed in this section and throughout the text. You seldom eliminate a longtime error tendency after a brief lesson or two, but by working on it throughout the text, you can make great progress.

RUN-ON SENTENCE REVIEW ACTIVITY 4.16

The following passage contains some run-on sentences. Rewrite the passage and correct the run-on sentences by separating complete sentences or joining them with coordinate or subordinate conjunctions. Separate longer sentences and join shorter, related sentences.

EXAMPLE	The teachers were upset. They had received no raise for three years they decided not to return to school in the fall without a decent contract.
REVISED	The teachers were upset. They had received no raise for three years, so they decided not to return to school in the fall without a decent contract.

Joe was placed in the state penitentiary, he had served time in other places. His first trouble came in grade school. He was caught sniffing glue. He stayed in detention for a night his parents refused to pick him up until morning. Six months later he was back in juvy for stabbing a boy in the shoulder with an ice pick. He got into three more fights with inmates while in detention, he was finally released, his parents had split up neither of them wanted Joe. He was sent to live with an aunt in Grace Falls. He kept out of trouble for over a year until he got involved with some older men. They robbed a liquor store, he drove the car, later they had him delivering drugs because he was a minor. He finally got caught and was sent to detention for two more years. When he got out, he ran away and melted into the street life of the city. His aunt didn't hear about him for two years until she got a call that he had been arrested for assaulting a junkie. He was a month over eighteen, so when he was convicted, he was sent to the state penitentiary, no one from his family visited him.

Fragments

As you learned in Unit Three, fragments are caused by separating a clause from the sentence it belongs with or by leaving out words that would complete the sentence.

EXAMPLE	I'm very tired this morning. Because I only got three hours of sleep last night.
CORRECTED	I'm very tired this morning because I only got three hours of sleep last night. *(because fragment is joined to sentence it belongs with)*
EXAMPLE	Walking to school this morning in the driving rain.
CORRECTED	I was miserable walking to school this morning in the driving rain. *(words added to form complete sentences)*

Fragments are most commonly created through punctuation errors and can be remedied by eliminating the period that separates them from the sentence they belong with.

FRAGMENT REVIEW ACTIVITY 4.17

Each of the following groups of sentences contains one fragment. Correct the fragment by adding it to the sentence that it belongs with.

EXAMPLE	Joe was late for work. Since others were also late. Joe had no problem.
REVISED	Joe was late for work. Since others were also late, Joe had no problem.

1. People are traveling more. Because gas prices aren't increasing. Hopefully, prices won't go up this summer.

2. Before you buy a car at Happy Harry's. Check it out carefully. He sells some real junk.

3. A nuclear accident is always possible. Unless nuclear energy plants are dismantled. Environmental groups continue to protest their existence.

4. Clean out your closet. When you finish. Give me the shirts you've out-grown.

5. The crowds used to be sparse at Minneapolis stadium. People are returning in large numbers. Because the Twins have started winning again.

6. Although the current recession is tough. It doesn't compare to the Great Depression. Ask people who have been through both.

7. Hanna is trusting. Because she believes in people. Her brother is the suspicious one.

8. Thanks for the great breakfast. Before I leave. Can I do the dishes for you?

9. The trip is on. Unless it snows. We'll go if it rains.

10. The choir practiced for hours. They sang the Messiah five times. Before they had finished for the night.

PUNCTUATION

In earlier units the three most common uses for commas were introduced: within series of words, before conjunctions in compound sentences, and after introductory groups of words. In this section, you learn three new uses for commas: to set off relative clauses (which were introduced earlier in this unit), interrupters, and ending phrases.

Comma Usage

Add the following rules for comma usage to those you learned in previous units.

1. *Relative clauses:* To punctuate relative clauses correctly, follow these basic rules:

    a. If the word modified by a *who* or *which* clause is clearly named or identified, the clause is set off by commas.

    Mary Garcia, <u>who owns the dress shop on "G" Street</u>, is my neighbor. (Mary Garcia *clearly names the person.*)

The Golden Gate Bridge, <u>which spans San Francisco Bay</u>, is painted annually. (Golden Gate Bridge *clearly names the bridge.*)

The new fish market on Oliver Avenue, <u>which opened its doors last Friday</u>, specializes in shellfish. (New fish market on Oliver Avenue *clearly identifies the market.*)

Matt Golden, <u>who drives a milk truck</u>, married Emma Blue, <u>who lives on his route</u>. (Matt Golden *and* Emma Blue *clearly name the people.*)

b. If a *who* or *which* clause is needed to identify clearly the word it modifies, don't set it off with commas.

The men <u>who work for my aunt</u> live in Trenton. (Who work for my aunt *identifies the men.*)

The directions <u>which you gave us</u> were easy to follow. (Which you gave us *identifies the directions.*)

I'd like to meet the woman <u>who painted that strange picture</u>. (Who painted that strange picture *identifies the woman.*)

c. Never use commas with relative clauses beginning with *that*.

The students <u>that sit in back of the room</u> are very talkative.

I'd like to see the watermelon <u>that weighs over fifty pounds</u>.

2. *Interrupters:* Set off incidental words and phrases that require reading pauses in a sentence.

<u>By the way</u>, what time are you going to class today?

I am interested, <u>of course</u>, in getting a good grade and in learning a lot about physics.

<u>Fortunately</u>, I did a lot of scuba diving before diving off the coast of Australia.

My father, <u>as you might know</u>, works with your father at the Lockheed Aircraft plant.

3. *Ending phrases:* To indicate a reading pause, insert a comma before an ending group of words that begins with an *ing*-word or the word *especially* or *particularly*.

Leticia sped through the multiple choice half of her physics test, knowing that the thought problems in the second half would take a lot of time.

Jonathan walked home disappointedly from the Department of Motor Vehicles, wondering if he would ever pass his driving test.

Washington, D.C., is beautiful in the spring, especially when the cherry blossoms are in bloom.

Shop at Martin's Boutique for floral arrangements, particularly if you like silk flowers.

COMMA ACTIVITY 4.18

Place commas in the following sentences according to all the rules you have learned. Some sentences won't require commas. When you finish, proofread your latest draft for correct comma placement.

EXAMPLE   In the early morning hours Mary prowls the house and waits for dawn to break.

REVISED   In the early morning hours, Mary prowls the house and waits for dawn to break. *(comma after introductory phrase)*

1. John and Henrietta decided to jog to school and back three times a week.

2. John Helen and Henrietta decided to jog to school and they later decided to jog back home as well.

3. Before you try the cornflakes in the cupboard check the packaging date on the box and see how old they are.

4. Samantha really enjoys playing strange characters in plays because the parts are so different from her personality.

5. After Gladys fixed the radiator hose on her Plymouth the fan belt and the smaller radiator hose broke.

6. Working on his stamp collection and watching old "Cisco Kid" reruns on TV are Albert's pastimes and he ignores everything else around him for weeks at a time.

7. For the week-long field trip to Death Valley we'll need picks and shovels tents and cots food and water and heavy jackets.

8. Harvey left third base at the crack of the bat and raced for home plate well ahead of the ball.

9. From the looks of that cut on your head and your bruised knees you'd better see a doctor and do it fast!

10. Louise and Mavis invited Teddie and Rumford to the Lucky Horseshoe Casino and then didn't show up.

11. If I had a dime for every time you had an excuse for being late for work I could retire early and live like a king.

12. Allyson thought about attending Mumsford College and even sent in an application but at the last minute she decided to attend a business college.

13. Rex Garcia who was born in Santa Fe, New Mexico is now the mayor of his hometown.

14. When I returned to my apartment I found Marian Weber an old high school friend waiting for me outside.

15. I wanted to sit in a floor seat at the Tina Turner concert but since all floor seat tickets are sold I'll settle for a balcony seat which costs $15.

16. My uncle by the way knows your family well.

17. I'm not interested in going to the debate especially since it doesn't start until 10:00 P.M.

18. Pao didn't worry about the language entrance exam knowing he could take it again before school started.

19. You'll have no trouble finding the library which is the only round building on campus.

20. Incidentally do you know who our new neighbors are?

CORRECT USAGE

Standard English follows basic rules of grammar that govern the way we write and talk. Such rules make it possible for people to communicate effectively anywhere in the world where English is spoken. Knowledge of these rules and their practical application to writing and speaking is essential to our functioning effectively within the world of educated people.

In this section you are introduced to a new area of grammar—pronoun-antecedent agreement—and you review what you learned about subject-verb agreement in Unit Three. Understanding and applying rules of agreement are fundamental to writing correctly.

Pronoun-Antecedent Agreement

Pronouns replace words that don't need repeating in a sentence or paragraph. To use pronouns most effectively, follow these basic conventions:

1. Replace a word with a pronoun instead of repeating the word unnecessarily.

AWKWARD	The building lost the <u>building's</u> roof in the tornado.
BETTER	The building lost <u>its</u> roof in the tornado.
AWKWARD	Betty was going to be late for class, so <u>Betty</u> called her teacher.
BETTER	Betty was going to be late for class, so <u>she</u> called her teacher.

2. A pronoun agrees in number and gender with the word it replaces: its *antecedent*. For example, if an antecedent is singular and female (Betty), the pronouns replacing it must be singular and female (she, her, hers). In the following examples, the antecedent is underlined twice; the pronoun replacing it is underlined once.

EXAMPLES   A <u>student</u> in dental assisting must take twelve units of science if <u>she</u> wants to get a degree. *(The antecedent* student *is singular, so the pronoun* she *referring to* student *is also singular.)*

<u>One</u> of the boys is missing <u>his</u> watch. *(The antecedent* one *is singular, so the pronoun* his *referring to* one *is also singular.)*

<u>Women</u> should never downgrade <u>their</u> abilities. *(The antecedent* women *is plural, so the pronoun* their *referring to* women *is also plural.)*

<u>Jays</u> are beautiful birds. <u>They</u> are a brilliant blue color in winter. *(The antecedent* jays *is plural, so the pronoun* they *referring to* jays *is also plural, even if it is in a different sentence.)*

3. The following pronoun forms agree with the following antecedents:

   a. singular female antecedent (woman, Barbara): she, her, hers, herself

   b. singular male antecedent (man, Roscoe): he, him, his, himself

   c. singular genderless antecedent (book, desk): it, its, itself

   d. singular male/female antecedent (a person, a student, one): he or she, his or her, himself or herself

   e. plural female antecedent (girls, women): they, them, their, theirs, themselves

   f. plural male antecedent (boys, men): they, them, their, theirs, themselves

   g. plural genderless antecedent (trees, boxes): they, them, their, theirs, themselves

h. others + yourself (John and I, the class and I): we, our, ours, ourselves

i. person spoken to ("Mary," "Felix"): you, your, yours, yourself

j. yourself: I, me, my, mine, myself

The following sentences show a variety of pronoun-antecedent agreement situations (the pronoun is underlined, and an arrow is drawn to the antecedent).

Rita lost her wallet, and she had twelve credit cards in it.

A twenty-dollar bill is lying on the kitchen table, and it had been there for a week.

Jack, Jonathan, and Sylvester all took their SAT tests last Saturday.

Marian and I always take our dirty clothes to the dormitory laundry service.

Clyde doesn't believe that he can maintain his current 3.4 GPA.

Thelma, you look stunning in your pink taffeta dress.

The students all took their compasses with them on the backpacking trip.

A student should always lock his or her car when it's in the parking lot.

PRONOUN-ANTECEDENT ACTIVITY 4.19

Substitute an appropriate pronoun for each word that is repeated unnecessarily in the following sentences, making sure that the pronoun agrees with its antecedent.

EXAMPLE   Mary brought Mary's baby brother with Mary to class Monday.

REVISED   Mary brought her baby brother with her to class Monday.

1. That building should have been torn down years ago. That building is a terrible fire hazard.

2. Gretchen used to weigh over 190 pounds, but now Gretchen is down to 130.

3. Marian and I used to shop at Macy's, but Marian and I don't shop there anymore.

4. The teachers at the high school are getting old, and the teachers seem bored with the teachers' jobs. A lot of the teachers should retire.

5. That blister on your heel looks sore, and that blister is going to get worse if you don't put medication on that blister.

6. Thelma should do Thelma a favor and get some sleep for a change.

7. John and I don't consider John and me close friends, but John and I do share a lot of interests.

8. My English book got my English book's cover torn off of my English book. Now my English book's pages are starting to come unbound.

9. The new movie playing at the Bijou is frightening. The new movie involves deranged killers on the loose on a college campus, and the college campus looks a lot like Hillcrest Community College.

10. Small earthquakes hit the valley a number of times last month, and although the small earthquakes caused little damage, the small earthquakes kept all of the neighbors on edge. Some of the neighbors are thinking about moving.

Indefinite Pronouns

Indefinite pronouns can cause agreement problems. They are always considered *singular* and therefore always require *singular* pronoun references:

anybody	everybody	nothing
anyone	everyone	one
each	everything	somebody
either	nobody	someone
every	no one	something

The following examples of pronoun-antecedent agreement involve indefinite pronouns. This is the most troublesome agreement situation because the incorrect plural pronoun references don't *sound* wrong to many people. Here are the correct and incorrect forms:

EXAMPLES

INCORRECT Everyone should bring <u>their</u> books to the room.

CORRECT Everyone should bring <u>his</u> or <u>her</u> books to the room.

INCORRECT Each person should finish <u>their</u> homework before taking a break.

CORRECT   Each person should finish <u>his</u> or <u>her</u> homework before taking a break.

INCORRECT   No one did <u>their</u> best in the marathon because of the oppressive heat.

CORRECT   No one did <u>his</u> or <u>her</u> best in the marathon because of the oppressive heat.

INCORRECT   Somebody must have completed <u>their</u> art project before the contest deadline.

CORRECT   Somebody must have completed <u>his</u> or <u>her</u> art project before the contest deadline.

PRONOUN-ANTECEDENT ACTIVITY 4.20

Fill in the blanks in the following sentences with pronouns that agree with their antecedents. Circle the antecedent for each pronoun. When you finish, proofread your latest draft for pronoun-antecedent agreement.

EXAMPLE   The mind can snap if too much stress is placed on <u>*it*</u>.

1. The opossum hangs upside down beside _____ mate.

2. The man who won the canned hams should bring _____ car to the alley.

3. Each of the women works for _____ room and board.

4. A woman from the Bronx left _____ purse in a Manhattan theatre.

5. One of the trucks lost _____ brakes. _____ careened downhill.

6. Those bags she carries weigh a ton, and _____ are huge.

7. Pronouns should always agree in number with _____ antecedents.

8. A person should never press _____ luck.

9. Every one of the politicians made a promise that _____ couldn't keep.

10. The geraniums are losing _____ flowers very early.

11. John told me that it didn't matter to his instructors if _____ came to class late if _____ homework was completed and _____ maintained an A average on all quizzes.

12. One of the male monkeys in the middle cage kept spitting on _____ sister who _____ shared a swing with.

JOURNAL ENTRY SIXTEEN

From this unit, relate in your journal what you learned about writing comparative papers—including prewriting, drafting, revising, and editing—that may help you with future writing.

WRITING REVIEW

In the "Writing Review," you apply what you have learned throughout the unit to a second writing assignment. To write your paper, follow the process provided, which summarizes the steps presented in this unit.

WRITING PROCESS

1. Write a paper for your classmates comparing two similar subjects: American and Japanese cars, renting or buying a home, leasing or buying an automobile, getting married or living together, attending a four-year or community college, American and foreign students, walking or jogging for fitness, dormitory or apartment living, two similar majors (for example, business and business administration), high school and college, high school and college students, two computer programs, college and professional basketball. Answer the following questions to help you decide on your topic:

    a. What topic am I interested in and knowledgeable about?

    b. What topic might be interesting to some of my classmates?

    c. What would my purpose be in writing about this topic?

    d. What conclusion might I draw based on the comparison?

STUDENT SAMPLE I think I'll do some kind of comparison with students. I could compare high school and college students, but the differences seem too obvious. I could compare different types of college students on campus—athletes, aggies, student council members, computer geeks—but I think I'd end up stereotyping groups since I don't know that much about them.

I have met a number of foreign students from Southeast Asia at school and have gotten to know some of them fairly well. They have a different perspective on going to college than most American students I know. I could compare foreign students and American students, or more specifically Asian students and American students. I think I'll give it a try.

Since most American students don't mix much with foreign students, and vice versa, I think my best reading audience would be college students in general. I'm not sure what my purpose would be yet.

2. In what important areas are you going to compare your two subjects? Follow these suggestions:

   a. Come up with four or five factors to compare your subjects on.

   b. Decide in what order you want to compare these factors in your paper.

   c. Evaluate your two subjects in each area before writing.

   d. Decide on your purpose, if you haven't done so.

STUDENT SAMPLE

Comparing Asian and American Students

1. attitude toward going to college

2. reasons for attending

3. difficulties faced

4. pressure to succeed

PURPOSE   Help classmates understand their Asian peers on campus better

3. Write the first draft of your comparison paper following these suggestions:

   a. Include a beginning, middle, and ending to your paper. Introduce your topic in the beginning, make your comparisons in the middle, and draw your conclusion for readers in the ending.

   b. Keep the reading audience—your classmates—in mind as you write, and tell them things that many of them may not already know. (In other words, don't just repeat what would be common knowledge for most students.)

   c. Draw a reasonable conclusion for readers in the final paragraph(s) based on your comparison.

American and Asian Students

STUDENT SAMPLE
DRAFT
America may be the great "melting pot," but at this college, not much "melting" has taken place yet with the newest wave of foreign students, most typically Southeast Asians. These students are easily distinguished from their American counterparts, both by the way they stick together on campus and by their relative seriousness. They seem to have a determination that is often lacking in American students.

   I've gotten to know a few Asian students, not very well, but at least enough to get beyond "How ya doin'?" One thing I've learned is that they don't take college for granted like Americans. In their countries, like Cambodia, Laos, and Vietnam, college was restricted to the well-to-do, so the opportunity for a college education is a great thing for them. While most Americans take college for granted, many foreign students consider it a rare opportunity that shouldn't be wasted.

Many foreign students are attending college for different reasons than American students. They have come to America with hope but little else. Many are living in overcrowded apartments, their parents eking out a living the best they can. These students realize that their passport out of poverty is a college degree, so they are highly motivated to succeed. Many American students come from relatively comfortable backgrounds, and they feel no urgency to change their living conditions or improve their lives. They want to eventually graduate, but in the meantime, life isn't so bad.

Foreign students are also going through tremendous transitions that American students can't relate to. While they are going to school, they are at the same time learning a new language, adjusting to a different culture, and trying to fit into a foreign society. It is little wonder that they stick together on campus and seem to be quiet and shy.

As my friend Latana said (in broken English), "You're never quite sure how Americans feel about you, so you feel uncomfortable a lot. You don't talk much because you feel you talk very poorly and are afraid of sounding stupid." On the other hand, American students have no such transitions to make. As Latana said, "Foreign students have to learn how to walk and run at the same time. American students have been walking all their lives."

A final difference between American and foreign students is the pressure they feel. With Asian students, according to math professor Dr. Lum Cho, there is first the traditional fear of failing in college and "losing face," causing the family disgrace. Second, there is pressure to succeed and help the family, who is counting on you. Third, there is pressure not to "blow" a great opportunity for an education, perhaps the only opportunity you will have. Most American students feel no such pressures, and without the pressures, they are more relaxed and carefree about school.

The more I get to know a few Asian students on campus, the more I like them. They are bright, funny, and very nice. And now that I've gotten beyond "How ya doin'," I can begin to understand their seriousness, their determination, their shyness, and their sense of isolation in a strange land. They don't have a lot in common with the typical American students of today who take education for granted. They probably have a lot in common with the children of earlier Irish, Italian, and German immigrants who were sent to college with their families' hopes. In a way I envy them. For foreign students, the American dream is still exciting and alive.

4. When you finish your first draft, set it aside for a while before evaluating it. Then read the draft and apply the following revision guidelines. When you are ready, write your second draft, including all revisions for content, organization, and wording improvement.

   a. Evaluate the strength of your opening. Do you introduce your topic in an interesting way? Do readers understand what you are comparing and why? Would they want to read further?

   b. Evaluate the effectiveness of your comparison. Have you compared your subjects in all important areas? Can readers clearly see the differences (and similarities) between subjects? Have you used appropriate details and examples to help readers understand each point of comparison? Have you organized your comparison to help readers follow it clearly?

   c. Evaluate the strength of your conclusion. Does it follow logically from the comparisons you have made? If appropriate, have you given readers the best possible advice for making a decision? Is your conclusion unqualified (same recommendation for everyone) or qualified (optional recommendations based on differences among readers)?

   d. Check your paragraphing to see if readers can move smoothly through your opening, middle, and conclusion. Do you present your points of comparison in different paragraphs? Are your sentences and paragraphs tied together with appropriate transitional wording? Do you have any overly long paragraphs that need dividing or short paragraphs that need combining or developing further?

   e. Read each sentence carefully to see if you can improve its smoothness, clarity, or conciseness. Also check to see if you have over-relied on certain sentence structures or joining words, and make revisions to improve sentence variety. Finally, check the lengths of sentences and, when appropriate, combine pairs or groups of very short sentences or divide overly long ones.

5. When you have completed all revisions, proofread your paper for any remaining errors by following these guidelines:

   a. Make sure you have a period at the end of each sentence. Check your paper carefully for run-on sentences that need punctuating or for sentence fragments that need attaching to the sentences they belong with.

b. Check word endings to make sure you have an *s* on all plural words and an *ed* on regular past tense verbs and that your present tense verbs agree with their subjects.

c. Check your spelling carefully, including your use of homonyms such as there/their/they're, know/no, your/you're, threw/through, it's/its, and right/write.

d. Check internal punctuation. Have you inserted commas in series of words, before coordinate conjunctions in compound sentences, after introductory groups of words, and to set off relative clauses, interrupters, and ending phrases? Have you used apostrophes (') in contractions and possessive words and quotation marks ("I") with direct quotations?

e. Have you used correct subject pronoun forms with compound subjects? (John and I, my mother and I, Rudy and she, the Joneses and they.) Do your pronouns agree in number and gender with their antecedents? (Everyone invited his or her mother to the graduation. The Smiths brought their children with them to the party.)

6. When you are ready, write or print out the final draft of your comparison paper and share it with classmates and your instructor.

WRITING ABOUT PROBLEMS AND SOLUTIONS

Problem solving is an everyday task for most people. Class is about to begin and you can't find a parking place anywhere near your building. Where to park? You have a cart-full of groceries and realize you don't have your credit card and have just a couple of dollars on you. What to tell the checker? You've run out of gas miles from any service station and you need to be at a meeting at work in a half hour. How to get to work? Your garbage cans are overflowing and due to a holiday, the garbage pick-up won't be for another week. How to relieve your garbage problem?

Problems confront us all of the time, some of them ongoing (not enough money, not enough time), and some of them unforeseen (unplanned pregnancy, layoffs at work, classes canceled). Effective problem solving is an important part of dealing with life and whatever it sends our way.

Writing about problems and solutions has a number of values. First, it requires serious analysis of the problem: exactly what is the problem, what are its causes, what are its effects, how, if possible, can it be solved or reduced, and what will happen if it isn't solved or grows worse? Second, in writing problem/solution papers, you learn new organizational schemes which are different from previous papers. Third, writing about problems and solutions can benefit the writer—who may find a new solution to a per-plexing problem—and to readers—who may face similar problems and benefit from the writer's analysis.

Problem solving is also a group activity, and solutions to difficult problems are often found by teams of people: engineers, scientists, board of trustees, student councils, family councils, social workers. It makes sense that many minds working on the same problem will generate the most ideas, and often the best solutions come from combining ideas from different sources. During the prewriting process, you do some problem solving in groups.

PREWRITING

For your unit writing assignment, you write about a problem that affects you personally, but that also may affect other people. For example, if you are working full-time and going to school, finding time to do everything you need to may be a problem for you, but also for many other students. If the escalating cost of textbooks is eating up most of your school budget, you can bet it's affecting other students. And if are in a relationship that is fraught with problems, you probably aren't alone.

Your first prewriting task is to decide on a problem to write about, one that you would like to eliminate from your life. Once you have selected a problem, you will do a problem analysis: how did it start, what are its causes, how is it affecting you, how may it be affecting others, how might it be solved? Next, you will consider a general organizational plan for your first draft. Then after considering the best reading audience for your paper and your purpose for writing, you should be ready to write your first draft.

Since problem solving is also a group activity, you will work in small groups to generate a number of problems to consider, and later you will bring your problem to the group to get opinions on possible solutions. Sometimes we feel that our problems are unique and that we are alone with them, but that is seldom the case, and working in groups helps us realize that.

TOPIC SELECTION

By this time, you may already have thought of a problem that is weighing on you that you may want to write about. That's great. However, sometimes the first problem that comes to mind may be the most immediate and short-lived: not having the money to buy tickets for an upcoming concert, having nothing to wear for Saturday's wedding, or having to share your car with your brother for a couple of weeks. Such problems are vexing, but they are relatively minor and soon pass.

For your writing assignment, choose a lingering problem that if not resolved, will continue to trouble you: not being able to find a part-time job; continually fighting with your spouse or girlfriend/boyfriend; not being able to control your drinking (or someone else's drinking); being without a major or career interest after two years of college. And if you are facing a particularly difficult problem, no doubt others in the class have had or continue to have a similar problem.

TOPIC SELECTION ACTIVITY 5.1

In small groups, brainstorm to come up with a number of problems for writing consideration: personal problems, family problems, school-related problems, relationship problems, health problems, community problems, environmental problems, etc.

When you brainstorm, share with the group whatever ideas come to your mind without considering their relative importance. The purpose of brainstorming is to get the most ideas possible on the table. Through this process, you will undoubtedly uncover some excellent potential writing topics.

Topic Selection Guidelines

After considering the problems generated in your group's brainstorming session, and other problems you have thought of, you should be ready to decide on a problem to write on. In selecting a topic, consider these guidelines:

1. Select a topic that is a thorny problem for you: a problem that is affecting your well-being in some manner, and that can't continue as it is.

2. Select a problem that other people may also be facing or have faced— the people who would ideally form your reading audience.

3. Select a problem that you don't already have a ready solution for. One purpose of this assignment is to seek solutions where none appear to exist.

4. Select a problem that you are comfortable writing about. If the problem is so personal and sensitive that you wouldn't want to share it with others, don't write about it.

5. Select a problem that no other students (or few students) are writing on. Your instructor may check on topic selection to avoid duplication.

TOPIC SELECTION ACTIVITY 5.2

Select the problem that will be the topic for your upcoming paper.

STUDENT SAMPLE   My girlfriend is pregnant, I found out about a week ago. It's a tough situation because we haven't been getting along that great for a while. I was working out of the area for a month, and then she called and I found out. She wants to get married, and I've said okay. But this isn't how I wanted to get married. And I don't know if I really love her, at least the way I did earlier. But the pregnancy's my fault. It's my responsibility, and I'd feel like a jerk not marrying her. She's a good person, there's nothing wrong with her. It's me—I found myself looking at other girls when I was away. I didn't think about her much. Maybe she's got doubts like me. It's a real problem.

STUDENT SAMPLE   The parking problem on campus is terrible. When I come in for my 9:00 class, I can't find a parking place anywhere. If I drive around and around waiting for someone to leave, I get really late for my class. If I park a half mile away on the street, I'm also late, and I worry about my car getting sideswiped by passing traffic or broken into. The school should have enough parking so all students can find reasonable parking. This is a real problem for me and a lot of other students. And our teachers get upset when we're late for class. One won't even let me in class if I'm like 10 minutes late.

PROBLEM ANALYSIS

Before writing about your problem, take some time to analyze the situation. Answer the following questions to help you investigate the problem, and to generate some ideas for your first draft.

1. What exactly is the problem? Try expressing it in one clear sentence.

   I'm late for class because there isn't adequate parking on campus at 9:00 A.M.

2. How did the problem get started, and what caused it?

   The size of the enrollment keeps going up, and more and more classes are offered. But the parking areas are the same as when the enrollment was quite a bit smaller. Off-campus parking is minimal and not that safe for the cars.

3. What effect(s) does the problem have on you?

   I'm often late for class. My teacher gets mad at me, and sometime won't let me in class. I worry about my car when I park away from campus. I have to rush to school after I drop my daughter off at daycare, but there's still no parking, even fifteen or twenty minutes before class. By the time I get to class, I'm always stressed.

4. What effect(s), if any, does the problem have on others?

   Other students face the same problem, and they complain like I do. Some come an hour earlier just to get a space, but a lot of us can't do that. It affects teachers too because they don't like students coming late all the time.

5. What are possible solutions to the problem?

   I think its clear that the school needs more parking for students on campus. But I haven't looked into it to know if that's possible or where we'd park or anything. I haven't talked to anyone or tried to do anything about it. I wouldn't know where to start. Maybe there are other solutions I haven't thought of.

FINDING SOLUTIONS

Solving difficult problems is seldom simple. Sometimes unresolved problems between a parent and child, a husband and wife, employees and management, or two neighboring countries can go on for years and poison relationships. Some problems have plagued our country for decades. Over the past twenty years, America's "war on drugs" has failed in large part to solve the country's significant drug problem. Experts can't even agree on the main causes of the problem or the best ways to eliminate them.

In seeking solutions to a problem, the following suggestions will help you consider different possibilities and evaluate their chances for success.

1. What exactly does it mean to "solve" the problem? What do you want to accomplish through its being solving? For example, the college parking problem may be considered solved when all students attending 9:00 A.M. classes can find on-campus parking and not have to walk farther than ten minutes to class.

2. What are the roots or causes of the problem? It may be impossible to solve a problem if you don't have a clear understanding of its causes. For example, experts believe that America's drug problem has a number of complex causes, including poverty, organized crime, easy access, profit motive, drug importation, lack of programs for addicts, and perhaps even its illicit status. A problem with multiple causes is often more difficult to solve.

3. Consider possible solutions that could attack these causes and either eliminate or reduce their impact. For example, a major cause of America's drug problem is the desire for drugs among millions of Americans. Many experts believe that if this desire is not reduced— through education and positive lifestyle alternatives—the drug problem will never be solved.

4. Consider both short-term progress towards solving the problem and longer term solutions. Success in the beginning may be improving a situation that will take a longer time to resolve. For example, professional baseball averted a strike in 2002 by each side making some concessions that would move baseball towards greater revenue sharing and salary caps, but there is still much to be done to solve baseball's financial problems.

5. Come up with as many solutions as possible, including those that may seem implausible or rather drastic. Often your first ideas are the most obvious and traditional, but not necessarily the best. For example, your first idea on improving a campus parking situation may be to build more lots. However, the more novel idea of having campus shuttles taking students to classes from off-campus parking areas may be worth considering.

6. Consider compromises in finding a solution to a problem. Oftentimes, particularly in relationships, the solution to a problem involves two or more parties finding a "middle ground," by each party giving up something to get something. Solutions are often not perfect, and in dealing with problems with others involved, the best solution is often one that satisfies no one completely.

7. Consider how time will affect the problem and its ultimate solution. For example, sometimes people have to ride out a difficult situation for a time, knowing that their circumstances will change. You may have an absolute "roommate from hell," but when the semester is over, or when the six-month apartment lease is up, or when you get a job so you don't need a roommate to help with expenses, your problem will go away with your roommate. While the adage "don't run away from your problems" is often good advice, solutions that help take you out of a bad situation are worth considering.

8. Talk to other people about the problem. Seldom are problems unique to individuals. Usually you can find people who either have the same problem or have worked through it in the past. Effective problem solving often is a collective effort, so don't feel that you have to solve a problem by yourself.

SOLUTION ACTIVITY 5.3

In small groups, have each classmate present the problem he or she is going to write on. Taking into consideration the eight points presented on solving problems, brainstorm possible solutions to the problem. The purpose is for the group to generate a number of solution alternatives for each classmate to consider. Your group may come up with some ideas that you hadn't considered, or you may realize that your problem is going to be very difficult to solve, and will require step-by-step progress towards an ultimate solution.

AUDIENCE AND PURPOSE

Before writing the first draft of your problem/solution paper, consider the following:

1. What reading audience would I want to share my paper with? Who might benefit from reading about it?

   Any student who has morning classes has a parking problem, but I'd also like the teachers and administration and campus police to know it's their problem too. I'd like to write to all of them.

2. What would my purpose be in writing for a particular audience?

   To get something done about the current bad parking situation. To get things changed. I guess I'd have to come up with a definite plan or solution and say, "This is what needs to be done, and this is how it can be done," something like that.

AUDIENCE ACTIVITY 5.4

Decide on a particular reading audience that you would like to read your paper. It may be your classmates, a particular group of students within your class (women with children, students who work and go to school, students who take day and night classes), or a completely different group of readers. Select your reading audience based on your topic, whom you think would benefit from reading your paper, and whom you would like to read it.

Next, decide on your purpose for writing to this audience. Why are you writing to them, and what do you want to accomplish?

JOURNAL ENTRY SEVENTEEN

In your journal, relate how the prewriting activities have helped prepare you to write your first draft. What, if anything, stands out as being most useful?

FIRST DRAFTS

Now that you have selected a topic for your problem/solution paper, analyzed the problem, its causes, and possible solutions, and considered your reading audience and writing purpose, you are ready to write the first draft. The following suggestions will help you get started.

DRAFTING GUIDELINES

1. As you write your first draft, consider using this basic organizational plan, which is easy for readers to follow.

   a. Introduce the problem, why you are concerned about it, and why, if at all, your readers should be concerned.

   b. Present the cause(s) of the problem. How did it start and develop?

   c. Present the effect(s) of the problem on you, and if applicable, on others.

   d. Present a single solution, alternative solutions that should be tried, short-term and longer term solutions, a compromise that could solve the problem, or anything else you have come up with to improve the situation. If you are dealing with a difficult problem, you may not be presenting a single, simple solution, but rather a more realistic way of dealing with the problem in different ways. Or if the problem may seem impossible to solve completely, you may be discussing ways to improve the situation.

   e. As you follow this plan, feel free to make changes in organization that better fit your particular topic and how you want to present it. For example, if it seems better to present the problem's effects on you before you get into its causes, reverse the order. Or if you feel it's important to let readers know in the beginning what your solution is (so they will have it in mind as they read), present it.

2. Paragraph your paper as you move to its different parts: introduction (presenting the problem and your concern with it), causes of the problem, effects of the problem, possible solution(s).

3. Keep your readers and purpose in mind as you write. What are you trying to accomplish by writing about this particular problem? What do you want your readers to take from the paper?

DRAFTING ACTIVITY 5.5

Before writing your draft, read the following draft and in small groups, identify each of the following: what the problem is, its causes, its effects, and the writer's solution. In addition, discuss the writer's organizational plan and how effective it is.

Athletes and Academia
by Theresa Worsley

After last semester, I don't really want any more athletes in my English class—at least freshman football players. Never have I seen such a spoiled, ill-prepared, obnoxious group of students in my life. I was in no way prepared for them, and they weren't prepared for me.

These athletes—they haven't earned the distinction "student-athletes" in my mind—didn't come to school for an education, they came to play football. They had no more interest in my class than in sewing doilies. They missed class, they were late, they talked while I was talking, they didn't do homework, and they didn't come prepared for class. They did what I suspect they've been doing in school for many years, and apparently getting away with it. They had gotten to college, after all.

They also considered themselves the elite, probably from years of being coddled as top high school athletes, and then being recruited by coaches who told them how great they were, and finally going where they were most wanted. They expected the girls in class to swoon over them and the teachers to let them do what they wanted, which was precious little. They had this unbelievably skewed vision of what college was—a place to hang out before football practice—and of their own value—lords of the campus to be catered and deferred to.

The reality was that most of the other students in class viewed them as either jerks or weird novelties. Most of the students were there to learn, many of them going to school, holding down jobs, and raising children simultaneously, and they had no patience for the oafish, immature behavior of the athletes. They did not like the athletes wasting class time with their antics, and the girls weren't amused by their "God's gift to women" attitudes. It was a terrible classroom environment for serious students.

As for the teacher, I turned into a high school disciplinarian, kicking athletes out of class, not allowing them in when they came late, shutting them up constantly, threatening them with the inevitable failing grades, and trying to make things one-tenth as miserable for them as they were for me. Of course, what I said and did ran off their backs since they didn't care about the class or what I thought of them. With most of the athletes, I made little progress during the semester, and although I thought that giving them their deserved failing grades would provide heart-warming retribution, it didn't.

Within a year, I saw few of the same athletes on campus. Most that were in my class either hadn't made it through their freshman year or hadn't returned the next year. They were absolute losers when it came to college, and football wasn't going to save their educational hides. But what went wrong with these kids didn't start yesterday; it began years ago as people swelled their heads about how great they were, and the teachers and administrators let them slide from year to year so they could play ball. In their minds, they were all going to be great college players and then play in the NFL, and apparently no one, including college coaches, disabused them of that dangerously false notion. So they're out of college and back home within a year or two, with nothing to show for it and a grim future ahead.

For some athletes, reality has gotten turned on its head. While their only real chance for a better future is education, they see no worth in it. While college sports represents only an opportunity to get an education, they see it as the key to their future. This monumental self-delusion is often fed by the very adults in their lives who should be starving it. Of course all athletes don't fit this mold, but if my class is an indication, plenty of them do.

Go to college for one year, carry a full student load, and make at least a C average. If it takes a second year to get to a C average, go for two years. Then you can participate in college sport. That's the new rule for athletic eligibility. Prove that you are a student first, and then you can earn the privilege of being a student athlete. If we really care about the youth of our country, we should make this critical collegiate rule change that puts education first for all students, particularly the educationally at-risk athletes who too frequently end up leaving college for the low-paying jobs of the uneducated, or worse. As a society, we love sport, and we idolize athletes, and we ruin, or help ruin, the lives of thousands of young people as a result. Education first. And second. And third.

DRAFTING ACTIVITY 5.6

Write the first draft of your problem/solution paper following the guidelines presented.

REVISIONS

When you write a first draft, you are probably thinking more about getting your ideas on paper than on how your reading audience will respond. Therefore, it is important to revise your draft with your readers in mind. The success of your writing depends on how it is received by readers, so it is useful to learn to read a draft as if through the eyes of others. It is also valuable to get feedback from readers to see what kind of an effect your draft is having.

REVISION GUIDELINES

When evaluating your first draft, consider these suggestions:

1. Evaluate the opening of your paper. Does it introduce your problem in some manner so that readers know what you are writing about? Do you present the problem in a way that creates reader interest? Is there anything you might add? Answer the question, "Based on my opening, what would inspire readers to want to read further?"

2. Evaluate the middle part of the paper: how well do you present the causes of the problem? How effectively do you show the effects that the problem has on you and on others? What might you add to help readers understand the problem better or make the paper more interesting?

3. Evaluate your conclusion. Do you present a realistic solution or possible solutions that deal with the problem's causes? Do you explain what this solution will do for you, and perhaps for others? The solution part of your paper is perhaps the most important since readers may discover something they hadn't considered.

4. Evaluate your paragraphing. Does it help readers move smoothly through the opening, middle, and ending of your paper? Have you used transitions (first, second, then, however, therefore, as you can see, for example, finally) to tie sentences and paragraphs together? Have you dealt with causes and effects in separate paragraphs, or introduced different causes or different effects in new paragraphs?

5. Evaluate the organization of your paper. Have you presented the different parts of your paper in the best order? Does a particular sentence or paragraph seem out of place where it is? What might you move to a different location where it would make more sense? (See the upcoming section on "Organization.")

6. Read each sentence carefully to see if you can improve its clarity, smoothness, or conciseness. Many first draft sentences can be improved through the revision process. In addition, make revisions to improve sentence variety, replace overused joining words, and combine pairs of short sentences. (See the upcoming section on "Sentence Revision.")

7. Read the draft from your readers' perspective. Have you presented a serious enough problem for readers to take an interest in? Have you written in a way that readers will clearly understand the problem and how it is affecting your life? Have you presented a solution or possible solutions that truly address the problem and give readers something to consider?

REVISION ACTIVITY 5.7

In small groups, evaluate the following student draft by applying the revision guidelines presented. Note suggestions for revision along with things that the writer does well.

Next, make copies of your draft for your group to read, and critique each student draft as you did the sample student draft to give each classmate some ideas for revision.

STUDENT DRAFT   My problem is that my boyfriend left me while I was still pregnant with my son. I think about him all the time, especially when I look at my son.

I wish I could get over him, but my son looks so much like him that it reminds me of all the time we spent together. However, I would not take him back or let him near my son.

The biggest problem is the fact that I am so heart broken because my son will never know his father. One reason is because his father will most likely never come back, and the second, I will never let him near my son.

I don't think he even cares about us anyway. I figure if he did, he would have called me by now to see how we are doing. He hasn't called me since the day he left, and I don't think he ever will. I keep hoping he would, but it is only hope and wishes that won't come true any time soon.

The only solution to my problem is I have to let go. I know that it will be hard at first, but with the help of my family and the love for my son, I can get through this. I just need to ask God for help along the way. I guess deep down in my heart I have always known what to do, but it was up to me to do it. Now I will do what I have to do, which is move on with my life, and with God's help, I will.

REVISION ACTIVITY 5.8

Evaluate your own draft a last time using the revision guidelines. (Your instructor may first have you go over the upcoming sections on organization and sentence revision.) When you are ready, write your second draft.

JOURNAL ENTRY EIGHTEEN

In your journal, record the improvements you made in your second draft. In what ways do you think the second draft is superior to the first?

ESSAY ORGANIZATION

The organization of any paper has something of an *organic* quality: it comes in part from the uniqueness of that particular paper based on your topic and what you want to accomplish. For example, while you have probably followed the organizational plan presented in this unit for a problem/solution paper—introduce the problem, present its causes, present its effects, present possible solutions—such a scheme may not be best for every problem/solution paper. As you write and reread your draft, you will develop a sense for what should come next, and what should follow that, based on your writing purpose and the most effective organization for achieving it.

As you read the first draft of your problem/solution paper to evaluate its organization, consider these questions.

1. Does it make sense to present my solution in the opening when I present the problem, or am I better off waiting until the end of the paper after I have presented everything else?

2. Might it be more effective to present the effects of the problem rather than presenting the causes first? Which is the most effective order based on my topic and what I want to achieve?

3. Assuming your problem has more than one cause and more than one effect, what is the most effective order for presenting the causes? For presenting the effects? What organization most effectively highlights the most important cause(s) and effect(s)?

ORGANIZATIONAL ACTIVITY 5.9

Read the following essay "Stunted Progress" by Andrew Arias and analyze its organization. In small groups, identify the problem the essay is presenting, its causes, its effects, and its solution. Evaluate the effectiveness of the essay's organization based on what you believe to be the author's purpose.

Stunted Progress
by Andrew Arias

There is good news for Latinos throughout the U.S. More Latinos, men and women, are going to college than ever before. In the last decade, the increase in the number of Latinos graduating from high school and attending college, or coming to college as adults after spending years in low-paying jobs, has been dramatic.

There is bad news too. All studies show that Latino college students, along with African Americans, are far more likely to drop out of college than white or Asian students. In addition, they most often drop out during their first or second year of college, and often during the first semester. A much greater percentage of Latino students who begin their third year of college end up graduating, and each semester they stay in, their odds of graduating get better. However, a recent national study revealed that over sixty per cent of Latino students who start college neither graduate nor receive vocational certificates. That alarming drop-out rate is steeper than the current high school rate for Latinos, and equally troubling.

While some college is better than none, it isn't much better. The majority of decent paying jobs requires at least a bachelor's degree. Students who drop out after a year or two are thrown back into the high school diploma job market, which is much smaller and poorer paying. Their career and life opportunities are severely stunted, their work choices reduced to a minimum. Sure, there are people who do fine in life without a college degree: successful salespeople, small business entrepreneurs, many city and county employees. However, there are many more who struggle throughout life with low-paying jobs, encountering the difficulties that often come with them: money problems, relationship problems, credit problems, inability to buy a home.

Many Latinos who drop out of college come from low-income families. They drop out when they can't afford the cost of books and tuition, or when they have to go to work to help support their families. Often the first in their family to attend college, they don't have role models to show them the real-life benefits of a college degree, nor college educated parents or siblings to help them through the inevitable tough times. There is also the call of the old neighborhood, the friends who aren't in college, and the allure of spending money available through minimum-wage jobs. They also don't understand the monumental impact that leaving college can have on their future.

The educational emphasis in Latino communities, and in high schools across the country, needs to change. The old mantra of "Go to college" needs to be replaced with the new mantra "Graduate from college." Many Latino students feel that just by going to college after high school, they have accomplished something. They believe that the "getting there" is in some ways an end rather than the beginning of a long and difficult journey. Attending college must become a given—something that is expected. Graduating from college must become the goal—something that no one wants to fall short of.

High schools have done a much better job in the past twenty years of encouraging Latino students to stay in school, providing programs and assistance to help them stay on track and develop the requisite language skills for success, and educating parents to the importance of education. Colleges must now exercise the same diligence in keeping Latino students in college and moving them towards graduation. Many community colleges are now doing a better job of counseling and tracking "at-risk" students, getting them into study skills classes, and employing intervention strategies with students who are struggling. Four-year colleges and universities aren't doing nearly as much, and they need to start.

No one needs reminding of the litany of problems that come with large populations of undereducated citizens: high unemployment, expanded welfare rolls, more crime, more drug use, fewer stable families. Yesterday undereducated may have meant not graduating from high school. Today it means not graduating from college. Our vast Latino population in the U.S., with assistance from our school systems, has come a long way in getting our youth to attend college. The next step is even more important: graduating them from college in record numbers. The emphasis must shift from entrance to exit.

ORGANIZATIONAL ACTIVITY 5.10

Read the following sample draft of a problem/solution paper and evaluate its organization. In small groups, discuss possible organizational changes that would make the paper more effective. Could some paragraphs be better located? Then read your latest draft and consider any organizational changes that would strengthen it.

SAMPLE DRAFT   My sister's toddler is turning into a very spoiled baby. When I'm around other babies her age, which is nineteen months, I realize how differently she acts. Of course, she doesn't know any better because she is just a baby, so it's not her fault. However, if my sister and her husband don't start taking control and teaching her how to behave now, she's just going to get worse and she'll suffer for it when she gets into school and has to mind a teacher and get along with other kids.

To be honest, my sister and her husband get invited a little less frequently to family get-togethers because we all know Samantha will run wild and make it hard on everyone. It's particularly hard on the rest of us relatives because we really want to discipline her for her own good, but with her parents there, it's almost impossible to do. And it's like they're totally oblivious to the problem. They just laugh at everything she does or ask her not to do something and when she doesn't mind, they ignore it. Samantha also keeps getting bolder as she gets older, and she thinks she can do anything. Since she has no limits, the time will come when she puts herself in danger—for example running out into the street—and her parents can only blame themselves.

Samantha is a beautiful, happy baby who could be a real joy to be around. However, she's out of control. She goes where she wants, she does what she wants, and she doesn't mind her parents at all. When she stands in her high chair and they tell her to sit down, or when they tell her to come here, or when they tell her "Don't do this" or "Don't do that," she ignores them, or she gives them a little smile and just keeps on going. And when she finally doesn't get her way, she pitches a huge tantrum, throwing herself on the ground kicking and screaming. But her parents don't like to see her throw tantrums, so they usually give in.

The problem is that my sister and brother-in-law think everything she does is cute. They idolize her, and they can't get mad at her for anything. They also want her to be happy all the time, so she is really the one in control, leading them all over the house where she wants to go, or all over the park or all over the neighborhood. She's in control, and she knows it. And when it comes to sharing, forget it. If there's a cousin around or a baby of a friend, Samantha goes and takes anything the other baby is playing with, and if someone tries to take something from her, she screams bloody murder. She is totally into herself and her needs, and her parents have let her become that way.

Finally, whenever I baby-sit Samantha, or when other relatives help out, we need to start doing what her parents haven't done: letting her know that as a baby, she isn't in control. I love her and want her to be happy also, but I'm not afraid to discipline her, and neither are some of my aunts. So we need to start being firmer when she's with us and her parents aren't around. If Samantha doesn't learn some self-control, she's going to be miserable as she gets a little older. Nobody likes a five-year old brat, and she's not going to be popular with anyone—her fellow students or teachers. There's still hope, because she's only nineteen months old— but it's time to get her going in the right direction, with my sister's help or not.

There are some really good books out there about setting limits for babies, and the consequences if you don't, so a sly way to perhaps get them thinking is to mail them, anonymously, two or three of these books. That may make them mad, but perhaps they'd get the message, especially if they think any number of people could have sent the books, which is possible. I also think our family needs to lay some "tough love" on them and just not invite them to some traditional family get-together that everyone gets invited to.

My sister doesn't realize it, but she's hurting her daughter when she thinks she's being a good mother. I can't say anything to her, because first I'm the younger sister who knows nothing, and second, I have no kids of my own, so what do I know? My mom is sometimes just about as bad as my sister, so she won't tell her anything. Besides, I don't think talking to her would help anyway. I think they believe everything is just fine.

SENTENCE REVISION

All writers share the task of revising first-draft sentences. The goal of such revision is to craft sentences that flow smoothly and express your thoughts clearly. Like most writers, you will continue to improve your sentence revision skills as long as you write.

Wording Problems Review

The first step in revising first-draft sentences is learning to identify sentences that need some work. Basically, you are looking for sentences that appear vague, awkward, or wordy. If a sentence doesn't look or sound right to you, it probably needs revising. When you locate a problem sentence, experiment with different wording options until you find the best combination. Here is an example:

First-Draft Sentence   With sentence revision, you are working with both improving the clarity of a sentence's content and the wording through which to express that content best.

    Revised   With sentence revision, you are improving both your clarity of thought and the wording through which that thought is expressed.

    Revised   Through sentence revision, you are clarifying your thoughts and improving the way you express them.

    Final revision   Through sentence revision, you clarify your thoughts and improve your wording.

Compare the first, second, third, and final drafts of the sentence. The first sentence struggles to get the writer's thoughts on paper; and the final draft expresses them clearly, smoothly, and concisely. Such revisions often occur over time throughout the drafting process.

SENTENCE REVISION ACTIVITY 5.11

For revision practice, rewrite the following paragraph to make the sentences clearer, smoother, and more concise. When you finish, read your latest draft and revise sentences that could be improved.

At first, I felt sorry for my roommate because she was lonely. I did things with her, tried to cheer her up when she was depressed, and my clothes she could borrow anytime. Nothing seemed to help out the situation for long though because I'd come back to the dorm after class and there she'd be just staring at the ceiling or just crying for no reason on the bed. I couldn't be with her all the time. One night a dance was put on by the college and I met a guy who seemed really nice. We started going out, and my roommate was made very angry by that. She wouldn't talk to me or say anything to me when I came back from dates. It was like as if she was being betrayed for having a boyfriend. On top of that, my clothes were now borrowed by her without asking, and she was even getting into my make-up. Finally, I'd had enough. Anxious to get out of that room, I asked the dorm adviser when another dorm room would become vacant. I moved out of that room and into a single room, and even though I had to pay more for it, having to pay the extra money was worth the freedom that I received from my old roommate. I hope some psychological counseling can be

gotten by her both for her own good and before she drives another roommate crazy.

Sentence Variety Review

In the sections on sentence variety, you use different sentence structures to
express yourself most effectively. Like many writers, you may sometimes
overuse favored structures and joining words, which can become boring to
readers. Working with different structures makes you more aware of your
options and more comfortable in using them.

SENTENCE REVISION ACTIVITY 5.12

Revise the following paragraph by combining sentences to form more
effective and informative ones. Your revised paragraph should include a
variety of simple, compound, and complex sentences, including some with
relative clauses beginning with "who," "which," "whose," or "that."
When you finish, reread your latest draft to evaluate your sentence variety
and use of joining words, and make revisions for improvement.

The drinking water in town is tasting awful. The city is chlorinating it.
They are doing this to kill bacteria. The bacteria count is higher than the
allowable level. The level is established by the county health department.
The water now has a strong aftertaste. It is safe. It is practically undrink-
able. Most people are opting for bottled water. They can buy it in any
supermarket. It costs about a quarter a gallon. There is another option.
Some people are installing water-treatment units. These units have carbon
filters. The filters take out all of the chlorine. The water tastes normal. It
tastes just like bottled water. Both options are better than drinking chlori-
nated water. I prefer the water-treatment unit. It's more convenient. It still
allows me to drink tap water. It's sad that the untreated city water isn't
safe enough to drink. This is the result of underground contaminants polluting the water system. The contaminants come from agricultural pesti-
cide spraying.

Other Structural Problems

Three specific sentence problems are covered in the "Sentence Revision"
section of the appendix: nonparallel construction, dangling modifiers, and
misplaced modifiers. Your instructor may refer you to those sections if
those types of problems occur in your writing.

JOURNAL ENTRY NINETEEN

In your journal, relate the kinds of sentence revisions that you make to
improve your wording. What are the most common flaws in your first
draft sentences, and how do you eliminate them through revision?

FINAL EDITING

The last step in the writing process is to give your draft a final proofreading for errors. Rather than scanning your draft for grammatical, spelling, and punctuation errors simultaneously, try concentrating on one area at a time. That way you are least likely to overlook a particular kind of error.

PROOFREADING GUIDELINES

When proofreading your draft, make sure to cover the following areas.

1. *Sentence endings:* Make sure you have a period at the end of each sentence, and correct any run-on sentences or sentence fragments. (If you have a particular problem with run-on sentences or fragments, see the upcoming review section.)

2. *Word endings:* Check to make sure plural words end in *s* or *es*, regular past tense verbs end in *ed*, and present tense verbs agree with their subjects. Also check for *er* and *est* endings on comparative and superlative adjectives. (See the upcoming section on comparative and superlative adjectives under "Correct Usage.")

3. *Spelling:* Check your spelling carefully, and look up any words you are uncertain of. Also check your use of homonyms such as there/their/they're, your/you're, no/know, through/threw, and its/it's.

4. *Internal punctuation:* Check your use of commas with words in series, before conjunctions in compound sentences, after introductory groups of words, and to set off relative clauses, interrupters, and ending phrases beginning with *especially, particularly,* and *ing-ending* words. (See the section "Comma Usage Review" later in the unit.) Check for apostrophes in contractions and possessives and for quotation marks around direct quotations. Finally, check your use of semicolons and colons (covered later under "Punctuation").

5. *Pronoun usage:* Check your subject pronoun usage (Marianne and I, my brother and he, we and they), and make sure that all pronouns agree with their antecedents. (See the upcoming section "Pronoun-Antecedent Agreement Review.")

ON-LINE ACTIVITY: PROOFREADING TIPS

Are you still having problems detecting errors in your drafts? For some on-line assistance, go to the Bowling Green University Writing Lab On-line: http://www.bgsu/edu/offices/acen/help_pages.html.

When you arrive, click on "Proofreading (short)." You will find some practical suggestions for proofreading your drafts effectively. Make note of the most useful suggestions, and apply them when you proofread your latest draft.

EDITING ACTIVITY 5.13

In small groups, proofread the following student draft for errors and make the necessary corrections.

STUDENT SAMPLE DRAFT

I've had obsticles threw out my life. One of my biggest problems. That I've incurred was when I had my divorce. I know that it effected my life completely. As well as my children. I got married at an early age of 15. It seemed hard to become a grown up at such an early age.

I became a very young mother, at fifteen and wasn't able to enjoy my childhood. But that was no one's fault but mind. I tried to become a responsiable mother. I worked hard and I became a responsiable parent for my child.

I knew that it wasn't going to be easy. But with lots of help from my family I was able to be strong. My plans when I was young were to live a happy life. But I guess that I followed the footsteps of my parents. I don't blame my parents because I guess just like my relationship, theirs wasn't meant to be.

I know that I tried to be a good wife to keep my relationship working. But when your husband don't cooperate it's impossiable to make anything happen. But we tried to work it out for nine years. We had our ups and downs but life seemed just seemed to work out its own way. But I guess everything happens for the best. Because we have gone our own different ways.

We have remained friends for our kids sake. I've remarried know and I'm happily married, I have know found my true husband, he has made me very happy. God is know part of my life and I have put a lot of my love into my relationship.

EDITING ACTIVITY 5.14

Proofread your latest draft for errors following the guidelines presented. Concentrate in particular on eliminating your personal error tendencies. (Your instructor may have you cover the upcoming punctuation and grammar sections before proofreading.)

When you have corrected all errors, write or print out the final draft of your paper to share with readers.

JOURNAL ENTRY TWENTY

In your journal, relate the progress you have made during the course on eliminating errors from your writing. In what areas have you made improvement, and how have your proofreading skills—your ability to identify existing errors—improved?

SENTENCE PROBLEMS

The following activity is for students who continue to have problems with run-on sentences and fragments. If you have such problems, do the activity before proofreading your draft.

RUN-ON AND FRAGMENT REVIEW ACTIVITY 5.15

The following passage contains run-on sentences and fragments. Rewrite the passage and correct errors by changing or adding punctuation, or by adding joining words to combine sentences.

EXAMPLE   The service at the restaurant was terrible. Because there was one waitress for ten tables. People got frustrated, they left without ordering.

REVISED   The service at the restaurant was terrible because there was one waitress for ten tables. People got frustrated, and they left without ordering.

This was the last semester that Charlotte would car pool. Because she had too many bad experiences. She had gotten in a car pool at the beginning of the semester with three other girls who lived nearby. When Ela drove, she was always five to ten minutes late, she always had elaborate excuses. Marsela, on the other hand, was always ten minutes early, tooting her horn and waking up the neighborhood. The third girl was totally unpredictable, she relied on her brother to pick her up. One day she was on time, the next day early, and the next day late, sometimes she wouldn't come at all. Since Charlotte was the only one with first-period classes, the others weren't concerned about the time. Next semester Charlotte will take a bus to school. Even though the bus stop is a mile from her house.

CORRECT USAGE

The following section introduces a new grammatical area that you should find useful: comparative and superlative adjectives. In addition, pronoun-antecedent agreement is reviewed.

Comparative and Superlative Adjectives

Writers frequently use adjectives to compare things: people, cars, colleges, movies, jobs, cities, or religions. They may use adjectives to compare the size of four brothers, the speed of two sports cars, the cost of tuition at a number of colleges, the endings of Steven Spielberg movies, the difficulty of different jobs, the crime rate in different cities, or the creation myths in different religions. Adjectives that are used in comparisons take particular forms which follow grammatical rules.

An adjective may be used to describe a single person or thing, to compare two people or things, or to compare one person or thing to many others. Here are examples of these three uses for adjectives and the three forms the adjectives take:

DESCRIPTIVE   Sally is <u>short</u>. (Short *describes Sally*.)

COMPARATIVE   Sally is <u>shorter</u> than Sue. (Shorter *compares the height of Sally to that of Sue*.)

SUPERLATIVE   Sally is the <u>shortest</u> person in her family. (Shortest *compares the height of Sally to that of all others in her family*.)

Notice that with the one-syllable adjective *short*, the *er* ending is added for comparing two things, and the *est* ending is added for comparing *more than two things*. Here are three more examples of the uses for adjectives with a longer descriptive word:

DESCRIPTIVE   Sally is <u>considerate</u>. (Considerate *describes Sally*.)

COMPARATIVE   Sally is <u>more considerate</u> than Sue. (More considerate *compares Sally to Sue*.)

SUPERLATIVE   Sally is the <u>most considerate</u> person in the class. (Most considerate *compares Sally to all of her classmates*.)

Notice that with longer adjectives (two syllables or more), a *more* is added before the adjective for comparing two things, and a *most* is added before the adjective for comparing more than two things.

Now that you have a general idea of the forms that adjectives take, the following rules for making comparisons with adjectives should help you use them correctly in your writing.

Comparative Form (Comparing Two Things)

1. Add *er* to *one-syllable adjectives.*

   I am <u>shorter</u> than you are.

   Sam is <u>smarter</u> than Phil.

   Mercury lights are <u>brighter</u> than florescent lights.

2. Add *more* in front of adjectives with *two or more syllables.*

   I am <u>more depressed</u> than you are.

Sam is <u>more graceful</u> than Phil.

Mercury lights are <u>more effective</u> than florescent lights.

3. Exception: Add *er* to two-syllable words ending in *y* or *ow* (drop the *y* and add *ier*).

I am <u>lonelier</u> than you are.

Sam is <u>sillier</u> than Phil.

Mercury lights are <u>prettier</u> than fluorescent lights.

The river is <u>shallower</u> today than last week.

4. The word *than* often comes after an adjective in sentences comparing two things. (See all of the examples from items 1, 2, and 3.)

5. Never use both *more* and an *er* ending with an adjective.

Wrong	You are <u>more smarter</u> than I am.
Right	You are <u>smarter</u> than I am.
Wrong	You are <u>more beautifuler</u> than ever.
Right	You are <u>more beautiful</u> than ever.

Superlative Form (Comparing Three or More Things)

1. Add *est* to *one-syllable adjectives*.

I am the <u>shortest</u> person in my family.

Sam is the <u>smartest</u> elephant in the zoo.

Mercury lights are the <u>brightest</u> lights for tennis courts.

2. Add *most* in front of adjectives with *two or more syllables*.

I am the <u>most dependable</u> person in the family.

Sam is the <u>most curious</u> elephant in the zoo.

Mercury lights are the <u>most expensive</u> lights on the market.

3. Exception: Add *est* to two-syllable words ending in *y* or *ow* (drop the *y* and add *iest*).

I am the <u>rowdiest</u> person in my family.

Sam is the <u>heaviest</u> elephant in the zoo.

Mercury lights give off the <u>loveliest</u> glow of any outdoor lights.

That is the <u>shallowest</u> that I've ever seen Lake Placid.

4. The word *the* often comes before the adjective in sentences comparing three or more things. (See all of the examples in items 1, 2, and 3.)

5. Never use both *most* and an *est* ending with an adjective.

WRONG	You are the <u>most smartest</u> person I know.
RIGHT	You are the <u>smartest</u> person I know.
WRONG	Francine is the <u>most remarkablest</u> artist in the school.
RIGHT	Francine is the <u>most remarkable</u> artist in the school.

ADJECTIVE ACTIVITY 5.16

Each of the following sentences compares two things. Fill in the correct *comparative* form of each adjective in parentheses. Count the number of syllables the adjective has, add *er* to one-syllable adjectives and two-syllable adjectives ending in *y* or *ow*, and add *more* in front of other adjectives of two syllables or more.

EXAMPLES   (quick) You are a *quicker* runner this year than last.

(beautiful) The nearby hills are *more beautiful* in the spring than in the summer.

1. (interesting) The first day of school was _____ than I thought it would be.

2. (friendly) The teachers were _____ than I imagined.

3. (fascinating) The lectures were_____ than my high school lectures.

4. (short) The classes were also _____ than usual, since it was the first day.

5. (fast) The whole day went by _____ than I expected.

6. (tedious) I thought college would be _____than it was.

7. (enthusiastic) Now I am _____ than ever about coming back tomorrow.

8. (long) However, tomorrow's classes will be much _____ than today's.

9. (difficult) The homework will definitely be _____ than today's.

10. (typical) Tomorrow will be _____ of a regular college day than today was.

ADJECTIVE ACTIVITY 5.17

Each of the following sentences compares three or more things. Fill in the correct *superlative* form of each adjective in parentheses. Count the number of syllables the adjective has; add *est* to one-syllable adjectives and two-syllable adjectives ending in *y* or *ow*, and add *most* in front of other adjectives with two syllables or more.

EXAMPLES   (quick) I felt the *quickest* today in track practice that I've ever felt.

(unusual) The antique knife display in the library is the *most unusual* display of the year.

1. (interesting) The first day of school was the _____ of the week.

2. (friendly) I met some of the _____ teachers I have ever met.

3. (fascinating) The lectures were the _____ I have ever taken.

4. (short) The classes were also the _____ I have ever attended.

5. (fast) It was the _____ day of school I've been through.

6. (tedious) I thought college would be the _____ part of my education.

7. (enthusiastic) Now I am the _____ I've ever been about going to school.

8. (long) Although the classes tomorrow will be the _____ I've had, I should still enjoy them.

9. (difficult) Although the homework will be the _____ I've done, I don't think I'll mind it.

10. (typical) Students say that the second week of college is the _____ week to judge school by, so I hope it goes as well as the first.

Pronoun-Antecedent Agreement Review

As you recall from the previous unit, pronouns must agree in number and gender with their antecedents:

John visited <u>his</u> grandparents in Florida by <u>himself</u>.

Melissa and I took <u>our</u> final a day early because <u>we</u> had to work the next day.

The boat tore <u>its</u> hull on some rocks, and <u>it</u> began sinking rapidly.

Writers sometimes have problems when an *indefinite pronoun* is the antecedent: each, one, everyone, someone, no one, somebody, everybody. Indefinite pronouns are singular and require singular pronoun references:

Everyone brought <u>his</u> or <u>her</u> blue book to the history final.

One of the boys lost <u>his</u> wallet at the baseball game.

Each of the mothers took <u>her</u> turn working at the school bake sale.

Nobody wants <u>his</u> or <u>her</u> name slandered by gossip.

PRONOUN-ANTECEDENT ACTIVITY 5.18

For more practice with pronoun-antecedent agreement, fill in the blanks in the following sentences with pronouns that agree in number with their antecedents. Circle the antecedent for each pronoun.

EXAMPLE   People can usually be trusted if *they* are given responsibility.

1. The old shack lost _____ tin roof in the hurricane.

2. Each of the girls has a room to _____ in the bungalow.

3. Two men from New Zealand left _____ passports at the airport.

4. A student needs to set _____ priorities straight before _____ can do well in college.

5. Every one of the geraniums got _____ bloom at the same time.

6. Hawaii is a favorite vacation spot for Japanese tourists. _____ is _____ island home away from home, and _____ flock there by the thousands.

7. Humans are _____ own worst enemy in destroying _____ environment. _____ must reverse the destructive process _____ have initiated.

8. Maria did _____ math totally by _____ for the first time in _____ life, and _____ was very proud.

9. A person in need of financial help should consult an expert, and _____ should stay away from _____ well-meaning friends no better off than _____ is.

10. Each cadet was instructed to do _____ own locker inspection, and no one was to leave the barracks before _____ had finished _____ chores.

11. The watches that I bought from the catalog have all lost _____ plastic covers because _____ weren't properly attached to the faces.

12. Skateboards are being seen on college campuses again. _____ lost _____ appeal to students in the late seventies, but now _____ are back in vogue as a means of transportation.

13. Either Sarah or Brunhilda left _____ beaker in the chemistry lab.

14. The presents that you bought me for my birthday lost _____ charm when I heard you paid for _____ with my credit card.

15. The women who got the best bargains at the garage sale did _____ shopping before 7:00 A.M., and the rest of us were left with what _____ had picked over.

PUNCTUATION

This section introduces two new punctuation marks that writers find useful: semicolons and colons. It also includes a review of comma usage.

Semicolons and Colons

The semicolon (;) and colon (:) allow writers to vary their sentence structure and add flexibility to their writing. Semicolons and colons are used in the following ways.

1. *Semicolon:* joins two complete sentences that are related in meaning and that are relatively short (used as an alternative to separating sentences with a period or joining sentences with a conjunction).

EXAMPLES   Marion should be at the checkout any minute; her ten-minute break is almost over.

Hank's health is his number one concern; in fact, nothing else seems important right now.

Melissa should never have tried to run a hard mile without warming up; she knows better.

2. *Colon:* (a) used after a *complete thought* to indicate that a series of items follows.

EXAMPLES   We need the following utensils for the picnic: knives, forks, spoons, spatulas, and a cheese grater.

Sandra has the characteristics of an outstanding athlete: intelligent, dedicated, coachable, goal oriented, and confident.

Note—A common misuse of the colon is after the words "such as," "like," and "includes."

WRONG   Tools we need to install the wall plug include: pliers, a screwdriver, and wirecutters.

RIGHT   Tools we need to install the wall plug include pliers, a screwdriver, and wirecutters.

RIGHT   We need the following tools to install the wall plug: pliers, a screwdriver, and wirecutters. (The colon now follows a complete thought.)

3. *Colon:* (b) used after a *complete thought* to highlight a single item that follows.

EXAMPLES   There's one virtue that Peter definitely lacks: patience.

The answer to Maria's financial problem is obvious: find a better job.

As a camp counselor, you've made one thing apparent: your concern for troubled children.

I've got something that you need: the keys to the house.

PUNCTUATION ACTIVITY 5.19

Add semicolons and colons to the following sentences where they are needed. Put a C in front of each correctly punctuated sentence.

EXAMPLE   You show a real aptitude for computer programming; you have a promising future.

1. ___ There's one class in college I've had trouble passing physiology.

2. ___ I know how to get from our dormitory to the downtown library I went there several times last semester.

3. ___ Everyone fails occasionally don't get discouraged.

4. ___ Freda replaced her computer's floppy disk system with a hard disk drive the new system is much faster and stores more information.

5. ___ Millicent has been taking aerobic dance four times a week for four years she started when she was forty-five years old.

6. ___ One attribute comes to mind when considering golfer Jack Nicklaus's years of unparalleled success mental toughness.

7. ___ The chain saw equipment in the garage should include two 16-inch Weber chain saws, a bag of extra chains, a gallon of gasoline, three cleaning rags, and four pints of chain saw oil.

8. ___ My aunt's cat Tiger is a fearless fighter her other cat Chubby prefers hiding behind the washing machine.

PUNCTUATION ACTIVITY 5.20

For practice, write five of your own sentences that require semicolons and five more that require colons, and punctuate them correctly. (Use the words *however* and *therefore* after the semicolons in at least two sentences, and write some sentences in which the colon is followed by a single word and others in which it is followed by a series.) When you finish, check your latest draft to see where you might use a semicolon or colon.

Comma Usage Review

The following review activity is for students who are still having some problems with comma usage.

COMMA REVIEW ACTIVITY 5.21

Following the comma usage rules presented in the text, insert commas where they are needed in the following essay.

My freshman year I really enjoyed the freedom that came with college. After having been in "prison" for four years of high school it felt great not having classes every hour of the day and even greater being able to miss a class now and then.

The problem was the "now and then" became more frequent as the semester went on. I mostly had large lecture classes and the teachers didn't take roll or worry about who was there and who wasn't. Therefore I started sleeping in more and more often and I often relied on the notes that friends would take in class.

My grades started slipping more and more but I was determined to make up for it all by doing well on my finals. The trouble was I had missed so much class and gotten so far behind that I tried to do about a month's studying in a few nights. I vowed to stay up all night studying before each final but it never worked out. I was hopelessly behind and I did terrible on my finals.

For the first semester I ended up with one C and the rest D's and F's. I was so ashamed that I lied to my parents and my friends. Basically I blew my first semester of college and I learned that the freedom of college was deceptive. In college they give you enough rope to hang yourself so that's what I did. If you don't learn to take the responsibility to go to class and put your free time to good use you'll end up in a hole. This semester I'm having to dig myself out including taking two classes over again. I'll also have to go to summer school if I want to end up with thirty units for the year. I'm going to class regularly taking my own notes and keeping up on my reading better. So far I'm doing okay but there's still twelve weeks to go. I hope I've learned my lesson especially since my parents are paying my tuition.

WRITING REVIEW

In the "Writing Review," you apply what you have learned throughout the unit to a second problem/solution paper. The following writing process summarizes the steps presented throughout the unit. While following the process, feel free to make changes in it that you have found helpful for writing other papers.

WRITING PROCESS

1. Select a problem to write about that affects most or all of the students in your class. It may be a school-related problem, a common type of personal or relationship problem, or a common work-related problem. Pick a problem that your classmates—your reading audience for the paper—will be interested in.

2. Before writing about your problem, take some time to analyze the situation. Answer the following questions to help you investigate the problem, and to generate some ideas for your first draft.

   a. What exactly is the problem? Try expressing it in one clear sentence.

   b. How did the problem get started, and what caused it?

   c. What effect(s) does the problem have on you?

   d. What effect(s), if any, does the problem have on others?

   e. What are possible solutions to the problem?

3. In seeking solutions to your problem, use the following suggestions:

   a. What exactly does it mean to "solve" the problem? What do you want to accomplish through its being solved?

   b. What are the roots or causes of the problem? It may be impossible to solve a problem if you don't have a clear understanding of its causes.

   c. Consider possible solutions that could attack these causes and either eliminate or reduce their impact.

   d. Consider both short-term progress towards solving the problem and longer term solutions. Success in the beginning may be improving a situation that will take a longer time to resolve.

   e. Come up with as many solutions as possible, including those that may seem implausible or rather drastic. Often your first ideas are the most obvious and traditional, but not necessarily the best.

   f. Consider compromises in finding a solution to a problem. Oftentimes, particularly in relationships, the solution to a problem involves two or more parties finding a "middle ground," by each party giving up something to get something. Solutions are often not perfect, and in dealing with problems with others involved, the best solution is often one that satisfies no one completely.

g. Consider how time will affect the problem and its ultimate solution. For example, sometimes people have to ride out a difficult situation for a time, knowing that their circumstances will change. Solutions that help take you out of a bad situation are worth considering.

h. Talk to other people about the problem. Seldom are problems unique to individuals. Usually you can find people who either have the same problem or have worked through it in the past. Effective problem solving often is a collective effort, so don't feel that you have to solve a problem by yourself.

4. Determine your purpose for writing to your classmates about this problem. What do you want to accomplish? What do you want your classmates to learn or understand?

5. Write the first draft of your paper following these guidelines:

a. As you write your first draft, use this basic organizational plan, which is easy for readers to follow.

1. Introduce the problem, why you are concerned about it, and why, if at all, your readers should be concerned.

2. Present the cause(s) of the problem. How did it start and develop?

3. Present the effect(s) of the problem on you, and if applicable, on others.

4. Present a single solution, alternative solutions that should be tried, short-term and longer-term solutions, a compromise that could solve the problem, or anything else you have come up with to improve the situation. If you are dealing with a difficult problem, you may not be presenting a single, simple solution, but rather a more realistic way of dealing with the problem in different ways. Or if the problem may seem impossible to solve completely, you may be discussing ways to improve the situation.

b. As you follow this plan, feel free to make changes in organization that better fit your particular topic and how you want to present it. For example, if it seems better to present the problem's effects on you before you get into its causes, reverse the order. Or if you feel it's important to let readers know in the beginning what your solution is (so they will have it in mind as they read), present it.

c. Paragraph your paper as you move to its different parts: introduction (presenting problem and your concern with it), causes of problem, effects of problem, possible solution(s).

d. Keep your readers and purpose in mind as you write. What are you trying to accomplish by writing about this particular problem? What do you want your readers to take from the paper?

My Problem as a Newlywed

STUDENT SAMPLE
DRAFT
The first years of our marriage, my husband and I were like travelers, going from here to there and there to here. My husband would come down and pick me up in Mexico and we'd come to the U.S. Once I would get tired of being in the U.S., I'd just tell him, "I want to go back to Mexico," and he would take me back. He would drop me off and return to the U.S. He did this many times and never complained for the first years of our marriage.

However, things did not stay like this because he eventually got tired. He told me he was not going to be picking me up and taking me back whenever I felt like it. I remember the last time he picked me up from Mexico. Everything was smooth as usual. Once we arrived in Texas, everything was fine until I again grew tired of being here and wanted to go back to my family. I began telling him one evening when he got home from work that I wanted to go back again.

I still remember how calmly he responded and his exact words. He said, "Ok, if you want to go back to Mexico, then go. I think that by now you know the route and are able to go alone because I'm not going to take you back and go get you whenever you feel like it anymore. Go ahead and leave and stay as long as you wish. Enjoy your stay and be happy, and when you decide to return, you know the way back. I just hope that by the time you decide to return you don't find the house occupied."

Even though he said this, I still left because I didn't believe he was serious. A month went by and then another, and I noticed he was becoming more distant and not calling as often. I still believed he would come for Christmas like he always did, but he didn't come. Then I thought he was waiting for New Year's, but still nothing. Finally I called him and told him how upset I was, and again he reminded me of what he had said. I still waited until February but when I realized he was serious, I knew I had to go back to him on my own.

This is the way I finally realized that I would have to start my married life here in the U.S. even if I didn't want to. It was very difficult for me to become accustomed to the new traditions and a new culture, but I realized that my life is here. I suffered a lot because I didn't and still don't have family members in this country. Even now I sometimes get sad and lonely, but I have maintained good communication with my sisters in Mexico.

Even though a part of me will always want to go back, I cannot because my husband and daughter are here, and I belong with them as their wife and mother. I had to grow up and realize that my place is with my husband and daughter, no matter how much I miss the rest of my family. I am also lucky that my husband was patient with me for many years and let me return to Mexico. And he was happy that I finally came back on my own for good.

6. When you finish your first draft, set it aside for a while, and then reread and evaluate your paper for possible revisions, following these guidelines:

   a. Evaluate the opening of your paper. Does it introduce your problem in some manner so that readers know what you are writing about? Do you present the problem in a way that creates reader interest? Is there anything you might add? Answer the question, "Based on my opening, what would inspire readers to want to read further?"

   b. Evaluate the middle part of the paper: how well do you present the causes of the problem? How effectively do you show the effects that the problem has on you and on others? What might you add to help readers understand the problem better or make the paper more interesting?

   c. Evaluate your conclusion. Do you present a realistic solution or possible solutions that deal with the problem's causes? Do you explain what this solution will do for you, and perhaps for others? The solution part of your paper is perhaps the most important since readers may discover something they hadn't considered.

   d. Evaluate your paragraphing. Does it help readers move smoothly through the opening, middle, and ending of your paper? Have you used transitions (first, second, then, however, therefore, as you can see, for example, finally) to tie sentences and paragraphs together? Have you dealt with causes and effects in separate paragraphs, or introduced different causes or different effects in new paragraphs?

   e. Evaluate the organization of your paper. Have you presented the different parts of your paper in the best order? Does a particular sentence or paragraph seem out of place where it is? What might you move to a different location where it would make more sense? (See the Essay section on "Organization" on page 162.)

   f. Read each sentence carefully to see if you can improve its clarity, smoothness, or conciseness. Many first draft sentences can be improved through the revision process. In addition, make revisions to improve sentence variety, replace overused joining words, and combine pairs of short sentences. (See the upcoming section on "Sentence Revision.")

g. Read the draft from your readers' perspective. Have you presented a serious enough problem for readers to take an interest in? Have you written in a way that readers will clearly understand the problem and how it is affecting your life? Have you presented a solution or possible solutions that truly address the problem and give readers something to consider?

7. Write the second draft of your paper, including all revisions you have noted to improve it.

8. When you have completed your latest draft, proofread it for errors following these guidelines, and make the necessary corrections:

a. *Sentence endings:* Make sure you have a period at the end of each sentence, and correct any run-on sentences or sentence fragments.

b. *Word endings:* Check to make sure plural words end in *s* or *es*, regular past tense verbs end in *ed,* and present tense verbs agree with their subjects. Also check for *er* and *est* endings on comparative and superlative adjectives.

c. *Spelling:* Check your spelling carefully, and look up any words you are uncertain of. Also check your use of homonyms such as there/their/they're, your/you're, no/know, through/threw, and its/it's.

d. *Internal punctuation:* Check your use of commas with words in series, before conjunctions in compound sentences, after introductory groups of words, and to set off relative clauses, interrupters, and ending phrases beginning with *especially, particularly,* and *ing-ending* words. Check for apostrophes in contractions and possessives and for quotation marks around direct quotations. Finally, check your use of semicolons and colons.

e. *Pronoun usage:* Check your subject pronoun usage (Marianne and I, my brother and he, we and they), and make sure that all pronouns agree with their antecedents. (See the section "Pronoun-Antecedent Agreement Review" on page 175.)

9. Write the final error-free draft of your paper to share with classmates and your instructor.

Unit 6

Writing About Issues

Writers write for a variety of reasons: to inform, educate, advise, analyze, problem solve, and entertain. Another common reason for writing is to influence readers' thoughts or actions, particularly on issues important to the writer. When you write to influence readers, you want them to agree with and support your position, which may mean changing their minds or getting them to take seriously something they hadn't considered.

People frequently write about issues in newspaper editorials, "letters to the editor," work-related communications, and letters to individuals that the writer wants to influence. A writer may try to convince readers to vote for a particular candidate, to help reverse the firing of the city's philharmonic orchestra conductor, to vote against the city bond measure requiring a tax increase, to support a city-wide curfew for minors, to oppose a tuition increase at the local college, or to contribute money to build a performing arts building at the college. A common purpose for writing about issues is to move people to action they would not otherwise take.

Your audience for issue-oriented writing can be a tough one: people who either don't agree with you or don't have an opinion. You obviously don't have to convince people who already agree with you on the issue, so your task is either to change other people's minds or to get them thinking about something they may know or care little about. Audience awareness is a crucial part of writing effectively about issues, and there is an interesting psychological component: what makes people change their opinions?

Writing about issues comes at the end of the text so that you can call upon all that you have learned through previous writing experiences. The skills you have developed to draw upon personal experience, to support an opinion effectively, to make valid comparisons and draw reasonable conclusions, to analyze problems, to organize your thoughts, and to word your thoughts clearly will all contribute to your writing about issues effectively.

PREWRITING

Writing about issues requires dealing with topics that people have different opinions on. If most people agree on something, like that ten-year-olds shouldn't be allowed to drive, there is nothing to write about. However, if there was a legislative bill in your state to raise the legal driving age to eighteen, or to lower the legal drinking age to eighteen, people would have different viewpoints, and much would be written on each issue.

You may already have definite opinions on some important issues. You may, for example, favor gun control, disagree with capital punishment, condone legalized abortion, support gay rights, support rent control, disagree with legalizing marijuana, or support an increase in the speed limit on freeways. Often the biggest challenge of writing about issues effectively is to *support* your opinion in ways that convince *skeptical* readers of its reasonableness and good sense.

In analyzing your opinion on an issue, you may discover that it is based more on emotion rather than reason, or on beliefs you hold but have never questioned. You may even find that the viewpoint isn't really yours, but rather that of parents or friends whose opinion you've adopted. None of this means that you should abandon your position on an issue, but you may need to examine it critically before writing about it.

Second, while it is easy to write for readers who agree with you, these people don't need convincing. Instead, you must engage readers who disagree or have no opinion in a way that keep them reading and thinking. Sometimes just getting a reader to think about an issue in a different way, or to question his or her viewpoint, means you have been successful. People seldom change their minds on important issues overnight, but you may plant a seed that gets them to question their thinking.

TOPIC SELECTION

For your writing assignment, you will select an issue that you and others feel is important enough to write about—one which people have different opinions about. When you take a position on an issue, you "make a case" for what you believe in a way that will influence readers. The purpose of writing about issues is to change people's minds, to move them to action, to cause them to think differently, or to get them to think seriously about something they haven't considered.

To select an issue to write about, consider the following:

1. Select a *controversial* topic—one that people have different positions on. It may be a local controversy—something related to your school or community—or a state, national, or international concern. It could be in the area of education, politics, sports, music, health, fashion, family, crime, etc.

2. Select a topic that you are knowledgeable about. You need enough knowledge about the issue, gained from experience, reading, or other sources, to write about it effectively. You may, of course, talk to others to get ideas or examples for your paper, to better understand opposing viewpoints, to test your own belief and reasoning, or to learn more about the issue.

3. Select an issue that you are interested in, that you feel is important, and that you would like to influence people about.

4. Select a topic that is specific enough to develop in a 400- 500-word paper. For example, gun control is a general topic that you might write a book on. Therefore, you might narrow that topic to something specific like "Banning Assault Weapons," "Gun Control and the Fifth Amendment," "Minnesota's Handgun Control Initiative," or "Guns in the Home: Protection or Liability?"

TOPIC SELECTION ACTIVITY 6.1

In small groups, brainstorm to come up with a number of issues that students may be interested in and want to write about. Consider issues in different areas: local school-related issues, local community issues, state issues, education issues, political issues, sports/athletic issues, health issues, exercise/fitness issues, music issues, fashion issues, family issues, legal issues, ethnic/racial issues, etc. Make a list of any issues that come to mind, neither evaluating nor discarding any issue.

After you have brainstormed a number of issues, go through the list and select ten issues that the group feels are most important or interesting. Be prepared to share your issues with the class.

TOPIC SELECTION ACTIVITY 6.2

Following the suggestions presented and considering the issues developed by your group and the class, select an issue to write about. Take your time thinking about different topics, and consider issues that affect (or may affect) you and people you know. Your instructor may want to approve topics to ensure that a variety of issues are covered by the class.

STUDENT SAMPLE ISSUE CONSIDERATION

What's controversial these days? There's a bill in the state legislature to increase community college tuition by 15% next year. That could hurt some students. In the local paper this morning it said the city council is debating whether to spend a couple hundred thousand dollars to "beautify" the downtown area, and some people think it's a waste of money; others think it's a good idea. On campus, there's a controversy on whether condom vending machines should be installed in the bathrooms.

There's the instant replay debate in professional football. What about steroid use? Does anyone disagree that it's bad? What about beer being sold in eating places at four-year colleges? Is that an issue anymore? On our campus there's concern over whether campus police should be allowed to carry guns. I don't know what I want to write about yet.

After more thinking, none of those topics really moved me. Then I remembered the rumor that the college newspaper may be shut down after this year. I checked it out and it's true. The school is planning on dropping the paper after next semester. I may want to write about that. It's going to be controversial, at least with some students.

POSSIBLE ISSUE FOR PAPER

Shutting down the college newspaper

PREWRITING CONSIDERATIONS

Before writing your first draft, consider the following prewriting plan.

1. Decide on a tentative *thesis* for the paper: the position you want to take on the issue and support in a paper. Consider your thesis carefully, for it will influence everything that you write.

THESIS STATEMENT EXAMPLES

TOPIC: GUN CONTROL

Banning assault weapons does not go far enough in curbing violence in America.

TOPIC: COLLEGE CAFETERIA

To improve the quality of food and reduce prices, the college cafeteria operation should be privatized.

TOPIC: GARBAGE PICKUP

The city's proposal to increase the garbage pickup in Rockport from once to twice a week should be supported.

Topic: Possible Iraqi war   U.S. military intervention in Iraq would be a big mistake.

Topic: Dormitory curfew   Since college students are adults, there should be no curfew for students living in the dormitories.

2. Decide on your reading audience: the people that should read about this issue and your position on it. Whom do you want to influence? Through what means can you best reach them? (letter to the editor of college paper? city paper? letters to the college board of trustees? personal letters to key individuals?)

Example   Topic Dormitory curfew: My audience would be the dormitory director, the dean of students, the college president, the board of trustees, and the student council, all of whom have a role in setting school policy.

3. Decide on your writing purpose: what you hope to accomplish with your readers. Do you want to change their minds? change their behavior? encourage them to support your position on the issue? take a particular action?

Example   Topic: Dormitory curfew   I want them to take an action: do away with the obsolete dormitory curfew that I guess few colleges in the country still have.

4. Generate a list of possible supporting points for your thesis position: reasons you believe the way you do. These reasons will provide the basis on which readers will evaluate your position.

Example   Topic: Dormitory curfew   reasons why the curfew should be discontinued

a. students are adults

b. no other college in the area has a dormitory curfew

c. current curfew doesn't work anyway

d. many students won't live in dorms due to curfew

e. discrimination against dormitory students

f. curfew distracts from serious dorm problems

5. Think of a few *opposing* arguments to your position on the issue: reasons why some readers might disagree with you. Also, consider how might you *refute* (tear down, disprove, prove illogical, neutralize) those arguments in your paper.

EXAMPLE   TOPIC: DORMITORY   reasons some people favor the curfew
                   CURFEW

a. parents' concern for students' safety

b. curfew reduces potential for bad behavior (late night drinking, vandalism, fights, etc.)

c. some students in dorms favor the curfew so students won't come in
   late and wake people up.

6. Besides what you already know about your topic, what else might you
   need to know to write the best possible paper? Talk with people who
   can provide the best information, and you may want to talk with
   people with an opposing viewpoint to understand their thinking.)

PREWRITING ACTIVITY 6.3

Following the suggestions just presented, do a prewriting outline for your
topic that includes the following:

1. Topic
   Dropping the school newspaper

2. Thesis (position statement)
   The school newspaper is too important to students to be dropped.

3. Audience
   The school board, who is considering eliminating the paper, and also
   the students, whose support is needed to keep the paper

4. Purpose
   Convince the school board not to drop the paper, and convince students to get involved.

5. Supporting points for thesis

   a. student enjoyment in reading paper

   b. only source of outside news for most students

   c. main source of information for college activities

   d. source of debates and discussion

   e. tradition of the college

6. Arguments against keeping newspaper

   a. budget problems at the college

   b. having trouble staffing paper with students

c. faculty advisor problems

7. Refuting arguments:

a. newspaper is a tiny part of school budget—not a big savings

b. newspaper could generate more income through more sales of advertising space

c. many small schools have some trouble with staffing, but they don't get rid of their papers

d. recruit journalism students like the college recruits athletes

e. make faculty advisor regular full-time faculty member rather than part-time person

8. Things to find out before writing:

a. Talk with some students on the newspaper staff to see if they have any good ideas for saving the paper.

b. Talk with faculty advisor to get budget figures for the newspaper.

PREWRITING ACTIVITY 6.4

In small groups, present your topic and what you plan to do with it. Evaluate group members' topics and plans, ask questions, discuss other positions on the issue, and make suggestions that might help each student prepare for writing.

JOURNAL ENTRY TWENTY-ONE

After having done prewriting work for several papers throughout the course, relate in your journal what you find to be the most effective prewriting process for you. In other words, what things do you like to help you write a first draft?

FIRST DRAFTS

Now that you have selected an issue and done some prewriting planning, you are ready to write the first draft. The following suggestions will help you get started.

DRAFTING GUIDELINES

1. Open the paper by introducing your topic and presenting your thesis: your position on the issue. Begin the paper in a way that will inspire

readers to continue. Let them know why they should take an interest in the topic.

2. In the middle paragraphs, present and develop your supporting points, and also present and refute (tear down, disprove, neutralize) one or two opposing arguments. To influence people, it helps to cast some doubt on their beliefs as well as support your own.

3. Keep your readers in mind as you write. Since you are trying to influence them, you don't want to alienate or offend them, which may occur if your tone seems very angry, or if you imply that their beliefs are inferior to yours. In addition, consider what you need to remember about your particular audience.

For example, if you are writing to a board of trustees, these are people who probably care about the college and the students, who are college graduates themselves, but who aren't involved enough in the day-to-day operation to know exactly what's going on. They probably aren't the enemy, but they may need educating on an issue.

4. In the conclusion, make your purpose clear to readers. Why did you write to them? What do you want them to do or think? How can you conclude your paper to best accomplish your purpose?

PREWRITING ACTIVITY 6.5

Before writing your first draft, meet in small groups to discuss how best to influence people who don't believe as you do on an issue. Answer the following questions to help you think of ways that people are influenced. Make a list of things that you might do in a paper to influence readers. Be prepared to share your ideas with the class.

1. When you really want something from someone (have someone do a particular favor for you, have someone help you with something), how do you best accomplish your purpose? How might that knowledge help you write your paper?

2. How can someone get you to change your mind about something of importance? How might this knowledge help you write your paper?

3. If you were going to talk to a group of high school seniors on the importance of practicing safe sex and avoiding pregnancies, what might be the best way to get them to take you seriously? How might this knowledge help you write your paper?

4. What would be the best "psychology" to use on a six-year-old to convince her to get a flu shot that she is unwilling to get? How might this knowledge help you write your paper?

5. You have a neighbor who belongs to the National Rifle Association and owns a number of guns. What do you think would be the best approach to get him to support legislation banning the ownership of handguns? How might this knowledge help you write your paper?

6. Divide your group, half in support of legalized abortion, half against (you may have to take a position you don't agree with). Listen carefully to the reasons the group members with the opposing position believe as they do, and try to understand their viewpoint. How might trying to understand the thinking and feelings of readers with opposing positions help you write your paper?

DRAFTING ACTIVITY 6.6

Read the following essay "Limiting Handguns" by Robert DeGrazia, who supports a ban on handguns, to get some ideas on openings, middle paragraph development, and conclusions, and to see how he dealt with his reading audience: people opposed to banning handguns.

Then write the first draft of your persuasive paper keeping in mind the guidelines presented.

Limiting Handguns
by Robert deGrazia

We buried Donald Brown in May. He was murdered by three men who wanted to rob the supermarket manager he was protecting. Patrolman Brown was 61 years old, six months from retirement. He and his wife intended to retire to Florida at the end of the year. Now there will be no retirement in the sun, and she is alone.

Donald Brown was the second police officer to die since I became commissioner here on Nov. 15, 1972. The first was John Schroeder, a detective shot in a pawnshop robbery last November. John Schroeder was the brother of Walter Schroeder, who was killed in a bank robbery in 1970. Their names are together on the honor roll in the lobby of Police Headquarters.

John Murphy didn't die. He was shot in the head last February as he chased a robbery suspect into the Washington Street subway station. He lived, but he will be brain-damaged for the rest of his life, unable to walk or talk.

At least two of these police officers were shot by a handgun, the kind one can buy nearly everywhere for a few dollars. Those who don't want to buy one can steal one, and half a million are stolen each year. There are forty million handguns circulating in this country; two and a half million are sold each year.

Anybody can get a gun. Ownership of handguns has become so widespread that the gun is no longer merely the instrument of crime; it is now a cause of violent crime. Of the eleven Boston police officers killed since 1962, seven were killed with handguns; of the seventeen wounded by guns since 1962, sixteen were shot with handguns.

Police officers, of course, are not the only people who die. Ten thousand other Americans are dead at the price of our promiscuous right to bear arms. Gun advocates are fond of saying that guns don't kill, people do. But guns do kill.

Half of the people who commit suicide do so with handguns. Fifty-four percent of the murders committed in 1972 were committed with handguns. Killing with handguns simply is a good deal easier than killing with other weapons.

Rifles and shotguns are difficult to conceal. People can run away from knife-wielding assailants. People do die each year by drownings, bludgeonings and strangulation. But assaults with handguns are five times more likely to kill.

No one can convince me, after returning from Patrolman Brown's funeral, after standing in the rain with hundreds of others from this department and others, that we should allow people to own handguns.

I know that many people feel deeply and honestly about their right to own and enjoy guns. I realize that gun ownership and self-protection are deeply held American values. I am asking that people give them up.

I am committed to doing what I can to take guns away from the people. In my view, private ownership of handguns must be banished from this country. I am not asking for registration or licensing or outlawing cheap guns. I am saying that no private citizen, whatever his claim, should possess a handgun. Only police officers should.

REVISIONS

While you should always revise with your readers in mind, it is particularly important to revise issue-oriented papers with the question in mind, "How will my readers respond to this?" For example, you may write a paper supporting euthanasia that people who agree with you would love but that your reading audience would find unconvincing. If such a draft isn't skillfully revised, it may miss its target audience: people whose minds you are trying to change.

REVISION GUIDELINES

When evaluating your first draft for possible revisions, consider these suggestions:

1. Evaluate the opening of your paper. Does it introduce your topic clearly and present your thesis so readers know your position on the issue? Is it interesting enough to keep readers engaged who may have a different opinion than yours? Do readers know why they should be interested in this issue?

2. Evaluate your middle paragraphs. Do you present some strong supportive points and develop each point effectively? (Read the upcoming section on "Paragraph Development" before revising your draft.) In addition, do you present and refute one or two opposing arguments to get readers to reconsider their own beliefs?

3. Evaluate your conclusion. Is it a strong part of your paper that leaves readers with something to think about? Does it clearly reveal your purpose so readers know why you have written to them? Do they understand what you would like them to think or do?

4. Evaluate your paragraphing. Does it help readers move smoothly through the opening, middle, and ending of your paper? Have you used transitions (first, second, then, however, therefore, as you can see, for example) to tie sentences and paragraphs together? Have you developed your supportive points in different paragraphs?

5. Read each sentence carefully to see if you can improve its clarity, smoothness, or conciseness. In addition, make revisions to improve sentence variety, replace overused joining words, and combine pairs of short sentences. (See the section on "Sentence Revision" later in the unit.)

6. Read the draft from your readers' perspective. Does it sound like it was written by a reasonable person who respects his or her readers although they may disagree? Was it written by a person whose viewpoint is based on a thorough knowledge of the issue?

REVISION ACTIVITY 6.7

In small groups, evaluate the following student draft by applying the revision guidelines just presented. Make note of what is done well in the essay and what might be improved through revision.

When you finish, evaluate each student's draft similarly, taking into account the audience that he or she is writing for. Have copies of your draft available for group members.

Keeping the School Newspaper (written for school board)

It is hard to believe the school board is thinking about dropping the newspaper. It's been around since the school began. It's as much a part of the school as the football team, the band, the student council or anything else.

I know a lot of students who read the school paper. In fact, that is the only paper they ever read, so they would be losing their one newspaper source. I know the paper isn't exactly the New York Times, but it serves a purpose. It keeps students interested in what's going on around school. We don't have much involvement in activities and government as it is. Without a newspaper keeping us in touch with sports, activities, meetings, and rallies, there would be even less involvement.

The newspaper also brings in some news of the outside world—things that are happening in education, some world events, things that are happening in state politics. As I said, it's not like major news coverage, but for me and other students, it is the only news we read regularly.

The paper also gives students a chance to express their viewpoints. I like reading letters to the editor and student editorials, and sometimes students do get involved in issues and take sides—for example, when they were considering changing the name of the college. There was some real student involvement, and a lot of it came out of the coverage the paper gave the issue. Students don't get involved in many issues at the college. Without the paper, they wouldn't know any issues to get involved in.

The paper also gives some people a chance for a little attention. It's fun getting your name or picture in the paper. I don't know any student who doesn't like that. A lot of students get their pictures and opinions in when they ask a weekly question like "How do you feel about the new early semester calendar?" That's one of my favorite weekly regulars in the paper, and a lot of others too.

The paper also provides some journalism training for a lot of students. Without a paper, where would the journalism majors go? That would wipe out a program, and our enrollment would drop.

Finally, the paper can't be a big expense. It doesn't look as though it's expensively done up. What's the big cost to justify dropping the program? Why don't you look for other things to cut that are less important? Why don't you look for ways to save the paper? I'd really miss the paper. It's important to the school. What's a school without a newspaper? Even my old junior high still runs a weekly newspaper. And this college can't?

REVISION ACTIVITY 6.8

After working through the upcoming section on "Paragraph Development," and considering your group's evaluation suggestions and your personal evaluation, write the next draft of your paper following the guidelines presented.

JOURNAL ENTRY TWENTY-TWO

In your journal, relate the most typical kinds of revisions you make during the drafting process. What do you tend to change, add, or delete in a draft as you revise? To what extent does your second draft of a paper differ from your first draft, and in what ways?

PARAGRAPH DEVELOPMENT

Effective paragraph development in an issue-oriented paper is important to accomplishing your purpose. Within your paragraphs, you answer skeptical readers' questions such as, How do you know that? How can you prove that? Why is that the case? or Why does that matter?

Providing Evidence

An important part of paragraph development in writing about issues is providing evidence that what you are saying is true or reasonable. Here are some examples of supportive points that need further development to convince readers.

EXAMPLES   Handgun control laws are working well in New Hampshire. (Give examples of how they are working well.)

Most people on welfare could be working. (Provide evidence. How do you know that is the case?)

The college bookstore is overcharging students for textbooks. (How can you prove that? Give examples.)

Yosemite Falls is a scenic wonderland. (How can the reader tell? Provide convincing details.)

The college newspaper budget is a fraction of the total school budget. (To convince readers, compare the cost of the newspaper to the school's budget and show the percentage of cost.)

For many students, a sixty dollar annual parking fee at the college can be a hardship. (How can readers be convinced? Provide examples of students affected by the fee.)

To make your supportive points most convincing to readers, follow these guidelines:

1. Provide evidence for all points in support of your thesis: your position on the issue.

   EXAMPLE

   THESIS   Community College transfer students are better risks for success at four-year schools than incoming freshmen.

SUPPORTING POINTS

a. Transfer students are more mature. (How are they "more mature"? How does being "more mature" help with success?)

b. Transfer students have already made the transition to college. (What does that mean? How does it affect success?)

c. Transfer students have already proven that they can handle college work. (How have they proven that? Give examples.)

d. Transfer students are by and large more serious about college. (How can that be proved? What evidence is there to support that claim?)

2. Provide evidence for any statement that readers wouldn't necessarily accept as true.

EXAMPLES   America is an ethnically diverse country. (No evidence needed—a true statement that readers would agree with.)

Today's immigrants create problems that earlier immigrants didn't. (Evidence is needed to support statement. What kinds of problems? What proof do you have? What examples can you give?)

America would be better off if it closed its borders to immigrants. (Evidence is needed to support statement. Why should we close our borders? How would we be better off? What proof do you have?)

3. For a particular supporting point, provide the most effective evidence to convince readers of its truth or reasonableness: facts, examples, details, statistics, explanations, or reasons.

EXAMPLES   Meredith Quiring is guilty of extorting money from her ailing grandmother. (Provide *facts* that support the claim.)

America's trade relationship with Japan is deteriorating. (Provide *examples* to support the claim.)

A standard car leasing agreement is too complicated. (Provide *details* that reveal its complicated nature.)

Our school district has a problem with unfunded equity. (Provide an *explanation* of what "unfunded equity" means, and then explain the problem.)

Children of divorced parents are more likely to divorce than children whose parents stay together. (Provide *statistics* to prove the alleged fact.)

Clayton would make a better governor than McWilliams. (Provide the *reasons* why Clayton would be a superior governor.)

PARAGRAPH ACTIVITY 6.9

Read the following essay "All America's Cultures" by Ji-Yeon Mary Yuhfill and determine the issue she is writing about and the essay's *thesis*: her position on the issue. In addition, note the types of examples, evidence, and details Yuhfill uses to make her points.

All America's Cultures
by Ji-Yeon Mary Yuhfill

I grew up hearing, seeing and almost believing that America was white—albeit with a little black tinged here and there—and that white was best.

The white people were everywhere in my 1970s Chicago childhood: Founding Fathers, Lewis and Clark, Lincoln, Daniel Boone, Carnegie, presidents, explorers and industrialists galore. The only black people were slaves. The only Indians were scalpers.

I never heard one word about how Benjamin Franklin was so impressed by the Iroquois federation of nations that he adapted that model into our system of state and federal government. Or that the Indian tribes were systematically betrayed and massacred by a greedy young nation that stole their land and called it the United States.

I never heard one word about how Asian immigrants were among the first to turn California's desert into fields of plenty. Or about Chinese immigrant Ah Bing, who bred the cherry now on sale in groceries across the nation. Or that plantation owners in Hawaii imported labor from China, Japan, Korea and the Philippines to work the sugar cane fields. I never learned that Asian immigrants were the only immigrants denied U.S. citizenship, even though they served honorably in World War I. All the immigrants in my textbook were white.

I never learned about Frederick Douglass, the runaway slave who became a leading abolitionist and statesman, or about black scholar W. E. B. Du Bois. I never learned that black people rose up in arms against slavery. Nat Turner wasn't one of the heroes in my childhood history class.

I never learned that the American Southwest and California were already settled by Mexicans when they were annexed after the Mexican-American War. I never learned that Mexico once had a problem keeping land-hungry white men on the U.S. side of the border.

So when other children called me a slant-eyed chink and told me to go back where I came from, I was ready to believe that I wasn't really an American because I wasn't white.

America's bittersweet legacy of struggling and failing and getting another step closer to democratic ideals of liberty and equality and justice for all wasn't for the likes of me, an immigrant child from Korea. The history books said so.

Well, the history books were wrong.

Educators around the country are finally realizing what I realized as a teenager in the library, looking up the history I wasn't getting in school. America is a multicultural nation, composed of many people with varying histories and varying traditions who have little in common except their humanity, a belief in democracy and a desire for freedom.

America changed them, but they changed America too.

A committee of scholars and teachers gathered by the New York State Department of Education recognizes this in their recent report, "One Nation, Many Peoples: A Declaration of Cultural Interdependence."

They recommend that public schools provide a "multicultural education, anchored to the shared principles of a liberal democracy."

What that means, according to the report, is recognizing that America was shaped and continues to be shaped by people of diverse backgrounds. It calls for students to be taught that history is an ongoing process of discovery and interpretation of the past, and that there is more than one way of viewing the world.

Thus, the westward migration of white Americans is not just a heroic settling of an untamed wild, but also the conquest of indigenous peoples. Immigrants were not just white, but Asian as well. Blacks were not merely passive slaves freed by northern whites, but active fighters for their own liberation.

In particular, according to the report, the curriculum should help children "to access critically the reasons for the inconsistencies between the ideals of the U.S. and social realities. It should provide information and intellectual tools that can permit them to contribute to bringing reality closer to the ideals."

In other words, show children the good with the bad, and give them the skills to help improve their country. What could be more patriotic?

Several dissenting members of the New York committee publicly worry that America will splinter into ethnic fragments if this multicultural curriculum is adopted. They argue that the committee's report puts the focus on ethnicity at the expense of national unity.

But downplaying ethnicity will not bolster national unity. The history of America is the story of how and why people from all over the world came to the United States, and how in struggling to make a better life for themselves, they changed each other, they changed the country, and they all came to call themselves Americans.

E pluribus unum. Out of many, one.

This is why I, with my Korean background, and my childhood tormentors, with their lost-in-the-mist-of-time-European backgrounds, are all Americans.

It is the unique beauty of this country. It is high time we let all our children gaze upon it.

REVISION ACTIVITY 6.10

The following paper contains a number of questionable statements that aren't supported by evidence. In small groups, read the draft and underline statements that most readers wouldn't accept without evidence. In addition, decide what kind(s) of evidence might be provided.

Next, read your draft to find supporting statements that you may provide little or no evidence for. Underline each statement and provide evidence (examples, facts, explanations, details, reasons) in the next draft that will convince readers of its believability.

Welfare Fraud

If you see someone driving around in a Cadillac, he may be a hard-working American who's made his money honestly. On the other hand, he may be a welfare recipient who receives taxpayers' money for doing nothing. Working Americans are getting ripped off by welfare cheaters, and it's time to dismantle the welfare system.

Most able-bodied men and women are on welfare because they are too lazy to work. The government literally pays them for being lazy. Most of these people are making more money sitting home doing nothing than they would make if they had a job. Something is wrong with a system that rewards laziness more than hard work.

What's more, they are producing another generation of welfare addicts: their children. They learn from their parents how to play the welfare game, and then they teach their own children through example. The vicious cycle goes on and on.

The system is further abused by government officials who get kickbacks from the welfare industry. By continuing to pass welfare legislation, they get a little welfare of their own from the welfare bureaucrats whose jobs are dependent on the system's survival. It's no wonder that few people on Capitol Hill question the tremendous abuses that pervade the welfare system.

I'm calling on all Americans to write their congressman and demand that legislation be implemented to dismantle our present welfare system. For every person it helps legitimately, there are ten people who take advantage of it. We need to get these welfare cheaters off their sofas and into jobs. Most of America's problems—crime, deteriorating cities, deteriorating families, drug use—are the results of our welfare system.

PARAGRAPHING REVIEW

By this time in the course, you should have a good understanding of basic paragraphing and its importance in helping you organize your ideas and convey them effectively to readers. This final review activity is for students who could benefit from some additional practice in paragraphing papers and using transitional wording.

PARAGRAPHING ACTIVITY 6.11

Divide the following essay into paragraphs by placing the paragraph symbol (¶) in front of each new paragraph. Change paragraphs each time the writer moves to a different aspect of his topic. Then evaluate the paragraphing of your latest draft, and make any changes that would make the paragraphing more effective for readers.

Down with the Greeks

Early Sunday morning, the whole place looked like a disaster area. Windows were broken out, bottles were strewn all over the floors, bodies were lying around, and a goat was on a sofa munching pretzels. The effects of an earthquake? A Chicago gangland massacre? A scene from a bombed-out Italian village in a World War II movie? None of the above. Just another Saturday night bash at the Sigma Nu frat house. Over the years, fraternities have completely lost sight of why they were created, if there were any good reasons in the first place. Today's fraternities represent a lot of the worst things about our society. They should be disbanded once and for all. First of all, fraternities are elitist outfits, each one catering to its own kind. For example, while I was at Landsford State, the Theta Chi's wanted nothing but doctors- and lawyers-to-be, the Sigmas wanted nothing but jocks, the SAE's nothing but rich party boys, and the Lambda Nu nothing but young Republicans. Each group hung around campus in a big clique, either ignoring or looking down their noses at outsiders. Fraternities aren't for everyone, as they would have you believe. Once in a fraternity, previously nice guys turned into egotistical snobs, including Tom Anderson from my old high school. Tom, a year ahead of me in school, had always been a friendly, decent guy. When I went to Landsford State as a freshman, I passed by Tom in his AGR sweatshirt with some of his frat friends, and he looked right through me, like I didn't exist. Later I asked a couple of other friends about good old Tom, and they said that he'd "gone frat" and was now a total jerk. So much for the myth that fraternities build character. Aside from the elitism, fraternities have become a place where bad behavior is valued. For example, the Sigmas have their annual March 31st belching contest, where the guy with the loudest, longest belch wins a case of beer. At the Theta house, there is the legend of Josh the Vomiter, the legendary Theta who came into a frat meeting totally bombed, walked to the front of the room, and regurgitated a half gallon of wine all over the visiting Grand Deacon from Klamath Falls. Then there's the cheating. I have seen the SAE "testing file" in their basement: a filing cabinet full of hundreds of stolen tests from every department on campus. The new pledge class each year shows their courage by stealing as many tests as possible, a great start on their fraternity careers. And the campus police have their records: over 80 percent of the vandalism reports in the college apartment area west of campus are traced back to fraternity houses, according to campus Police Chief George Shrum. A lot of the fraternities' problems occur because of all the drinking. Fraternities are basically boozing clubs, and by the fraternities' own admission in the school newspaper, over 200 kegs of beer are consumed in fall pledge week activities alone. Most of the social fraternities have at least three parties a week: a mid-weeker to kill the boredom, a TGIF, of course, and an elaborate drunk on Saturday nights. With all the emphasis on partying and drinking, it's not surprising that the overall GPA for frat members at Landsford State, according to the school registrar, is a 2.15, just high enough to stay in school. And the school president, Dr. Kirtch, had this to offer after the latest police raid on a frat party: "If some fraternities put half as much effort into encouraging studying as into encouraging drinking, they could do their members some good." Fraternities are sexist, racist organizations, and the facts speak for themselves. First, women cannot belong to fraternities, but each fraternity has a "little sisters' auxiliary," which is used, according to an ex-little sister, to clean up after parties, to get members dates, to console them when they're depressed, and to be their hostesses at parties. They are college geisha girls, in other words. As to racism, at Landsford College, 96 percent of the frat members are white, 2 percent are oriental, and 2 percent are black. And that is with a school population that is 70 percent white, 20 percent black, and 8 percent oriental. It is no wonder that the Black Student Union on campus has petitioned the college to start a new fraternity; they know the present fraternities aren't for them. I know what happens to many fraternity types when they get older. We have a number of service clubs in town and one club called the Order of the Eagles. They aren't civic minded; they just like to party: an open bar at every meeting, plus casino nights, stag nights, and trips to Las Vegas. And they don't care about their public image. In fact, they're proud of it. So fraternity types never die; they just join the Order of the Eagles somewhere and continue their self-centered, purposeless ways. If Landsford abolished all fraternities tomorrow, I wonder what negative effects that might have on students or the college. After two hours, I'm still thinking.

SENTENCE REVISION REVIEW

This final review section gives you more practice revising first-draft sentences to improve their wording and structural variety. Sentence revision is a critical part of the writing process, and your revising skills will continue to grow as long as you write.

Wording Problems

To help you improve first-draft sentences, here is a summary of the different kinds of sentence problems that writers often revise.

1. *Wordiness:* Sentences often contain more words than necessary to express a writer's thoughts. These sentences contain repeated words and phrases or unnecessarily complicated wording to make simple statements. To revise wordy sentences, eliminate unnecessary words and replace complicated phrases with simpler ones.

    WORDY SENTENCE   We were out in the rays of the sun for six hours of sentence daylight, but we didn't burn due to the fact that we wore a sunscreen that kept us from burning.

    REVISED   We were out in the sun for six hours, but we didn't burn because we wore a sunscreen.

2. *Awkward phrasing:* First-draft sentences often contain awkward wording that occurs when a writer first tries out his or her thoughts on paper. If a sentence sounds odd to a writer, it will probably give a reader problems. To correct awkward wording, find a better way to express the thought. Changing a word or two may make the difference, or you may have to revise the entire sentence.

    WORDY SENTENCE   There is a square cement floor with trees and bushes that are around the cement.

    REVISED   Oak trees and a few bushes surround the cement patio.

3. *Poor word choices:* First-draft sentences sometimes contain words that don't say quite what the writer wants. You can often tell when you've used a word in a first draft that doesn't sound right, but you can't think of a better choice. On returning to a draft after a few hours or days, the poorer word choices stand out even more, and often, better choices will come to you. To correct poor word choices, replace them with more appropriate words.

| Poor word | The clown made the boy full of fear instead of enjoying choice him. |
| Revised | The clown frightened the boy instead of entertaining him. |

4. *Concrete language:* Vague, general wording should be replaced by concrete language that *shows* the reader what the writer sees, hears, and feels.

| Vague wording | The boy works one part of the year. |
| Revised | My ten-year-old neighbor, Jim Jones, works all summer at his father's feed store. |

SENTENCE REVISION ACTIVITY 6.12

The following paragraph needs revising for sentence improvement. Rewrite the paragraph, making each sentence as clear and smooth as possible.

It was a hot day for a parade. The band of the school had a five-mile walk through the middle of the town. Before the parade began, the band members standing at attention for an hour. Most band members were wet with sweat before they had walked one step. One tuba player he passed out from the heat and is taken to the hospital. Finally, the band began marching and starts playing "When the Saints Go Marching In." Every one of the members of that band was sick of that song "When the Saints Go Marching In" before they got even halfway through the parade route they were marching along. By the time the band reached the judges' stand, their lips were too parched to suck, their march was a stagger, and their white uniforms are colored by sweat. The band finally went to the park and on the lawn collapsed. They stripped off their hats, coats, and shoes that they wore for the parade. They drank gallons of lemonade and compare blisters on their feet and compare scuffed up shoes.

Sentence Variety

Here is a summary of what you have learned about sentence variety in your writing.

1. Writers sometimes have a tendency to overuse certain sentence structures and joining words, which can lead to monotonous prose.

2. Check your first-draft sentences to see whether you have relied too heavily on a particular structure, for example, simple sentences (one subject, one verb) or compound sentences joined primarily by *and, but,* or *so.*

3. Vary sentence structures to include a combination of simple, compound, and complex sentences, and vary joining words by using many of the following: and, but, so, for, yet, or, when, before, after, while, as, until, since, although, unless, if, because, who, whose, which, that.

4. Writers sometimes tend to string pairs or groups of short sentences together, or to write overly long, involved sentences.

5. Check your first draft to find short sentences that could be effectively combined or overly long sentences that could be divided by inserting periods and eliminating some joining words.

SENTENCE VARIETY ACTIVITY 6.13

Revise the following first-draft sentences in different ways: combine sentences with joining words and eliminate unnecessary words; group similar words; and divide overly long sentences by inserting periods and deleting joining words. Vary your sentence structures and joining words, and don't try to squeeze too many sentences uncomfortably into a single sentence.

EXAMPLE   Melba likes to listen to her stereo. Thad likes to listen to his. They both enjoy using their headphones. They are brother and sister.

COMBINED   Melba and Thad, <u>who are brother and sister,</u> enjoy listening to their stereos and using their headphones.

1. Sheri is an interesting girl. She is a freshman in college. She is a practicing minister. She is an assistant manager of a shoe store.

2. The spaniel ran all over the hills. He was delighted to be in the open. He is owned by Mr. Jacobs. Mr. Jacobs turned him loose for an afternoon.

3. The old Keystone Building, which is on 52nd Street, is going to be demolished, and it will be replaced by a high rise, which will be built by the end of summer and have thirty stories.

4. Some children in town will be bused to school. They live on the northeast side of town. This will only be for one semester. Their school is being refurbished. It was damaged in an earthquake.

5. Clyde rushed to school. He opened his locker. He removed his notebook. He ran to his biology lab. He was late.

6. We found thousands of cockroaches in the old house, and we found them behind the refrigerator, and we found them this summer, but they were dead, for they had starved to death.

7. Greta is young. She is naive. She is impressionable. She is quick to learn.

8. The house is for sale. It's a dark brown. It's on the east corner of 5th Street. It's listed for $55,000. That is a real steal.

9. Jonathan, who is a nineteen-year-old fireman, is going bald, but he couldn't care less about going bald because he is not vain, and his fiancee loves him the way he is.

10. Ann rooms with Helen. Marie rooms with both of them. They are sophomores from Natchez. They live in off-campus housing. They live there during the semester. They move home in the summer.

11. Freda is friendly. She acts this way with everyone. She has no close friends. She moves often with her job.

12. Harley contemplates his future. He sits in his room. He forgets his past. It is troubled.

13. Mary likes to win. She isn't afraid of losing. She is the captain of the lawn bowling team. The team is from Friar Hill.

14. Teddy is my brother. He is younger than I am. He is bigger than I am. He doesn't weigh as much.

15. Harold has trouble with allergies, so he carries a box of tissues in his car, and he goes through the box in a day, and he does this in the springtime, for this is when his allergies are the worst.

16. Mattie found her first grade class picture. She found it in the attic. It was among boxes of old albums. She was rummaging around for an old sweater.

17. Think of a way to get out of health science today. Come up with something new. Make it ingenious. I'm not prepared for the test. Neither are you.

18. Alexandra had to make a choice. She had to choose between beauty college and art school. She had to decide in the next week. Both schools enrolled students on Monday.

FINAL EDITING

By this time in the course, you may need little guidance in proofreading your drafts and correcting errors. You may have even worked out your own error detection process. Undoubtedly, you are aware of your personal error tendencies and conscientiously scrutinize your drafts in those areas.

For those of you relying on the proofreading guidelines in the text, a final summary is provided. In the future, you need to internalize such guidelines to use them for any writing you may do.

PROOFREADING GUIDELINES

1. Check to make sure you have a period at the end of each sentence, and correct any run-on sentences, comma splices, or sentence fragments.

2. Check your word endings to make sure that plural words end in *s* or *es,* regular past tense verbs end in *ed,* one-syllable comparative and superlative adjectives end in *er* and *est,* respectively, and present tense verbs with singular subjects end in *s.*

3. Check your spelling carefully, looking up any words you are uncertain of. Also check your use of homonyms such as there/their/they're, know/no, its/it's, your/you're, and threw/through.

4. Check your comma usage in words in series and compound sentences, after introductory groups of words, and to set off relative clauses, interrupters, and ending phrases beginning with *especially, particularly,* and *ing-ending* words. Also check your use of apostrophes, quotation marks, semicolons, and colons.

5. Check pronoun usage to make sure you are using the correct subject pronouns in compound subjects and that all pronouns agree in number and gender with their antecedents.

EDITING ACTIVITY 6.14

In small groups, proofread the following student draft and correct any errors you find.

When you finish, proofread your latest draft following the guidelines presented. Correct any remaining errors, and then write or print out your final draft and share it with your classmates and instructor.

Abortion

STUDENT SAMPLE DRAFT I am writing about one of the most important problems in our society, legalized abortion. This problem is very controversial for many reasons and many people believe that abortion is a good solution to a woman or a couples problems. Other believe that if a woman has an abortion it is a crime.

Today abortion is legal in the United States however, I think abortion should be made illegal because I do believe it is a crime. The killing of a fetus is the taking of a human life weather it is in the mothers womb or not it is a live human being, and no one has the right to take its life but God.

If a woman doesn't want to have a baby, she should take precautions before having sex. For example, she has available many birth control measures, pills, shots, condoms, or other devices that prevent pregnancy. The better way to prevent pregnancy is don't have sex at all, this could help lower the abortion rate in our country greatly.

This problem of abortion is worse among adolescents because they do not have enough information about birth control and abortion. Sometimes the adolescent has little or no communication with her parents, for these reasons, they become pregnant when they are teenagers later they decide to abort because they this it is the best solution for their lifes. They prefer abortion to taking responsiability for a baby.

Abortion is a big problem in the U.S. and a crime in my opinion. Women have different options than abortion, for example, they can study and enroll in programs that can help them with the baby such as free day care and continuation school, or they can give the baby up for adoption, many couples are looking to adopt babies. In my opinion women in the U.S. should take these different options before having an abortion, abortion should be made illegal and the law should be changed.

JOURNAL ENTRY TWENTY-THREE

In your journal, relate how your proofreading and error correction has improved during the course. What do you do better now than you used to? What if anything do you need to continue working on? What have you found most valuable in helping you eliminate errors from your writing?

SENTENCE PROBLEMS REVIEW

The following review activity is for students who still have some problems with run-on sentences, comma splices, or fragments. Punctuating sentences correctly is fundamental to effective writing, so if run-ons or fragments still persist in your writing, keep working on the problem whenever you write.

PROOFREADING ACTIVITY 6.15

Proofread the following paragraphs for run-on sentences and sentence fragments. Separate run-ons and comma splices with periods or join the sentences to form compound or complex sentences. Attach fragments to the sentences they belong with or add words to form complete sentences.

Community colleges have both advantages and disadvantages compared to four-year schools. One advantage of community colleges is their cost. Throughout the country, community college tuition is less expensive than for four-year colleges, ranging from $300 to $600 per year. Most community college students also live at home, saving on the cost of room and board. Four-year colleges, on the other hand, range in tuition from $1,500 a year for some state-operated colleges to $15,000–$25,000 a year for private schools on top of that, most four-year college students live away from home. Spending $5,000–$8,000 per year on room and board. It is not surprising that many students choose to spend two years at a community college. Before transferring to a more expensive four-year school.

On the whole, community colleges are not as difficult as four-year colleges. Studies show that GPAs for community college transfer students drop in their third year while those of four-year college students do not. Surveys also indicate that most community college transfer students find their four-year college courses more difficult and time-consuming than community college courses. Therefore, it appears that community colleges may not prepare students as well as four-year colleges do, some community college students may find themselves at a disadvantage when they transfer.

Community colleges also don't have the activities that four-year colleges do. Since community colleges are by and large "commuter" schools. With students living at home, participation in campus activities is much lower than at four-year schools with their live-in dormitory populations. Participation in school government and on-campus clubs is limited student attendance at football and basketball games often numbers a hundred or fewer. Community college students on the whole miss out on the excitement and social involvement that can be an important part of the college experience.

CORRECT USAGE REVIEW

The first five units covered grammar usage situations in which writers sometimes make errors: past tense verbs, subject-verb agreement, subject pronoun usage, pronoun-antecedent agreement, and comparative and superlative adjectives. This section provides a final proofreading activity to help you recognize and correct such errors in your writing.

PROOFREADING ACTIVITY 6.16

Proofread the following paragraphs for grammar errors involving subject-verb agreement, subject pronouns, pronoun-antecedent agreement, or superlative and comparative adjectives. Make the necessary corrections.

The thing I like least about the apartments I live in are the topless dumpsters sitting in front of the west bank of apartments. First, it creates a bad smell. In the summer when it is full of garbage and used diapers, a putrid odor sweeps across the apartments when the afternoon breeze come up. Second, it is too small to accommodate a week's supply of trash. The garbage that gets piled up on top fall out, and dogs and the wind scatter them all over the driveway and lawn. By Friday before pickup time, the place is a littered mess.

The most worst problem are the flies. The garbage in the open dumpsters attract thousands of flies in warm weather, and they take up residence at the apartments. If you are outside, you constantly have to swat them off your face and body. They also find his or her way indoors, congregating in the kitchen while you eat and attacking your face while you sleep at night. From May to September, you can always hear flies buzzing somewhere in the apartment. They are the terriblest health problem at the apartments.

Obviously, the apartments need new dumpsters, ones that is covered to keep the flies away and the stench in, and ones that is large enough to hold a week's worth of garbage. It should also be moved to the east side of the apartments so that the breeze will carry the odor away from the buildings. If the owner isn't willing to pay a little more for decent covered dumpsters, I think the health department should be called. Some of the neighbors and me are prepared to do just that.

PUNCTUATION REVIEW

This final section provides a proofreading activity covering everything you have learned about using commas, apostrophes, quotation marks, semicolons, and colons in your writing.

PROOFREADING ACTIVITY 6.17

Proofread the following paragraphs for punctuation omissions, and insert commas, apostrophes, quotation marks, semicolons, and colons where they are needed.

The Inequity of College Grants

When I walk through the business services office at school I often notice a line of students getting their grant checks for the month. I don't begrudge them their checks because I know they need the money but when I see them Im reminded that I applied for every local and state grant I could and I didn't qualify for anything.

Because I get no financial aid I have to work at least thirty hours a week to help pay for my college and living expenses. I work at least four hours a day during the week and ten hours on weekends. With the colleges expenses so high, something needs to be done for lower-middle-income students like myself who are caught in between too "well off" for aid but too poor to survive without working long hours. I often ask myself why are people in my situation not given help?

As an example my mother and fathers combined income is $25,000. That may sound pretty good, but when there are four kids in the family house payments and the usual bills theres not much left for college expenses. My parents can't come close to paying for my tuition books fees and living expenses yet because of their salary bracket I didn't qualify for any grants. To stay in school I have to make at least $500 a month.

Having to work long hours I'm at a real disadvantage. Most students on grants don't work a lot and many students from middle- and upper-income families don't work at all. While I'm working thirty hours a week they can be putting those hours into studying. I never feel there's enough hours in the day to get my reading and studying done.

Another problem is I usually end up taking only the 12-unit minimum per semester to maintain a full-time students status I don't have time for more classes. This means I'll have to put in an extra semester or year of college to graduate or go to summer school every summer which is even more expensive than regular semesters. I also have to cram all of my classes into the morning hours so I can be at work by one o'clock on weekdays limiting my choice of courses and instructors.

The most aggravating thing is I know I could do so much better in school. When I was at home and going to high school my grades were good because I only worked a few hours a week. Now I feel like I have two full-time jobs and I don't have the time or energy to do my best in school. I end up settling for C's when I know I could be getting A's and B's. If I decide one day to apply for graduate school my grades are going to be a problem.

However I know I'm not in this alone. There are a lot of students caught in the same dilemma who tell me I have the same problems that you have. It just doesn't seem fair that going to college has to be made so much more difficult for some students than for others. In America everyone has the right to a college education but having the right and being given a fair opportunity to succeed are two different things. With some financial aid and a reduced work load I know I could succeed.

In the future I don't realistically see college expenses going down. Therefore I feel that for students like myself the salary limit for grant qualification should be raised. Im not saying I should have the full grant status that poorer students have but I feel that I should be entitled to at least a partial grant. Why couldnt someone in my position receive a half or quarter grant rather than being shut out completely? And why has the salary qualification level remained the same the last four years when the cost of college has gone up tremendously? One thing should be raised automatically with increased college expenses: the ceiling on grants.

JOURNAL ENTRY TWENTY-FOUR

In your journal, provide your opinion on the small group activities you have done throughout the course. How do you feel about the small group work in general, and why? What kinds of group activities in particular did you find most useful? What recommendations, if any, would you make for improving the small group activities?

WRITING REVIEW

In the "Writing Review," you apply what you have learned throughout the unit to a second issue-oriented paper. The following writing process summarizes the steps presented throughout the unit. Follow the process as presented or a more individualized process that works best for you.

WRITING PROCESS

1. Write about an issue that you would like to see people take action on: a situation that needs changing. Follow these suggestions:

   Pick an issue that is important—something that you would definitely like to see changed.

   Decide on your thesis for the paper: the position you will take on the issue.

   Decide on your reading audience—the people that can help change the situation—and on your purpose: what you want them to do to help change it.

2. To help plan your paper, do the following prewriting work:

   a. List some supporting points for your thesis: reasons that you are taking this position on the issue. Then decide what kind of evidence (facts, examples, details, explanations, personal experiences) you might use to substantiate each point.

   b. List one or two opposing arguments—reasons people might disagree with you—and decide how you might refute those arguments in your paper.

STUDENT SAMPLE   Something that I think needs changing is the college's practice of overscheduling courses each semester and then canceling course sections that get lower enrollments. I've had three or four classes canceled, which really messed up my schedule a couple of semesters.

Topic	The college's overscheduling of courses
Thesis	When the college overschedules and then cancels courses, students get hurt.
Reading audience	Students, administrators, admissions department
Purpose	Convince the school to stop the practice and offer only those classes that have a good chance of making enrollment.

Support points for thesis:

- My own experience with canceled courses (Provide example from last semester.)

- Students believe their schedules are set. (Explain why.)

- Students have to change their entire schedules. (Give examples.)

- Students often can't get into other classes. (Explain why.)

- Classes often aren't canceled until second or third week. (Explain effects on students in canceled classes.)

- Practice can jeopardize students' full-time status. (Explain negative effects.)

Opposing points to refute:

- Cost effective for school to maintain only high enrollment classes. (Refute: What's good for school is bad for students in this case. Offer fewer courses to begin with and put them in prime times for maximum enrollment.)

- Can schedule faculty most effectively this way. (Refute: College is here for the students, not for the convenience of teachers.)

3. When you complete your prewriting, write the first draft of your paper following these suggestions.

   a. In the opening, introduce your topic and thesis in a way that will engage your reader's interest or concern.

   b. In the middle paragraphs, present and develop your supporting points, and present and refute one or two opposing arguments.

   c. In the conclusion, make your purpose clear and provide whatever final thoughts you feel would best accomplish your purpose.

   d. Keep your readers in mind, and write in a way that you feel will produce the desired response.

Scheduling Woes

STUDENT SAMPLE
DRAFT Last semester I was lucky enough to enroll in all five classes that I needed for general education requirements. All the course sections I had in my schedule were still open when I registered. I didn't have to worry about back-up classes since I figured my schedule was set.

By the end of the second week of the semester, three of my five classes had been canceled, due to a lack of the "necessary" enrollment. Then I was forced, along with many other students, to scrounge around for other classes, which was frustrating and difficult. I ended up getting into only two other courses, neither of which I would have taken by choice. Clearly, there's something wrong with the scheduling practice at the college, and students are suffering.

For the second semester now, the college has scheduled significantly more sections of general ed courses than have been "made." It appears the school, or deans, or whoever makes the enrollment decisions waits to see which sections reach the magic minimum of twenty enrollees, and then cancels all those with fewer than twenty. Students caught in the smaller classes are then compelled to seek out other sections or courses, with no guarantees that they'll be allowed in.

To make matters worse, sometimes smaller sections are "carried" through the second week in hopes of late enrollments, leaving students desperately seeking classes in the third week of the semester. Some instructors have a policy of not accepting any students after the second week of the semester, and the students are often treated as if they have no business trying to get into classes late!

The effects of sections being canceled are obvious. First, students are lulled into believing that their schedules are set for the semester, so they don't worry about "double enrolling" in additional courses to cover themselves, a practice the college frowns on. Second, they are left, often for two weeks into the semester, with the uncertainty and anxiety of not knowing which of their classes will "make" and which will be canceled. Third, once classes are canceled, students are left with the responsibility of finding other classes to fill their schedules, and the college guarantees them nothing. Finally, and most damaging, they often end up taking classes they didn't want or need, and taking fewer classes than they had planned, which could jeopardize their grant eligibility and lengthen their stay at the college.

I'm sure the college has its reasons for overscheduling sections of courses. It can see which sections fill and then cancel the smaller sections that are more costly. It can also list the instructors for most sections as "staff" and then place teachers in sections where there are the best enrollments. And the college knows that with many small sections being canceled, the enrollment in the sections that "make" will only get better. In short, the administrators are doing what's best financially for the college at the expense of the students.

The college's current practice of overscheduling sections of courses is very unfair to students. The number of sections offered any semester should reflect the number of classes that realistically should fill with at least twenty students. That number can be pretty well determined by checking the number of sections of a course that "made" the same semester of the previous year. A two- or three-year study, taking college enrollment fluctuations into account, might provide an even more accurate indicator. The excuse that the college can't really predict how many sections to offer in any given semester just doesn't wash.

Last semester, according to the college admission's office, twenty-four sections of general ed pattern courses were canceled due to small enrollment. That is a scandalously high number. I think anyone could understand four or five sections needing to be canceled or added, based on enrollment fluctuations, but twenty-four canceled sections indicates a clearly intended practice of overscheduling and canceling classes, strictly for the financial benefit and convenience of the school and at the expense of the students.

This practice needs to be stopped immediately, and I am asking the administration to meet with a student committee before next semester's schedule is published. We want to ensure that all of the classes scheduled, based on current overall enrollment, have a realistic chance of reaching minimum enrollment figures. When that occurs, students' registration schedules will accurately reflect their load for the semester, students won't be forced to scrounge for classes after the semester begins, and students will have a better chance of getting the classes and the units they need. After all, the college is here for the students, and not the other way around.

4. Set your draft aside for a while, and then evaluate it for possible revisions. Follow these guidelines:

   a. Evaluate the strength of your opening. Are your topic and thesis clearly presented? Does your reader have a good idea why you are writing?

   b. Evaluate your middle paragraphs. Do you have some strong supportive points for your thesis? Do you provide evidence to substantiate each point? Have you effectively refuted an opposing argument or two that your reader may have?

   c. Evaluate the strength of your conclusion. Will the readers clearly understand your purpose? Have you told them what needs to be done? Do you conclude in a way that will elicit a positive response from them?

    d. Revise sentences to make them clearer, smoother, and more concise and to vary sentence structures and joining words.

    e. Read the draft from your readers' perspective, and make any final changes that you feel will make the person more responsive to your message.

5. Proofread your latest draft for errors following these guidelines:

    a. Make sure each that sentence ends with a period and that you correct any run-on sentences, comma splices, or fragments.

    b. Check word endings to make sure that plural words end in *s* or *es,* regular past tense verbs end in *ed,* present tense verbs agree with their subjects, and comparative and superlative adjectives have appropriate *er* and *est* endings.

    c. Check your spelling carefully, including your use of homonyms such as there/their/they're, your/you're, know/no, its/it's, and through/threw.

    d. Check your internal punctuation: commas, apostrophes in contractions and possessives, quotation marks around direct quotations, and semicolons and colons, if needed.

    e. Check your pronoun usage: correct subject pronouns in compound subjects (Joan and I, my mom and she, we and they) and pronouns that agree with their antecedents (A person should do *his or her* best in life. Mal and I did *our* projects by *ourselves.)*

6. Write the final draft of your letter and share it with the person it is intended for and your instructor.

APPENDIX

This appendix contains a number of writing activities that individual students may find useful. As your instructor becomes familiar with your writing needs, he or she may assign specific activities from the Appendix on a diagnostic basis. For example, if you struggle with irregular verb tenses, dangling modifiers, or punctuation of possessive words, you will find help in the Appendix.

The Appendix is intended to be used as an ongoing supplement to the rest of the text. The material has not been relegated to the Appendix because it is less important, but because all students will not use it similarly. For example, one student may find the "Spelling" section valuable while another may have no need for it. Putting such writing elements in the Appendix makes them available to students without overloading the units and distracting students from the writing process.

SENTENCE REVISION

Sentence revision is a task shared by all writers. This section will help you write and revise sentences more effectively by broadening your sentence repertoire and making you aware of common structural problems.

COMBINING SENTENCES

The best way to get rid of short, monotonous sentences in a draft is to combine pairs or groups of sentences to form more informative and interesting ones. Here are ways to combine short sentences:

1. Eliminate unnecessary words that are duplicated in the sentences.

2. Move descriptive words in front of the word they describe.

3. Join similar sentence parts with an *and, or,* or *but.*

Here are examples of groups of short sentences that have been combined in the revised versions following the methods just described.

EXAMPLES

DRAFT	Joanie is a student. She is a very good one.
REVISED	Joanie is a very good student.
DRAFT	Fernando bought a shirt. It was red. It was long sleeved.
REVISED	Fernando bought a red, long-sleeved shirt.
DRAFT	Alan went to the barbecue. Felicia went with him.
REVISED	Alan and Felicia went to the barbecue together.

COMBINING ACTIVITY 1

Each pair or group of short sentences below can be combined to form one improved sentence. Combine the sentences into single sentences by eliminating and moving words around and by joining similar words or groups of words with *and, or,* or *but.*

EXAMPLE	Gwen went to school. Maria went to school. They went with Bob.
REVISED	Gwen and Maria went to school with Bob.

1. The frog leaped onto the log. He plopped into the water. He disappeared.

2. Harry was tired. He was thirsty. He wasn't hungry.

3. Ellie got a B on her term paper. She got the same grade on her algebra test. She flunked her pop quiz in German.

4. Your X rays could be in the drawer. They could be on the shelf. They could be almost anywhere in the house.

5. The kitten was fat. It was fluffy. It was playing with a grasshopper. The grasshopper was badly injured.

6. Marge finally got a letter. It was from her parole officer. She was relieved.

7. The week was long. It was boring. It was almost over. Julian was very happy.

8. Susan's clothes were plain. They were cheap. They were also stylish. They were also in good taste.

9. The car spun toward the wall. It crashed. It burst into flames. The driver wasn't injured. He was lucky.

10. That puppy is very cute. It is black and white. It has droopy ears. It is in the pet store window. It isn't for sale.

A second way to combine shorter sentences is to join two complete sentences with *coordinate conjunctions* to form *compound sentences*. These are the most commonly used coordinate conjunctions:

    and   but   for   or   so   yet

The following are examples of two first-draft sentences joined by coordinate conjunctions to form single compound sentences. Notice that different conjunctions show different relationships between the two sentences they join. The conjunctions are underlined.

EXAMPLE	The Rolling Stones were popular in the 1960s. They are still popular today.
REVISED	The Rolling Stones were popular in the 1960s, <u>and</u> they are still popular today. (And *joins the information together.*)
EXAMPLE	Divorce statistics are rising. Couples are marrying in record numbers.
REVISED	Divorce statistics are rising, <u>but</u> couples are marrying in record numbers. (But *shows a contrast; something happened* despite *something else.*)
EXAMPLE	Rita may go to a movie tonight. She may stay home and read a mystery novel.

REVISED	Rita may go to a movie tonight, <u>or</u> she may stay home and read a mystery novel. (Or *shows a choice; alternatives are available.*)
EXAMPLE	James makes his own shirts. He enjoys sewing.
REVISED	James makes his own shirts, <u>for</u> he enjoys sewing. (For *means* because; *something occurs because of something else.*)
EXAMPLE	Working and going to school is difficult. Many students do both.
REVISED	Working and going to school is difficult, <u>yet</u> many students do both. (Yet is *similar to* but; *it shows a contrast.*)
EXAMPLE	The air is moist and cold. We'd better bundle up for the parade.
REVISED	The air is moist and cold, <u>so</u> we'd better bundle up for the parade. (So *is like* therefore; *one thing leads to another.*)

As you can see, different conjunctions serve different purposes. Being able to use a variety of conjunctions at appropriate times makes your writing more effective.

COMBINING ACTIVITY 2

Combine the following pairs of shorter sentences with conjunctions to form compound sentences. Use the conjunction that best joins each sentence pair: *and, or, but, so, yet, for.* Put a comma before the conjunction.

EXAMPLE	The weather is miserable today. It should be better tomorrow.
REVISED	The weather is miserable today, but it should be better tomorrow.

1. Jogging is a popular exercise. Some doctors don't recommend it.

2. You can take typing this semester. You can take it next semester.

3. Ms. Avery is an unpopular teacher. She lectures too fast.

4. Jodie didn't like the foreign movie. It was praised by the critics.

5. The smells from the cafeteria were wonderful. The food was disappointing.

6. Rain collected in jars on the back porch. We used the water to test for acid rain.

7. Freddie may be at the Pizza Palace. He may be at the roller derby with Lucinda.

8. Lupe joined the swim team. She wanted the exercise and the units.

9. Sam tried to return the defective smoke alarm. The store was closed.

10. Alicia couldn't study for the essay test. She got a good night's sleep instead.

A third way to combine sentences is to join two complete sentences with words called *subordinate conjunctions* to form *complex sentences*. Subordinate conjunctions may be placed between the two sentences or at the beginning of the first sentence. The following subordinate conjunctions are most commonly used in complex sentences.

after	if	whenever
although	since	where
as	unless	whereas
because	until	wherever
before	when	while

The following examples show two first-draft sentences joined by subordinate conjunctions to form complex sentences. Notice the different relationships that the subordinate conjunctions show and their use at the beginning or in the middle of the complex sentence. The subordinate conjunctions are underlined.

EXAMPLE   You are going to be late for biology class. You should contact your teacher.

REVISED   <u>Since</u> you are going to be late for biology class, you should contact your teacher.

EXAMPLE   Fred's friends took him home. They went out for pizza.

REVISED   <u>After</u> Fred's friends took him home, they went out for pizza.

EXAMPLE   I'm cleaning up your mess. You are watching television!

REVISED   I'm cleaning up your mess <u>while</u> you are watching television!

EXAMPLE   You have worked very hard. You have gained everyone's respect.

REVISED   <u>Because</u> you have worked very hard, you have gained everyone's respect.

EXAMPLE   George wants to pass the geography test. He will have to identify six mountain ranges.

REVISED   <u>If</u> George wants to pass the geography test, he will have to identify six mountain ranges.

EXAMPLE   Joanna refuses to exercise. She would like to be in shape.

REVISED   Joanna refuses to exercise <u>although</u> she would like to be in shape.

As you can see, subordinate conjunctions can show different relationships: time (*when, as, after, while*), cause and effect (*since, because, if,
unless*), place (*where, wherever*), or contrast (*although, even though,
whereas*). You may use them at the beginning or in the middle of a complex sentence depending on what you want to emphasize. Using complex
sentences adds variety to your writing and helps you express a wide range
of relationships between ideas.

COMBINING ACTIVITY 3

Join the following pairs of shorter sentences with appropriate subordinate
conjunctions to form complex sentences. You will begin some sentences
with subordinate conjunctions and use others between sentences. When
you begin a sentence with a subordinate conjunction, put a comma
between the two sentences you are combining. (Some sentence pairs won't
go together well until they are combined with a subordinate conjunction.)

EXAMPLE   The party was over. Ruby drove around until dawn.

REVISED   After the party was over, Ruby drove around until dawn.

EXAMPLE   The dog limped along the road. It had a thorn in its paw.

REVISED   The dog limped along the road because it had a thorn in its paw.

1. You leave for school tomorrow. Please pick me up at the corner.

2. Jim dropped his gymnastics class. He had a time conflict.

3. The economy improves greatly. The unemployment rate will climb.

4. Gina spent a lot of time reading romances. She still did well in school.

5. You believe everything Harley says. You are very naive.

6. I told you before. I'll be glad to water your ferns this weekend.

7. Ms. Howard is a fascinating teacher. She uses slides, movies, and field
   trips in her anthropology class.

8. The electricity is off in the apartments. Everyone is buying candles.

9. The shower door was broken. Manuel moved into the dormitory.

10. You've had experience with electrical work. Don't try to change that
    outlet.

COMBINING ACTIVITY 4

Rewrite the following passage. Combine sentences by adding joining words, moving words and phrases around, and eliminating unnecessary words. Combine the fourteen sample sentences into a few well-crafted ones.

EXAMPLE   Nona moved into her apartment today. She paid her rent a week ago. She was living alone. She was looking for a roommate to share expenses.

REVISED   Nona moved into her apartment today, but she paid her rent a week ago. Although she was living alone, she was looking for a roommate to share expenses.

Corrine collects records from the fifties and sixties. She has over one thousand 45 rpm discs. Her brother is a disc jockey. She buys duplicate records from his station cheaply. She enjoys the music of the eighties. She prefers the sound of early rock 'n' roll. She has every record Buddy Holly ever recorded. He was her favorite singer. She'll invite her friends over. They'll listen to old songs for hours. She's heard them hundreds of times. She never gets tired of them. She never considers her collection complete. She'll spend the weekend looking for records by Bo Diddley and Danny and the Juniors.

COMBINING ACTIVITY 5

Combine the following sentences to form single sentences using the combining methods you have learned.

EXAMPLE   The bed is below the picture. It has a walnut headboard. It is a single bed.

REVISED   The single bed with the walnut headboard is below the picture.

EXAMPLE   Jane got to the museum early. She still had to wait in line for an hour.

REVISED   Jane got to the museum early, but she still had to wait in line for an hour.

EXAMPLE   Sam had a good time at the drag races. He thought they would be boring.

REVISED   Sam had a good time at the drag races, although he thought they would be boring.

1. The gymnast was short. She was slender. She was strong for her size. She was determined.

2. The seats were slashed. They were in the back of the theatre. A gang of girls did it. They did it maliciously.

3. I met a man on the train. He was very friendly. He was very tall. He was going to Memphis. He was from Cleveland.

4. Marge was having trouble breathing. She went to the infirmary. The doctor kept her there overnight. He wanted to observe her.

5. We are planning on taking a ferry to Falcon Island. Our plans for Saturday could change. They could stay the same.

6. Jacques often missed class. It was history. His instructor seldom noticed. Jacques sat in the back of the room. He was very quiet.

7. Marsha was tired of wearing her shirt. It was an old sweat shirt. She bought a new one. It was just like her old one.

8. The large sailboat battled the wind for hours. It was off the coast of North Carolina. It finally capsized. No one was hurt.

9. Gilda was awakened by thunder. She couldn't go back to sleep. She tossed and turned. She did this until morning.

10. Max was a great clown. Holly was a great clown too. Ralph was a lousy clown. Marvin was a lousy clown. They all had fun.

COMBINING ACTIVITY 6

Combine the following sentences to form single sentences using the combining methods you have learned. Here is an example of each method:

DRAFT   The desk is in the corner. It is walnut. It is for studying. It is twelve years old.

REVISED The walnut study desk in the corner is twelve years old. *(repeated words eliminated, modifying words moved in front of word they describe)*

DRAFT   I never had problems with my hearing. Lately I don't hear the television well.

REVISED I never had problems with my hearing, but lately I don't hear the television well. *(compound sentence formed by using coordinate conjunction* but *to join sentences)*

DRAFT   She is really tired of school. She'll stick it out for her last semester.

REVISED Although she is really tired of school, she'll stick it out for her last semester. *(complex sentence formed by adding subordinate conjunction* although *to join sentence)*

DRAFT   Josephine finally went to an acupuncturist. She was bothered by nagging headaches.

REVISED   Bothered by nagging headaches, Josephine finally went to an acupuncturist. *(introductory phrase used in place of second sentence and unnecessary words eliminated)*

1. The lake is full of golden trout. It lies at the foot of Mt. Cirano. They will rise to any bait.

2. I don't think anyone was injured in the accident. I could tell from the looks of the cars involved. I couldn't say for certain.

3. Maria is tired of working. She is looking forward to school. Helena feels the same way as Maria. Joleen is enjoying working. She isn't looking forward to school.

4. The debate team swept through every match. They did it easily. They were from Des Moines. They competed against some of the best teams in the state.

5. You can take English 6 this semester. You can wait for summer school. It's easier in the summer. You don't learn as much.

6. Hilda is very friendly. She is generous with her time. She is generous with her money. She doesn't like to be used.

7. My German shepherd is six months old. It is being trained as a Seeing Eye dog. The Nunnley School for the Blind is training it. They will place it with a blind person. They will do this when the training is completed.

8. Freddie got a C- on his biology report. He worked very hard on the report.

9. The liquidambar is a tree. It is a good source of shade. It grows well in most climates. It fares best in warm weather. It fares worst in cold weather.

10. Please get ten more boxes of gingersnaps. Get the same brand. Do it this morning. Do it before I leave for work.

11. Mary has a terrible toothache. It's keeping her from eating. She should see a dentist. It could get even worse.

12. That man is mysterious looking. He has a patch over his left eye. He keeps looking at you. He seems to know you.

SENTENCE PROBLEMS

Three structural problems that may occasionally creep into your sentences are *nonparallel constructions, dangling modifiers,* and *misplaced modifiers.*

This section will help you identify and eliminate such problems in your writing.

Parallel Construction

One sentence problem that leads to awkward and confusing wording involves *parallel construction.* It is not uncommon for a writer to join two or more groups of words together in a sentence. For the sentence to be clear, these groups of words need to be very similar, or *parallel,* in structure. Here is an example of a sentence with parallel construction. The groups of words joined together are underlined.

EXAMPLE   Last night we ate outside, sat by the river, and listened to the frogs.

The underlined groups of words are parallel because they follow the same structure: past tense verb followed by modifying words. Now read the same sentence with some problems with parallelism.

EXAMPLE   Last night we ate outside, by the river sat, and listening to the frogs.

This sentence is very awkward. In the second group of words, the order of the past tense verb and the modifying words is changed, and in the last group, the verb has the wrong ending. The resulting sentence would bother any reader.

   Here are other examples of sentences with nonparallel constructions followed by revised corrected versions.

EXAMPLE   Joleen is tall, slender, and brown hair. (Brown hair *isn't parallel with* tall *and* slender.)

REVISED   Joleen is tall and slender and has brown hair.

EXAMPLE   I leaped across the creek, landed on the bank, and back in the water did slip. (Back in the water did slip *is not parallel with the first two parts.*)

REVISED   I leaped across the creek, landed on the bank, and slipped back into the water.

EXAMPLE   Swimming, jogging, and a tennis game are good forms of exercise. (A tennis game *is not parallel with* swimming *and* jogging.)

REVISED   Swimming, jogging, and tennis are good forms of exercise.

EXAMPLE   The MG is metallic blue, has four speeds, and racy. (Racy *isn't parallel with the other parts.*)

REVISED   The MG is metallic blue, has four speeds, and is racy.

REVISION ACTIVITY 7

The following sentences have problems with parallel construction. Rewrite each sentence and improve the wording by correcting the nonparallel part of the sentence.

EXAMPLE   John looked out the window, scanned in all directions, and no one.

REVISED   John looked out the window, scanned in all directions, and saw no one.

1. I enjoy skating, reading, to swim, and the sport of hockey.

2. Claude is short, stout, intelligent, brown eyes, and generosity.

3. We walked through the field, finding hundreds of acorns, and bring them home in baskets.

4. You may check out the periodical or in the library you may read it.

5. Doing dishes, cleaning her room, homework, to baby-sit her brother, and the flossing of her teeth were chores Eileen avoided.

6. Mildred walked into the class, does one hundred push-ups, and out the door.

7. You can chew gum in Kaser's class, but gum chewing in Bowie's class you can't do, and no gum in Borafka's class.

8. Not only is college harder than high school but also greater is the cost and more is the difficulty.

9. The news about the earthquake was terrible, the reports being shockingly graphic, the death count is tragically high, and more bodies being uncovered still.

10. Georgia is willing to organize activities for her sorority but no more tutoring pledges for their finals, and not willing to chair the pledge meetings.

Misplaced and Dangling Modifiers

Two common wording problems that can confuse readers involve *misplaced* and *dangling modifiers*. While the misplaced modifying phrase is located in an awkward position in a sentence, a dangling modifying phrase has nothing in the sentence to modify.

Follow these suggestions for identifying and correcting problems with misplaced and dangling modifiers.

1. A misplaced modifying phrase is usually some distance from the word it modifies, creating confusion about what the modified word is supposed to be.

EXAMPLES   (MODIFYING PHRASES UNDERLINED)

The man applied for a job in Chicago <u>from Toledo</u>.

The students can't hear the lecture <u>sitting in the back of the room</u>.

The house is for sale for fifty thousand dollars <u>across the street</u>.

The girl chased the elephant through the house <u>in pigtails</u>.

The young man was brought into the emergency room <u>bitten by a snake</u>.

2. To correct most misplaced modifiers, place the phrase directly after the word it modifies. Occasionally the phrase will fit more smoothly directly before the modified word.

EXAMPLES   The man <u>from Toledo</u> applied for a job in Chicago.

The students <u>sitting in the back of the room</u> can't hear the lecture.

The house <u>across the street</u> is for sale for fifty thousand dollars.

The girl <u>in pigtails</u> chased the elephant through the house.

The young man <u>bitten by a snake</u> was brought into the emergency room.

3. Dangling modifiers usually begin sentences, often start with words with *ing* and *ed* endings, and are followed by a subject they don't modify. The modifiers are "dangling" because they clearly don't modify the subject.

EXAMPLES   (DANGLING PHRASE UNDERLINED)

<u>Driving to work yesterday</u>, the road was very slippery. *(The subject,* road, *can't drive.)*

<u>Worried about her daughter's whereabouts</u>, the police were called immediately. *(The subject,* police, *weren't "worried about her daughter's whereabouts.")*

<u>Grounded for three weeks for bad grades</u>, John's sister got to use his car. *(The subject,* sister, *wasn't the one who was grounded.)*

<u>Running through the park</u>, the cool breeze felt great on our faces. *(The subject,* breeze, *can't run through the park.)*

4. To correct a dangling modifier, either (a) change the subject of the sentence so that it goes with the modifying phrase or (b) add a subordinating conjunction and subject to the modifying phrase to form a complex sentence.

EXAMPLES   Driving to work today, I noticed how slippery the road was.

or

While I was driving to work today, the road was very slippery.

Worried about her daughter's whereabouts, Gretchen called the police immediately.

or

Because Gretchen was worried about her daughter's whereabouts, the police were called immediately.

Grounded for three weeks for bad grades, John couldn't drive his car so his sister got to.

or

Because John was grounded for three weeks for bad grades, his sister got to use his car.

Running through the park, we felt the cool breeze on our faces.

or

As we were running through the park, the cool breeze felt great on our faces.

REVISION ACTIVITY 8

Each of the following sentences has a misplaced modifier. Rewrite each sentence and put the misplaced modifier in a more appropriate location. The result will be clearer, smoother sentences.

EXAMPLE   The girl showed up in a trench coat from the dorms.

REVISED   The girl from the dorms showed up in a trench coat.

1. The movie is very dull showing at the drive-in.

2. I was born in New Mexico of about one hundred families in a small town.

3. He didn't know that well how to drive a stick shift.

4. The cigarette that you finished smoking for your health is very bad.

5. He is a man used by God of many talents, for he is a pastor.

6. The girl was very wet from perspiring from Texas after the race.

7. The van was stolen from the front of the gym belonging to the school.

8. The jelly is from your knife in the peanut butter.

9. The candy bars have melted with nuts in the heat.

10. The patient has great courage in room 301.

REVISION ACTIVITY 9

Each of the following sentences begins with a dangling modifier. Rewrite the sentence to correct the problem either by changing the subject so that it goes with the modifying phrase or by adding a subordinating conjunction and subject to the dangling phrase to form a complex sentence. In each case, use the correction method that generates the smoothest, clearest sentence.

EXAMPLE	Working in the backyard all morning, my clothes got very dirty.
REVISED	While I was working in the backyard all morning, my clothes got very dirty.
EXAMPLE	Thrilled by his semester grades, everyone John knew got a phone call.
REVISED	Thrilled by his semester grades, John phoned everyone he knew.

1. Sitting on the sofa in the living room, my feet got very cold.

2. Bothered by a sore throat, Mary's doctor suggested that she stay home.

3. Angered over an unfair speeding ticket, the judge got a lecture from Ned.

4. Driving down Manning Avenue, the grape vineyards are beautiful in the spring.

5. Locked out of the house, the only way for John to enter was through a window.

6. Waiting for a taxi on "G" Street, four taxis drove right by me.

7. Bored by the movie on TV, the channel was changed by Gladys.

8. Trying for a school record in the high jump, the bar was raised for Marie to 5 feet 10 inches.

CORRECT USAGE

This section is for students who have problems with past tense verbs: omitting the ed ending or using incorrect irregular verb forms.

PAST TENSE VERBS

Not all of your writing is done in the present tense. You use *past tense* verbs when writing about an event that has already occurred, whether it happened a minute or a decade ago. The most common errors involving past tense verbs include leaving off the *ed* ending on *regular* past tense verbs and using incorrect *irregular* verb forms.

Regular Past Tense Verbs

Most verbs form their past tense by adding ed to the regular verb. Here are examples of regular past tense verbs:

Verb	Past Tense Form	Verb	Past Tense Form
answer	answered	instruct	instructed
ask	asked	kick	kicked
borrow	borrowed	learn	learned
climb	climbed	part	parted
count	counted	question	questioned
detail	detailed	rush	rushed
edit	edited	sail	sailed
fish	fished	scale	scaled
flood	flooded	talk	talked
head	headed	walk	walked

Regular verbs that end in certain letters offer slight variations to the basic *ed* verb ending.

1. Verbs already ending in *e* just add the *d*.

Verb	Past Tense Form
believe	believed
create	created

Verb Past   Tense Form (continued)

hate	hated
invite	invited
love	loved
receive	received

2. Verbs ending in *y* preceded by a *consonant* change the *y* to *i* and add *ed*.

Verb Past   Tense Form

bury	buried
carry	carried
marry	married
rely	relied
reply	replied
tarry	tarried

3. Verbs ending in *y* preceded by a *vowel* merely add *ed*.

Verb	*Past Tense Form*
annoy	annoyed
betray	betrayed
delay	delayed
destroy	destroyed
relay	relayed

4. A number of short regular verbs ending in consonants preceded by vowels with a *short vowel* sound (plăn, bŭg, fĭt) double their last letter before adding *ed*.

Verb	*Past Tense Form*	*Verb*	*Past Tense Form*
acquit	acquitted	knit	knitted
admit	admitted	mar	marred
bat	batted	plan	planned
bug	bugged	ram	rammed
can	canned	scan	scanned
cram	crammed	slug	slugged
fit	fitted	tar	tarred

VERB ACTIVITY 10

Write the past tense form for the following regular verbs. Some verbs will add *ed*, some will change *y* to *i* and add *ed*, and some will double the final letter and add *ed*.

EXAMPLES   slice *sliced*   cry *cried*   plan *planned*

1. betray

2. flood

3. cite

4. learn

5. plan

6. deny

7. marry

8. announce

9. save

10. annoy

11. time

12. dam

VERB ACTIVITY 11

The following passage is written in the present tense. Rewrite the passage changing the verbs to the past tense. Make sure to add ed endings to all regular past tense verbs.

EXAMPLE   Gertrude likes mustard on her rice.

PAST TENSE   Gertrude liked mustard on her rice.

Tonight the moon looks strange. Wispy clouds cover its surface, and a huge halo that looks perfectly round encircles it. Moisture drips from the air, and the moon glistens behind the veil of clouds. It appears eerie and beautiful. I watch the moon from my window and then drift to sleep. I enjoy enchanted dreams about hidden moon caves and moonmaids that lure sleepers into their caverns.

Irregular Verbs

Many verbs do not form their past tense with the regular *ed* verb ending. Instead, they form their past tense in different, *irregular* ways that involve changes within the verb instead of the addition of an ending. Although certain groups of irregular verbs form their past tense in similar ways, there are no rules to follow like the *ed* rule for regular verbs; therefore, you must memorize irregular verb forms to have them at your command.

The following is a list of frequently used irregular verbs whose forms are often confused. The verbs with similar forms are grouped as much as possible. The third column, "Past Participle," contains the irregular verb forms used with *helping verbs* such as *has, have, had, was,* and *were*. Here are examples of sentences containing the past tense and past participle verb forms:

EXAMPLES

John <u>flew</u> cross-country in a single-prop Cessna. *(past tense, action completed)*

John <u>has flown</u> cross-country many times. *(past participle + helping verb* has; *action continuing into the present)*

Lillie <u>sang</u> beautifully at the graduation ceremony. *(past tense, action completed)*

Lillie <u>has sung</u> at many graduation ceremonies. *(past participle + helping verb* has; *action continuing in present)*

Lillie <u>had sung</u> at many graduation ceremonies. *(past participle + helping verb* had; *action completed)*

Present Tense	Past Tense	Past Participle
become	became	become
come	came	come
run	ran	run
begin	began	begun
drink	drank	drunk
ring	rang	rung
sing	sang	sung
swim	swam	swum
fly	flew	flown
grow	grew	grown
know	knew	known
throw	threw	thrown
burst	burst	burst
cut	cut	cut

Present Tense	Past Tense	Past Participle (continued)
quit	quit	quit
set	set	set
choose	chose	chosen
drive	drove	driven
eat	ate	eaten
get	got	gotten
give	gave	given
rise	rose	risen
speak	spoke	spoken
take	took	taken
write	wrote	written
bring	brought	brought
build	built	built
catch	caught	caught
has	had	had
lead	led	led
sit	sat	sat
do	did	done
go	went	gone
see	saw	seen
lay	laid	laid *(to place or set something down)*
lie	lay	lain *(to recline or rest)*

VERB ACTIVITY 12

Fill in the blanks with the correct past tense and past participle forms of the irregular verbs in parentheses. Use the past participle form when a helping verb (such as has, have, was, were) comes before it.

EXAMPLES   (get) She has _gotten_ good grades on her math quizzes.

(run) George _ran_ into a brick wall.

1. (write) Ted has _____ more this semester than ever before.

2. (lead) The winding path _____ to a gazebo among the pines.

3. (drive) You have _____ me wild with your accusations.

4. (sit) Grace _____ on a stump contemplating her future.

5. (eat) Have you _____ the stuffed peppers in the cafeteria?

6. (build) Ted has _____ model planes since he was in grade school.

7. (begin) It has _____ to drizzle outside.

8. (throw) Mia _____ her back out in aerobic dance class.

9. (know) Hal has _____ some very strange people.

10. (set) Judy _____ her collection of figurines on the mantel.

11. (fly) We've _____ with six different airlines.

12. (drink) You have _____ enough coffee to last you a month.

13. (see) No one _____ or heard from Ezekiel for over two months.

14. (choose) You have _____ the most expensive brand of panty hose.

15. (come) By the time Ames had _____ home, everyone was asleep.

16. (become) You have _____ very proficient at archery.

17. (go) Mattie has _____ to collect dry firewood by the lake.

18. (bring) Grover _____ swamp mud in on his shoes.

19. (give) Reading has _____ Louise great pleasure for years.

20. (swim) Have you _____ across the lake by yourself yet?

21. (lie) Yesterday I _____ down at noon and awakened at 6:00 P.M.

22. (lay) Where have you _____ your pipe?

23. (lie) Have you ever _____ in a hammock?

24. (lay) The construction crew _____ five miles of asphalt in a day.

25. (see) Has anyone _____ my red pajamas?

VERB ACTIVITY 13

Here is more practice using irregular verbs. Write sentences using the following irregular verbs in the tenses indicated.

EXAMPLES   run (past)   Last night John ran past my house at 3:00 A.M.

eat (past participle)   You have eaten all of the cherries I was saving for the picnic.

1. fly (past participle)

2. burst (past)

3. choose (past)

4. fly (past participle)

5. drink (past participle)

6. write (past participle)

7. set (past)

8. rise (past)

9. take (past)

10. see (past)

11. lie (past participle)

12. swim (past participle)

13. drive (past participle)

14. become (past participle)

15. ring (past participle)

16. bring (past)

17. lead (past)

18. lay (past)

19. throw (past participle)

20. drive (past participle)

VERB ACTIVITY 14

Fill in your own choices of past tense and past participle verb forms to complete the following sentences. Spell correctly.

1. Freda _____ angry last night when her roommate _____ her bed.

2. The Gomez family has _____ all the way from Florida for their son's graduation.

3. It seems that we have _____ out of things to argue about.

4. It _____ raining early this morning.

5. Have you ever _____ as much cider as you _____ last night?

6. Jacqueline _____ across the lake and back in three hours.

7. That fifty-pound pumpkin was _____ with a special fertilizer.

8. Have you _____ the table for lunch yet?

9. I have _____ all along that you were a special person.

10. The balloon _____ high in the air and then _____ on a tree limb.

11. You have _____ to be very obnoxious with your Al Capone impressions.

12. Fran _____ her new car around town and _____ up boys.

13. Your father has _____, and that is the end of that!

14. Have you _____ good care of your health this semester?

15. The criminal was finally _____ to justice after years of evading the law.

16. Have you _____ all of your math homework?

17. Sammy _____ to the movies last night and _____ *Attack of the Killer Tomatoes.*

18. Have you ever _____ on a sharp tack that someone _____ on your seat?

19. You have _____ everyone with your time and patience.

20. The new Chevies aren't _____ to last like the older ones.

21. You _____ your history test easily, but you _____ your P.E. physical.

22. They _____ the missing painting and _____ it to its owner.

23. Ms. Hornsby _____ your story about little green men, but I _____.

24. Have you _____ your dear mother lately, or have you _____ her?

25. Henrietta _____ a mean saxophone at the party, and everyone _____.

26. Ito invited you to tea, but I _____.

27. Trudy has _____ twenty-three units of pottery classes and has _____ six of them.

28. The roses have _____ their flowers because you haven't _____ them.

29. Sam _____ the tree, _____ from a branch, and _____ his tongue out at a sparrow.

30. I have _____ to help you but you haven't _____, so I've_____ up hope that you'll ever become a sword swallower.

VERB ACTIVITY 15

The following passage is written in the present tense. Rewrite the passage in the past tense by adding *ed* to regular past tense verbs and by using the correct past tense and past participle forms for the irregular verbs.

EXAMPLE	Clyde buys his shoes at Zody's and wears them for years.
REVISED	Clyde bought his shoes at Zody's and wore them for years.

The campus goes berserk at Halloween. Boys sneak into girls' dormitories, hide in the closets, and scare them when they return from the cafeteria. Students bombard motorists' cars with water balloons, and there isn't a person asleep anywhere on campus. An army of dorm students attacks its rivals across campus. The students capture the dorm president and spray his body with green paint. They steal the dorm banner and hide it in a car trunk. Students from off campus begin a shaving cream war with on-campus students. They quit when the campus police finally intervene at 3:00 A.M. Then everyone is quiet for about a half hour, but the wildness begins again when the police leave.

SPELLING

This final section is for students who struggle with their spelling. It covers contractions and possessive words, commonly misspelled words, and homonyms that cause writers problems.

POSSESSIVES

One of the most frequently omitted punctuation marks is the apostrophe that is needed in possessive words. A *possessive* word is usually followed directly by something *belonging to it*. Here are some sentences with the possessive words correctly punctuated with apostrophes. The possessive words are underlined.

EXAMPLES	My <u>mother's</u> brother owns a fruit stand in the country.
	<u>Today's</u> weather looks menacing with those dark clouds in the east.
	I am going to <u>Celia's</u> surprise party tomorrow night.
	The <u>men's</u> room at the Forum is flooded.

My three <u>brothers'</u> cars are all 1974 Plymouths.

The <u>ladies'</u> club holds its meetings at the Howbarth Tavern.

As you can see, the word directly following the possessive word belongs to it: mother's *brother,* today's *weather,* Celia's *surprise party,* men's *room,* brothers' *cars,* and ladies' *club.* Notice that sometimes the apostrophe comes before the *s* and sometimes it comes after the *s.* Here are the rules for showing possession.

1. *Singular possessive word:* Add apostrophe and *s* to the word:

   a boy's dog, the tree's bark, May's hair

2. *Plural possessive word:* Add the apostrophe *after* the *s:*

   three boys' dogs, all the trees' bark, many girls' hair

   There are two exceptions to the possessive rules:

1. Plural words that form their possessive without adding s (man/men, woman/women, child/children, goose/geese) are punctuated as singular possessives (*'s*): men's hats, women's shoes, children's lessons, geese's feathers.

2. Possessive pronouns such as *yours, theirs, his, ours,* and *hers* do *not* require apostrophes since the form of the pronoun itself indicates possession.

POSSESSIVE ACTIVITY 16

Put apostrophes in the following possessive words to show singular and plural possessive forms.

EXAMPLES   a dog's life

                  the boys' club

1. the banks vault

2. a childs prayer

3. my uncles wife

4. six countries treaties

5. thirty books covers

6. the geeses feathers

7. a mans opinion

8. omens strength

9. twenty schools fight songs

10. four doctors nurses

11. Tuesdays child

12. the wars effect

POSSESSIVE ACTIVITY 17

Write your own sentences showing the possessive relationship that is given for each sentence. Follow the rules for adding 's or s'. Make sure the possessive word is followed by the thing belonging to it.

EXAMPLE   a dog belonging to Mark

REVISED   Mark's dog is a cocker spaniel.

EXAMPLE   the bones of all the dogs in the neighborhood

REVISED   All of the dogs' bones are hidden in the lot behind my house.

1. the hamster belonging to Mary

2. the snow of this morning

3. the lockers belonging to the men

4. the right to an education belonging to a student

5. the socks belonging to your grandmother

6. the station wagons belonging to six families

7. the great force of the ocean waves

8. the diagnosis of a doctor

CONTRACTIONS

A *contraction* is a word formed by combining two words and inserting an apostrophe to replace omitted letters. The most common contractions combine pronouns with verbs (I'm, he's, you've, we're) and verbs with the word *not* (isn't, wasn't, don't, won't, aren't).

Here are examples of common contractions and the word pairs from which they are formed:

Contraction	Word Pair	Contraction	Word Pair
I'm	I am	aren't	are not
you're	you are	wasn't	was not
he's	he is	weren't	were not

Contraction	Word Pair	Contraction	Word Pair
she's	she is	don't	do not
they're	they are	doesn't	does not
we're	we are	won't	will not
he'll	he will	wouldn't	would not
we'll	we will	hasn't	has not
they've	they have	haven't	have not
I've	I have	there's	there is
it's	it is	here's	here is
isn't	is not	who's	who is

CONTRACTION ACTIVITY 18

Write contractions for the following pairs of words. Don't forget the apostrophes.

EXAMPLE   he is <u>he's</u>

1. they are _____

2. it is _____

3. do not _____

4. does not _____

5. she is _____

6. I am _____

7. there is _____

8. they have _____

9. will not _____

10. are not _____

11. has not _____

12. you are _____

APOSTROPHE ACTIVITY 19

Put apostrophes in all of the contractions and possessive words that require them in the following sentences.

EXAMPLE   Theyre not going to the firemens ball Friday.

REVISED   They're not going to the firemen's ball Friday.

1. The chipmunks buried a years supply of nuts in the trees hollow.

2. Were supposed to be at the Smiths home for dinner, arent we?

3. The womens tennis team and the mens team were defeated in the leagues championships.

4. Havent you found your sisters new sweater or your four brothers fishing poles yet?

5. Megs response to Jacks question wasnt at all surprising to the groups leaders.

6. Cant you figure a way to curb Fredas appetite for anchovy pizza and lasagna?

7. No ones frame of mind is any better than Howies when he isnt drinking.

8. The dogs and the cats arent supposed to be in Mr. Grumbleys study.

9. The governments belief in the economys recovery isnt accepted by Willies grandfathers.

10. Youve had a difficult time with Newtons law of gravity, havent you?

COMMONLY MISSPELLED WORDS

Misspelled words account for the largest number of writing errors. Spelling errors are a nuisance to the reader, and final drafts should be free of them. Spelling is a minor problem for many writers, but it is a big problem for others. This section introduces some of the most commonly misspelled words and gives you a few basic spelling rules to follow; however, if you have serious spelling difficulties, you might seek further assistance from your instructor.

The following is the first of a number of word lists that appear throughout this section. Each list groups words that follow similar spelling rules.

Spelling List One: Words Ending in *ing*

beginning	kidding	putting	stopping
boring	letting	riding	studying
coming	living	running	swimming
dying	planning	sitting	taking
flying	playing	slipping	writing
hitting			

Words ending in *ing* are frequently misspelled. Here are the basic rules that will help you decide what to do when adding *ing* to a word.

1. *Verbs ending in e:* Drop the *e* and add *ing* (boring, coming, riding, raking).

2. *Verbs ending in y:* Keep the *y* and add *ing* (studying, playing, flying).

3. *Verbs ending in a* short vowel *followed by a single consonant:* Double the last letter and add *ing* (beginning, hitting, kidding, letting, planning, running).

4. *Verbs ending in a* long vowel *followed by a consonant:* Add *ing*, but do *not* double the final letter (dreaming, eating, sleeping, cheating). *Note:* Writers have few problems with this rule, so the words were not included in this spelling list.

SPELLING ACTIVITY 20

Following the spelling rules for adding ing to words, add the ing ending to the following words from Spelling List One.

1. come _____	5. study _____	9. ride _____	13. live _____
2. hit _____	6. run _____	10. stop _____	14. begin _____
3. play _____	7. write _____	11. bore _____	15. swim _____
4. plan _____	8. kid _____	12. put _____	16. let _____

Here is the second list of words that writers frequently misspell. Each list contains words that are similarly misspelled.

Spelling List Two: Words with *ie* and *ei*

achieve	field	neither
believe	friend	receive
deceive	grieve	relief
eight	height	review
either	neighbor	their

As you can see, each of these words contains either an *ei* or an *ie* vowel combination. Many writers misspell these words by turning the two letters around. Here are the basic rules for when to use *ie* and when to use *ei*.

1. In most words, the *i* goes before the *e* unless it follows the letter *c*. Then the *e* goes before the *i* as in *receive*, *deceive*, and *perceive*.

2. If the *ei* has a long a vowel sound, the *e* comes before the *i* as in *neighbor, eight,* and *freight.*

3. You need to memorize some exceptions to the *i* before *e* rule: *height, either, neither.*

SPELLING ACTIVITY 21

Write eight sentences using any two of the Spelling List Two words in each sentence. Use all fifteen words in the eight sentences. Spell the words correctly.

EXAMPLE   You can <u>achieve</u> more in life if you <u>believe</u> in yourself.

The words in Spelling List Three are grouped together because writers often misspell them in the same way: by leaving out a letter.

Spelling List Three: Left-Out Letters

again	opinion	stereo
always	restaurant	straight
clothes	schedule	surprise
familiar	separate	whether
February	several	which
finish	similar	while
interest	sophomore	

Thus, *again* is misspelled as *agin, February* as *Febuary, interest* as *intrest, clothes* as *cloths,* or *whether* as *wether.* The letters are often left out because of the way many people pronounce the words. Three-syllable words such as *interest, restaurant, sophomore,* and *several* are often pronounced and spelled as two-syllable words: *in-trest, rest-rant, soph-more,* and *sev-ral.* The *wh* words are frequently pronounced and spelled without the *h* sound: *wether, wich,* and *wile.*

Because there is no spelling rule to cover the range of List Three words, you will need to memorize them. The best tip for helping you learn them is to *pronounce* the words correctly so that you won't leave out letters by omitting syllables or sounds.

SPELLING ACTIVITY 22

Write ten sentences, including two different words from Spelling List Three in each sentence. Use the words in any order you wish, and spell them correctly. Underline the spelling words.

EXAMPLE   I <u>always finish</u> my English assignments five minutes before class.

Spelling List Four contains words that are grouped together because they all contain double consonants that can cause confusion. The writer is not always certain which letters to double. Unfortunately, there is no rule similar to the rules covering words in List One and List Two to tell you which letters to double. You need to memorize the words in List Four so that you can easily visualize their correct spelling. Because these words are commonly used, you should know them well by the time you complete this course.

Spelling List Four: Double-Letter Words

across	dinner	parallel
arrangement	embarrass	success
attitude	immediate	surround
business	impossible	terrible
different	occasion	tomorrow
difficult	occurred	

SPELLING ACTIVITY 23

Write nine sentences using any two of the words in Spelling List Four in each sentence. Use all seventeen words in your sentences.

EXAMPLE   Sarah made a business arrangement with her banker for a loan.

Spelling List Five: Words Ending in *ly*

actually	finally	lovely
busily	fortunately	naturally
completely	hungrily	really
easily	lively	unusually
especially	lonely	usually
extremely		

Writers who misspell *ly* words get confused about whether to drop a letter before adding the *ly* or whether to add an extra *l* to form an *lly* ending. The following simple rules should clear up the problems.

1. Add *ly* to the root word. Do *not* drop the last letter of the word (*lovely,* not *lovly, fortunately,* not *fortunatly*). An *lly* ending results only when the root word ends in *l* (*real/really, unusual/unusually, natural/naturally, actual/actually*).

2. If a root word ends in *y* change the *y* to *i* and add *ly* (*busy/busily, easy/easily, hungry/hungrily*).

SPELLING ACTIVITY 24

Add *ly* to the root words listed here, following the rules just covered for adding the *ly* ending.

Examples   clumsy *clumsily*

sane *sanely*

1. natural _____   8. fortunate _____
2. live _____   9. lone _____
3. hungry _____   10. complete _____
4. special_____   11. actual_____
5. busy _____   12. final _____
6. unusual_____   13. easy _____
7. real _____   14. love _____

SPELLING REFERENCE LIST

The following list includes more than one hundred of the most frequently misspelled words. You may use it as a convenient spelling reference when proofreading your drafts for errors. You may also want to select five to ten words per week to work on until you can spell every word on the list correctly.

accommodate	appearance	chief
achievement	approach	comparative
acquaintance	argument	conscience
acquire	attendance	controversy
actual	beginner	convenience
against	believe	criticism
alleys	benefit	dealt
amateur	boundary	dependent
amount	business	describe
apparent	certain	despair

disappoint	led	practical
disease	leisure	preferred
divine	license	prejudice
efficient	loneliness	preparation
embarrass	loose	principal
exaggerate	lose	principle
exercise	luxury	privilege
existence	maintenance	probably
expense	marriage	procedure
experience	meant	prominent
explanation	mere	promise
extremely	naturally	psychology
fascinate	necessary	pursue
forty	ninety	really
friend	noticeable	receive
government	obstacle	recommend
grammar	occasion	repetition
guarantee	occurrence	sense
height	operate	separate
heroes	opinion	shining
huge	original	similar
ignorant	paid	studying
imaginary	parallel	success
immediately	particular	surprise
independent	performance	tries
intelligent	personal	truly
interest	physical	villain
interrupt	piece	weather
knowledge	planned	whether
laid	possess	writing

HOMONYMS

Homonyms are words that sound alike but are spelled differently and
have different meanings. The three homonyms most commonly confused
by writers are *there*, *their*, and *they're*, which we cover in the next section.

There/Their/They're

Writers frequently confuse the words *there*, *their*, and *they're*. Once you
understand the use of each word, you will have little trouble distin-
guishing among them. However, you should always proofread your drafts

for *there*, *their*, and *they're* errors because they appear occasionally in most writing.

Here is the meaning of each word:

THERE	An introductory word often preceding *is*, *are*, *was*, and *were*
	There are five goldfish in the pond. I think there is room for you in the bus.
	A location
	Your books are over there. There are the books I've been looking for.
THEIR	Possessive pronoun (belonging to them)
	Their car was vandalized. Joe took their picture.
THEY'RE	Contraction for *they are*
	They're going to get married on Sunday. I think they're beautiful slides of Rome.

SPELLING ACTIVITY 25

Fill in the blanks with the correct word: *there*, *their*, or *they're*. Select the word or words that fit each sentence.

EXAMPLES   *They're* going to break the snail-eating record.

Their patience is waning.

There are four hummingbirds in the bird bath.

1. _____ are thousands of wheat fields in Kansas.

2. _____ webbed feet help mallards cruise across the pond.

3. _____an unusual breed of turkey.

4. _____ is a need for voters to mail _____ ballots by June.

5. _____ coming at 9:30, but _____ will be no one home.

6. _____ new sofa will be at _____ house by morning.

7. Plant the marigolds _____, _____, and _____.

8. _____ learning algebra faster than _____ cousins did.

9. Is _____ a phone in _____store?

10. _____ taking _____ time in _____.

SPELLING ACTIVITY 26

Write your own sentences using *there, their,* and *they're* as directed.

EXAMPLE   a sentence beginning with *their*

Their schedules for the fall semester are full of errors.

1. a sentence beginning with *there*

2. a sentence beginning with *their*

3. a sentence beginning with *they're*

4. *there* and *their* in the same sentence

5. *there* and *they're* in the same sentence

6. *their* and *they're* in the same sentence

7. *their, there,* and *they're* in the same sentence

8. *there* three times in the same sentence.

SPELLING ACTIVITY 27

Here is more practice using the words *there, their,* and *they're* correctly. Remember, *there* is an introductory word or shows location, *their* is a possessive pronoun (belonging to them), and *they're* is a contraction for *they are.* Fill in the correct form in each blank in the following paragraph.

EXAMPLE   *Their* shoes are new, but *they're* not bragging about it.

_____ is no doubt that Henrietta and Hank are nervous taking the test. _____ hands are shaking, and _____ frowning intently. _____ pencils are moving rapidly over the test booklet. _____ backs are hunched in effort. _____ working at a feverish clip, but _____ is a good chance they won't finish. It is a long and difficult test. _____ are one hundred multiple-choice questions and five essay questions. Finally, Henrietta and Hank stop at the bell, put _____ pencils down, and relax _____ minds. They've done _____ best, and _____ satisfied.

Confusing Duos: List One

A number of word pairs often confuse writers. They can slip erroneously into anyone's paper. The problem is not misspelling a word but using the wrong word in the wrong place. Here are some of the more commonly confused pairs with some information to help you tell them apart. (This is the first of two lists of confusing duos.)

ACCEPT	to receive (I <u>accept</u> your gift. Joy <u>accepted</u> the award.)
EXCEPT	to exclude, leave out (Everyone is going bowling <u>except</u> Millicent.)
A	comes before words beginning with a *consonant* (<u>a</u> book, <u>a</u> slug, <u>a</u> dog, <u>a</u> cat)
AN	comes before words beginning with a *vowel* or *vowel sound* (<u>an</u> apple, <u>an</u> orange, <u>an</u> answer, <u>an</u> herb)
ADVICE	what is *given* to someone (Joe gave me some very good <u>advice</u> about my major.)
ADVISE	the verb meaning to give advice (Joe <u>advised</u> me to major in computer technology.)
AND	conjunction joining words or groups of words (George is going, <u>and</u> so am I.)
AN	comes before words beginning with a *vowel* or *vowel sound* (<u>an</u> apple, <u>an</u> orange, <u>an</u> answer, <u>an</u> herb)
ARE	present tense of *to be* for plural subjects (The gifts <u>are</u> on the table.)
OUR	possessive pronoun, belonging to us (<u>Our</u> plans are uncertain. We'll go <u>our</u> separate ways.)
IT'S	contraction for *it is* (<u>It's</u> going to snow today. <u>It's</u> a rough exam.)
ITS	possessive pronoun (The tire lost <u>its</u> tread. <u>Its</u> flowers are drooping.)
KNOW	to have knowledge, to understand (I <u>know</u> the answer. He <u>knows</u> his limits.)
NO	none, negative (No one minds. There is <u>no</u> smoking in the library. I say "<u>no</u>.")
MINE	possessive pronoun, belonging to me (That book is <u>mine</u>. <u>Mine</u> is the red jacket.)
MIND	to behave, to oppose (The dog <u>minds</u> well. I <u>mind</u> your eating my lunch.)
PAST TIME	gone by (In the <u>past</u>, you have always done well. Your <u>past</u> is your business.)
PASSED	(You <u>passed</u> my inspection. His fever <u>passed</u> hours ago.)

SPELLING ACTIVITY 28

Fill in the blanks with appropriate words from the list of confusing duos.

EXAMPLE   <u>No</u> one cares where we sleep tonight.

1. Mattie paid _____ way into the park last night.

2. For breakfast I'd like _____ apple, _____ omelet, _____ and _____ banana.

3. Everyone seems to be having a good time at the party _____ you.

4. If Shandra takes my _____, she'll forget about working.

5. Do you know why _____ so foggy this month?

6. We are planning to spend _____ honeymoon in Tulsa.

7. I don't _____ if you borrow my sweater tomorrow.

8. I enjoyed studying with you this morning, _____ I hope we can do it again.

9. Fenway was too tired to be good company to _____ guests.

10. Do you _____ if we take up where we left off yesterday?

11. Jack would _____ you to take _____ aspirin and _____ hot bath.

12. Your case is _____ exception to _____ rule.

Confusing Duos: List Two
Here is a second group of confusing word pairs to add to your list.

CHOOSE   present tense verb (I <u>choose</u> the present with the green bow.)

CHOSE   past tense of *choose* (Yesterday I <u>chose</u> to stay home from work.)

QUIT   not to finish, to give up (John <u>quit</u> his job with General Motors.)

QUITE   completely, wholly (Are you <u>quite</u> certain of the time? That was <u>quite</u> a show.)

QUIET   opposite of noisy (Please be <u>quiet</u> in the hospital. I would like a <u>quiet</u> moment.)

THIS   singular word that identifies or locates (<u>This</u> is a great story. <u>This</u> table is new.)

THESE   plural of *this* (<u>These</u> are the best stories I've read. <u>These</u> tables are new.)

To	preposition of many uses (We went <u>to</u> the game. Look <u>to</u> your leader. Sheila belonged <u>to</u> the Modernes. <u>To</u> my knowledge, no one is missing.)
Too	also, in excess (We are going to the game <u>too</u>. You have done <u>too</u> much work for one person.)
Were	past tense form of *to be* with plural subjects (They <u>were</u> here a minute ago!)
Where	indicates location (<u>Where</u> are you going? Do you know <u>where</u> the dishes are?)
Through	preposition of movement or passage (<u>Through</u> the years, you've grown more lovely. We glanced <u>through</u> the book.)
Threw	past tense of *throw* (He <u>threw</u> the ball through the window. Mildred <u>threw</u> out her boyfriend.)
Your	possessive pronoun, belonging to you (<u>Your</u> books are a mess.)
You're	contraction for *you are* (<u>You're</u> the first person to call since the trial.)
Then	indicates time (<u>Then</u> you can go home. I did my work, and <u>then</u> I slept.)
Than	indicates comparison (You are smarter <u>than</u> I am. I saved more money this year <u>than</u> last.)

SPELLING ACTIVITY 29

Fill in the blanks in the following sentences with appropriate words from the list of confusing duos.

EXAMPLE   Last night you *chose* to be by yourself.

1. _____ pickles from Julio's Deli are the spiciest I've eaten.

2. _____ do you think _____ going with my anteater?

3. _____ dog was found in the neighbor's flower garden.

4. I am not _____ ready to _____ on the project.

5. _____ _____ you when we needed relief?

6. I think _____ taking _____ test too seriously.

7. Jody went _____ the races three hours _____ early.

8. I enjoy a _____ evening at home listening to_____ records.

9. I hear _____ not sure _____ tapes _____ left at school.

10. We went _____ the motions of reading our lines, but we didn't _____ have the feeling needed _____ move our audience.

11. Fred felt better _____ he had expected after the race, but _____ the exhaustion started setting in.

SPELLING ACTIVITY 30

Here is a list of all the confusing duos covered in this section. Using the words correctly, write one sentence for each confusing duo. Underline the words.

EXAMPLES   your/you're

You're going to the library, but your brother isn't going.

are/our

Are you going to take our advice about taking vitamin C?

1. choose/chose	16. mine/mind
2. quit/quite/quiet	17. past/passed
3. this/these	18. then/than
4. through/threw	19. bury
5. to/too	20. believe
6. were/where	21. instruct
7. your/you're	22. reply
8. there/their/they're	23. fund
9. accept/except	24. inflate
10. a/an	25. cheat
11. an/and	26. hurry
12. advice/advise	27. bellow
13. are/our	28. admit
14. it's/its	29. cap
15. know/no	30. decide

CREDITS

Andrew Arias
"Stunted Progress" by Andrew Arias. Reprinted by permission of the author.

Margaret Atwood
"Canada Through the One-Way Mirror" by Margaret Atwood. Copyright ©Margaret Atwood, 1986. Reprinted by permission of the author.

Robert DeGrazia
"Limiting Handguns" by Robert DeGrazia from the *New York Times*, January 1, 1974. Copyright c 1974 by The New York Times Co. Reprinted by permission.

Thomas French
"Long Live High School Rebels" by Thomas French from *The St. Petersburg Times*, November 22, 1987. Copyright ©1987 St. Petersburg Times. Reprinted by permission.

David Good
"Science" by David Good. Reprinted by permission of the author.

Thomas Jones
"Down With Jogging" by Thomas Jones. Reprinted by permission of the author.

Larry King
"The Old Man," by Larry King. Reprinted by permission of the author.

INDEX